MW00907313

BUILDING

the TOTAL

ATHLETE

Strength Training and Physical Conditioning for Junior and Senior High School Athletes

Mike Koehler
Bruce Hanson

PRENTICE HALL
Englewood Cliffs, New Jersey 07632

Library of Congress Cataloging-in-Publication Data

Koehler, Mike.
   Building the total athlete : strength training and physical conditioning for junior and senior high school athletes / Michael D. Koehler, Bruce Hanson.
      p.   cm.
   ISBN 0-13-304379-7
      1. Physical education and training.   2. Physical fitness.   3. Muscle strength.
   I. Hanson, Bruce.   II. Title.
   GV711.5.K64   1995   95-3933
   613.7'11—dc20   CIP

© 1995 by Michael D. Koehler

All rights reserved. Permission is given for individual coaches to reproduce the various forms and worksheets contained herein for individual program and team use. Reproduction of these materials for an entire school system is strictly forbidden.

Printed in the United States of America

10   9   8   7   6   5   4   3

This book contains techniques, ideas, and suggestions relating to exercise and diet but is not intended to substitute for proper medical advice. The Publisher suggests that you consult a physician or other health care professional prior to starting any fitness regime. The Publisher and the Author specifically disclaim any liability, loss, or risk, personal or otherwise, which is incurred as a consequence, directly or indirectly, of the use or application of any of the contents of this book.

ISBN 0-13-304379-7

ATTENTION: CORPORATIONS AND SCHOOLS

Prentice Hall books are available at quantity discounts with bulk purchase for educational, business, or sales promotional use. For information, please write to: Prentice Hall Career & Personal Development Special Sales, 113 Sylvan Avenue, Englewood Cliffs, NJ 07632. Please supply: title of book, ISBN number, quantity, how the book will be used, date needed.

PRENTICE HALL
Career & Personal Development
Englewood Cliffs, NJ 07632
A Simon & Schuster Company

On the World Wide Web at http://www.phdirect.com

Prentice-Hall International (UK) Limited, *London*
Prentice-Hall of Australia Pty. Limited, *Sydney*
Prentice-Hall Canada Inc., *Toronto*
Prentice-Hall Hispanoamericana, S.A., *Mexico*
Prentice-Hall of India Private Limited, *New Delhi*
Prentice-Hall of Japan, Inc., *Tokyo*
Simon & Schuster Asia Pte. Ltd., *Singapore*
Editora Prentice-Hall do Brasil, Ltda., *Rio de Janeiro*

DEDICATION

To Eric and Cassie Hanson.
You are loved.

ACKNOWLEDGMENTS

The authors would like to acknowledge Shari Mueller for her frequent help with the nutrition and weightlifting sections. She is an invaluable source of information and help. We would like to thank Jill Akey for being so unselfish with her assistance; Al Vermeil for his input; Nikki Roberg for her artistic ability; Mike Penrod for his knowledge of weightlifting; Win Huppuch and connie Kallback for their encouragements; Jane Jordan Browne for sticking with us through fits of pique; and last—but certainly far from least—Pat Koehler and Carrie Hanson for their patience.

ABOUT THE AUTHORS

Mike Koehler played fullback for Marquette University and the University of Nebraska, coached high school football for 31 years, counseled high school students for 25, and has been an adjunct professor of educational administration and supervision since 1974. Currently, he is devoting all his time to writing, teaching at the university level, and consulting with schools on supervision and student athletes. Mike is the author of scores of articles for professional journals, a nationally syndicated radio show, a newspaper column, and the videotape, *The ABCs of Eligibility for the College-Bound Student Athlete,* which is being marketed by the College Board. Mike also has written ten books, *Building the Total Athlete* being the most recent.

Bruce Hanson was an All-State high school athlete who attended Eastern Illinois University on a wrestling scholarship. While at EIU, Bruce studied Health Sciences and wrestled for four years. After college, he joined his brother as a personal fitness trainer, working with professional athletes, actors and actresses, judges, and a variety of people ranging from high school athletes to senior citizens. His continued studies have involved a graduate degree with emphasis in histology, kinesiology, and nutrition. Bruce and wife Carrie have two children, Eric Michael and Cassidy, and live in Brooklyn Heights. Bruce currently co-directs the Hanson System, a popular fitness center located in the So-Ho section of New York City.

ABOUT THIS BOOK

The purpose of a strength training and physical conditioning program for junior and senior high school athletes is to give coaches a comprehensive program for improving the strength and conditioning of young men and women in all areas of athletics. Only a few schools today involve their athletes in comprehensive programs, and most of these are at the university level. Yet the dividends from such programs are twofold. They help athletes maximize their performance and minimize their injuries.

Most junior and senior high schools fail to realize these benefits because they lack a comprehensive conditioning program. On the one hand, many coaches are unfamiliar with recent technical and scientific advances that have been made in the field of physical conditioning. Time constraints and an inability to break with tradition prevent them from changing current practice. On the other hand, their willingness to change is often compromised by limited resources and equipment.

Even where such resources could be available, administrators tend to funnel dollars into more visible equipment and program needs. They are usually unfamiliar with the reduction of serious injury which results from improved fitness levels. Section 10 of this book provides statistics demonstrating the effects of improved fitness on reduced injuries. Personal anecdotes that illustrate the value of total conditioning are included. The purpose is to sell even the most tightfisted administrator on the benefits of such a program in his or her school.

Building the Total Athlete also provides strategies on selling the program to your athletes. All too often, athletes become preoccupied with appearance and less concerned with performance and possible injury. Looking good on the beach is an outgrowth of conditioning that has more immediate value for them than performance on the field or court. The heads-up coach establishes programs that provide for aesthetic as well as strength increases. This book was written, therefore, to introduce to junior and senior high school coaches and students a total conditioning program that emphasizes improvement in cardiovascular efficiency, strength training, flexibility, and nutritional habits.

We realize that weightlifting accommodates only a part of the strength needs of athletes. The body mass so essential to peformance on the football field, for example, involves energy demands that can exhaust players in the fourth quarter. When coaches incorporate cardiovascular exercises into their conditioning programs, they observe immediate improvements in the strength outputs of players in the fourth quarter. Similarly, wrestlers improve their oxygen uptake in the third period, basketball players fast-break to the final buzzer, and distance runners avoid "hitting the wall" as they approach the tape.

Section 4 discusses a complete aerobic program that increases cardiovascular efficiency for all athletes. It provides sample workouts and reproducibles that detail the desirability of both aerobic and anaerobic running. Wind sprints improve form and explosiveness but increase lung capacity only marginally. An emphasis in this section, therefore, is on distance running within proper aerobic ranges. It also discusses anaerobic running in relation to cardiovascular conditioning and an increased tolerance for muscle fatigue.

Section 2 emphasizes the importance of improved flexibility both as an aid to performance and in the reduction of injuries. Stretching to enhance a complete range of motion helps quarterbacks, discus throwers, high jumpers, field hockey players, pitchers—anyone who wants to maximize muscle strength and avoid the muscle tears that result from tightness.

Sections 5 and 6 consider the specifics of strength training, from appropriate warming-up exercises to proper technique for working on specific muscles or muscle groups to cooling down exercises that avoid lactic acid buildups. A highlight of the section is the discussion of weightlifting exercises for specific sports. Charts are provided that relate specific exercises to the needs of individual athletes by sport. The reproducibles in this section alone make the book an essential for every coach. The section also provides a process for using the computer to individualize workouts for each athlete in your program.

Building the Total Athlete discusses power lifting for the development of bulk, high-repetition lifting for endurance, and speed lifting for explosive movement and improved reaction time. Such programs, which will be outlined in detail, provide advantages for all athletes and involve health habits that they will probably maintain through life.

Section 7 emphasizes proper nutrition as one of life's most important health habits. It discusses the importance of carbohydrates, especially before and during strenuous workouts and competition. It provides several reproducibles regarding diets for strength building, weight reduction, and before-game meals. It underscores the importance of lots of water during any kind of strenuous activity, and it dispels several myths about simple carbohydrates, salt tablets, fat, and other nutritional "facts."

Additional health habits are emphasized in sections 7, 8, and 9, which discuss smoking, drugs (including steroids), proper nutrition, sleep, and even stress reduction. Section 3 touches on the importance of academics and athletics and provides reproducibles that explain the coach's expectations and responsibilities to athletes and parents. It includes sample letters to parents, handouts to athletes, and forms for securing signatures.

We have provided a booklet of reproducibles in the appendix that can be duplicated and distributed to each of your athletes. It will become their conditioning "bible," something to have on hand at all times and review whenever they have questions about technique or safety points. You will use it with them as a teaching tool, and they will use it during the summer and other times when they don't have access to a coach.

All coaches seek the optimal performance of athletes through strength training and improved flexibility. The concepts outlined in *Building the Total Athlete* and provided in the booklet are important for coaches in all sports because they do much the same thing but go several steps further. They provide a wide range of diversified activities that focus on the unique requirements of different sports, and they provide a comprehensive aerobic and anaerobic program, flexibility exercises, and a nutritional emphasis that result in optimal performances for longer periods of time.

Most important, the student athletes discover the value of good habits, personal discipline, and plain old hard work. They feel good, and they feel good about themselves. For junior and senior high school students, good physical condition and its several benefits result in a willingness to participate in athletics, more energy for studies, increased responsibility, and an improved self-image.

Michael Koehler, Ph.D.
Bruce Hanson

CONTENTS

ABOUT THE AUTHORS   IV

ABOUT THIS BOOK   V

SECTION 1:   1
THE BENEFITS OF TOTAL CONDITIONING

WHAT IS PHYSICAL FITNESS?   2

CONSIDERING THE DEVELOPMENT OF TOTAL FITNESS GOALS   2
    Figure 1-1. Why Physical Fitness? 3
   Why Physical Fitness? 4

CONSIDERING THE ENTIRE FITNESS PROGRAM   4
    Figure 1-2. Understanding Physical Fitness 6
   Providing Feedback 5

HOW GOOD DOES THE ATHLETE WANT TO BE?   7
    Figure 1-3. Physical Fitness and Sports 9

RECOGNIZING PLAYER LIMITATIONS: HOW GOOD CAN THE ATHLETE BE?   8

IMPORTANT DIFFERENCES BETWEEN JUNIOR AND SENIOR HIGH SCHOOL ATHLETES   8

GETTING EVERYONE INVOLVED   10

LOOKING AT CURRENT CONDITIONING LEVELS   11

ASSESSING BODY FAT PERCENTAGE   11

PHYSICAL FITNESS IS NOT THE IMPOSSIBLE DREAM   12
    Figure 1-4. You and Your Body Fat   13
    Figure 1-5. A Word About Competition   14

FOSTERING THE GROWTH OF SELF-DISCIPLINE   15

TRAINING SMART FOR THE PREVENTION OF INJURIES   16
    Emphasizing the Need to "Slow Down Time"   16

LET'S WRAP IT UP   17

SECTION 2:   **19**
STRETCHING FOR PERFECTION

WHY FLEXIBILITY?   19
    Figure 2-1. Why Flexibility?   20
    The What and Why of Flexibility   21
    Figure 2-2. Flexibility Exercises   22
    Figure 2-3. The Key Word Is Safety   27

WARMING UP TO INCREASE BLOOD FLOW   28

WARMING UP THE WELL-CONDITIONED ATHLETE   28

KNOWING WHEN TO STRETCH   29
    Precompetition Flexibility   30
    Flexibility During Competition and Practice   30
    Postcompetition Flexibility   31
    Figure 2-4. Maintaining Your Flexibility   32
    Figure 2-5. The Cool Down   33

TEN TIPS FOR EFFECTIVE STRETCHING   31
    Figure 2-6. Ten Tips for Effective Stretching   34

STRETCHING WHENEVER YOU FEEL LIKE IT   35

AN INTERVIEW WITH CAROL MYERS   35

LET'S WRAP IT UP   37

SECTION 3:
THE COACH'S PLEDGE
39

CLARIFYING THE PURPOSES OF THE CONDITIONING PROGRAM AND THE COACH'S ROLE   40

EXPLAINING THE RELATIONSHIP BETWEEN TRAINING RULES AND GENERAL FITNESS   40
    Figure 3-1. Being a Total Athlete   41
   Process Is the Thing   42
    Figure 3-2. Some Straight Talk About Training Rules   43

THE ATHLETE'S PLEDGE   44
    Figure 3-3. The Athlete's Pledge   45

THE COACH'S PLEDGE   44
    Figure 3-4. The Coach's Pledge   46

MODELING THE RIGHT WAY   47

KEEPING THE PARENTS PLUGGED IN   47
   Early Notification   48
   Ongoing Notification   48
   End-of-the-Year Notification   48
    Figure 3-5. Sample Letter of Invitation   49
    Figure 3-6. FITNESS-Gram   50
    Figure 3-7. What PHYSICAL FITNESS Can Accomplish   51

MAINTAINING PERSPECTIVE   52

AN INTERVIEW WITH GEORGE KELLY, COACH OF FOUR NATIONAL CHAMPIONSHIP FOOTBALL
   TEAMS AT THE UNIVERSITIES OF NEBRASKA AND NOTRE DAME   52

LET'S WRAP IT UP   54

SECTION 4:
STRENGTHENING THE HEART AND LUNGS
55

HOW IMPORTANT IS CARDIOVASCULAR EFFICIENCY?   55
   A Word About Proper Equipment   57
   The Specifics of Aerobic Training   57
   Distinguishing Between General Fitness and Competitive Training   58

RELATING AEROBIC TO ANAEROBIC CONDITIONING   59
    Figure 4-1. Fitness Training: For What Purpose?   60
   A Reminder About Warming Up   61

AEROBIC ACTIVITY FOR WEIGHT REDUCTION   62

    Figure 4-2. Is Weight Loss Your Goal?   63

    Figure 4-3. Burning Off the Calories   65

    Avoiding Dramatic Weight Changes   66

TRAINING AEROBICALLY   67

    Aerobic Training and the Total Athlete   67

INTERVAL TRAINING   68

    Figure 4-4. Interval Training   69

STAYING FIT AEROBICALLY   70

    Figure 4-5. Off-Season Workout: Soccer, Football, Field Hockey   71

    Figure 4-6. Off-Season Workout: Basketball, Volleyball, Badminton, and Track   72

    Figure 4-7. Off-Season Workout: Baseball, Softball, Field Events   73

    Figure 4-8. Off-Season Workout: Wrestling, Gymnastics, and Swimming   74

REPLACING BODY FLUIDS   75

    Figure 4-9. Complementary Exercises got Both In- and Off-Season Workouts   76

    Figure 4-10. Your Need for Water   78

A REMINDER TO THE JUNIOR HIGH COACH   79

LET'S WRAP IT UP   80

SECTION 5:   81
STRENGTH TRAINING: EXPLANATIONS AND PROGRAMS

INTRODUCTION   81

MUSCLES PLAY A BIG ROLE   82

ALWAYS WARM UP   82

THE WHAT AND WHY OF BELTS   83

LET'S CUT DOWN ON INJURIES   83

    Figure 5-1. Warming-Up Exercises   84

    Figure 5-2. Use a BELT!!   86

    Figure 5-3. Pain vs. Fatigue   88

    Figure 5-4. Athletic Permit Card   89

PROPER FORM CREATES SUBSTANCE   92

    Proper Form to Increase Strength   92

A WORD ABOUT BREATHING   93

CONSIDERING NEEDS OF JUNIOR HIGH STUDENTS   94

STRENGTH TRAINING WITHOUT WEIGHTS: MANUAL MOVEMENTS   94

Figure 5-5. Exercises for the Abdominals   95

Figure 5-6. Your Complete Workout   101

WHERE YOU ARE AND WHERE YOU WANT TO BE   108

Figure 5-7. Where Do You Want to Be?   109

WHAT ARE AEROBIC AND MAXIMAL MUSCLE STRENGTH?   110

Determining Maximums   110

WEIGHT TRAINING FOR IMPROVED PERFORMANCE   111

Figure 5-8. Weightlifting Programs   112

REGARDING THE PROGRAMS   116

Level A   116

Level B   116

Level C   116

Level D   116

LET'S WRAP IT UP   117

SECTION 6:   **119**
STRENGTH TRAINING: FOCUSING ON THE ACTUAL EXERCISES

DESCRIPTIONS OF EXERCISES   119

Figure 6-1. Descriptions of Exercises   120

THE DOWNSIDE OF BODY MASS   136

CAN ATHLETES OVERTRAIN?   136

THE COMPUTER IS YOUR FRIEND   137

SPORT-SPECIFIC CHARTS   137

Figure 6-2. Sport-Specific Exercises   138

A WORD ABOUT MYTHS   150

WHAT ARE THE OTHER ELEMENTS OF THE COACH'S ROLE?   151

Figure 6-3. Something to Think About   152

LET'S WRAP IT UP   153

Figure 6-4. If You Want Total Conditioning, You Need   154

SECTION 7:   **155**
EATING YOUR WAY TO SUPERIOR PERFORMANCE

HOW DOES NUTRITION FIT INTO THE BIG PICTURE?   155

Rethinking the Importance of Nutrition   156

THE CHEMISTRY OF EATING AND EXERCISING 156
Using Common Sense with Nutrition 157

Figure 7-1. Eating Your Way to Improved Performance 158

WHAT COACHES MUST KNOW 159
Understanding Nutrients 159

Proteins Help Balance The Diet 160

A Word About Amino Acids 160

Figure 7-2. Proteins and Protein Supplements 161
What About Amino Acid Supplements? 162
How Much Protein Is Enough? 163

BULKING UP THE RIGHT WAY 163

THE FLIPSIDE: LOSING WEIGHT THE RIGHT WAY 164
The Reality of Eating Disorders 165

THE DIET DURING STRENUOUS EXERCISE 165

THE PREGAME MEAL 166

A FEW MYTHS ABOUT NUTRITION 166
Figure 7-3. Practice and Diet 167

Figure 7-4. The Pregame Meal 168

LET'S WRAP IT UP 170

SECTION 8: **171**
DRUGS: KEEP SAYING NO

WHAT IS A DRUG? 172

DON'T BE THE VICTIM OF SOMEONE ELSE'S NEEDS 172
Peer Group 173

Figure 8-1. A Few Words About Peer Groups 174
Parents 175
The Community 175

TOBACCO AND ALCOHOL ARE DRUGS 175

WHY ARE SOME DRUGS HARMFUL? 176
Figure 8-2. Alcohol and Tobacco: Something to Think About 177

THE CASE AGAINST COCAINE 178
Figure 8-3. Taking a Closer Look at Marijuana 179

Figure 8-4. The Case Against Cocaine and Other Drugs 180

OTHER DRUGS AND WHY THEY HURT PERFORMANCE 181

THE CASE AGAINST STEROIDS — 182

HOW WIDESPREAD ARE STEROIDS? — 182

A FEW WARNING SIGNS — 182
   Figure 8-5. The Warning Signs of Drug Use   184

WRITTEN REFERRALS — 185

WHERE DOES THE SCHOOL STAND ON DRUG USE? — 185
   Figure 8-6. Writing Referrals   186

GOOD COMMUNICATION IS A MUST — 187

WHERE DO THE ATHLETES STAND? — 188

SELF-WORTH AS A DETERRENT TO SELF-INDULGENCE — 189

LET'S WRAP IT UP — 189

SECTION 9:
BEYOND ATHLETICS — **191**

TOTAL CONDITIONING AS A WAY OF LIFE — 192
   Figure 9-1. Interested in Total Fitness?   193

TAKING A CAREFUL LOOK AT STRESS — 194
   Self-Talk   195

LOOKING AT EXERCISE AND SLEEP — 195

THE DOWNSIDE OF SUNTANNING — 196
   Figure 9-2. Getting Enough Sleep?   197
   Figure 9-3. Think Twice About That Suntan!   198

A WORD ABOUT VISUALIZATION — 199
   How Thinking Improves Performance   199
   Figure 9-4. Need Practice Time? Visualize It!   200

LIFELONG FITNESS FOR ENDURANCE — 201

BEYOND ATHLETICS TOWARD SELF-DISCIPLINE — 202

LET'S WRAP IT UP — 202
   Figure 9-5. Fitness: Exhilaration, Not Exhaustion   203

SECTION 10:
SELLING THE PROGRAM — **205**

INTRODUCTION — 205

FIRST THINGS FIRST: SELLING THE PROGRAM TO STUDENTS — 205

Making Fitness Necessary and Fun   205

Taking Responsibility for Your Own Life   207

Making the Right Kinds of Friends   207

Figure 10-1. Take Control of Your Life   208

These Statistics Don't Lie   209

Figure 10-2. New Kid on the Block?   210

Teenagers Are Especially Susceptible   211

Figure 10-3. Everything in Moderation!!   212

ADVERTISING PREVENTION AND TREATMENT OF INJURIES   213
Selling Total Fitness   213

A Word About Treatment   214

Promoting Maintenance of Fitness   214

Talking About Playing Through Pain   215

When Athletes Imagine or Fabricate Pain   216

Maintaining an Objective Approach   216

Figure 10.4 DON'T Play with Pain!   217

AVOIDING ONE-SPORT ATHLETES   218

SELLING THE PROGRAM TO ADULTS   219
Reduction of Injuries   219

Figure 10-5. The Athlete's Need for Total Fitness   220

Needs of Female Athletes   221

GETTING INTO THE COMMUNITY   221
Figure 10-6. Community Contact   223

Figure 10-7. Contacting Businesses   225

Keeping the Program Visible   224

LET'S WRAP IT UP   226
Figure 10-8. Press Release   227

APPENDIX: TOTAL FITNESS BOOKLET

Section One

THE BENEFITS
OF TOTAL CONDITIONING

First, a quick story. To lead, we must first learn to obey. This is especially evident in sports, where leaders, both adolescent and adult, must model the self-discipline and restraint that result in personal and team growth. Because most adolescents are groping through the developmental tangle of their lives to find a sense of who they are, they have problems with this notion.

Their problems sometimes involve an inability to distinguish between leadership and power; some have never learned that control of others is impossible without control of self. We worked with a gifted young wrestler one year who maintained only a passing acquaintanceship with his textbooks but developed a personal relationship with the dean of students. To him, school was an interlude between aggravating the bus driver in the morning and frustrating his opponents on the mat in the afternoon.

Fortunately, his coach realized that the boy's enthusiasm for sports was the tool to accomplish a little "attitude adjustment." It was easy convincing him that a total conditioning program would make him a better wrestler. It was somewhat harder convincing him that his grasp of participial phrases and simple equations was as important as his best wrestling hold. Even more difficult was getting him to reflect the sensitivity and restraint that define genuine toughness.

So his coach took him to a local university during the off-season to see the weight room, to watch a workout, to tour the athletic study halls, to meet the coach, and to talk to a couple of wrestlers. The coach followed the tour with a conversation with the athlete and his parents and was pleased to observe a change in his behavior the following school year. Much of the change resulted from his commitment to a total conditioning program. The self-discipline that resulted spilled over into his studies and personal behavior.

The change didn't occur overnight and resulted as much from simple maturation as the coach's continued vigilance, but a lot sprang from the university visit, the influence of other coaches and athletes, and the self-discipline that issues from hard work and commitment. A total conditioning program, therefore, considers the entire student athlete, defines strength from a variety of perspectives, and emphasizes its wise use.

What Is Physical Fitness?

There is no single best definition of physical fitness, primarily because we seek it for so many different reasons. The fitness requirements of a world-class marathoner are a whole lot different from those of a middle-aged schoolteacher. The exercises we do, therefore, will vary, depending upon our individual needs.

The term also differs from "good health" to the extent that good health suggests a simple absence of illness, and physical fitness implies the energy and strength levels to seek and find our goals in life. Physical fitness certainly contributes to good health, but good health doesn't guarantee physical fitness and its opportunites to accomplish the activities that are so important to us.

Physical fitness, therefore, is a way to realize our values and to influence our self-perceptions—not just to feel good, but to feel good *about* ourselves. The work it involves can have an effect as significant on the self-concepts of young athletes as on their strength levels. Let's define physical fitness, then, as a *condition of general health that provides the energy and strength needed to work hard, and to pursue and achieve personal goals.* For some, these goals may relate to a demanding academic program or a stressful career. For our purposes, however, they relate primarily to appearance and athletic performance.

Considering the Development of Total Fitness Goals

Obviously, the attainability of a young athlete's goals is an important first consideration. "Shooting for the moon and settling for the top of the barn" is appropriate for all young athletes. Others, however, won't settle for anything less than the moon. Such youngsters sometimes reflect a serious departure from reality. Most youngsters use occasional dreams to brighten a drab daily routine or to visualize a likely future. Others use them to fortify weak self-concepts. In both instances, dreams can serve a very important purpose by providing a desirable and perhaps realistic alternative to a current reality.

Some few, however, confuse dreams with reality; they live in the proverbial "dream world." Such students require the attention of coaches and others in the building to estabish realistic expectations of themselves. The weight room is no place for grandiosity. Coaches must work closely with their athletes during conditioning activities, therefore, to guarantee exercises appropriate to their strength and developmental levels. The reproducible in figure 1-1 can be very useful in this regard. Coaches should distribute it early each season.

Figure 1-1

WHY PHYSICAL FITNESS?

INTRODUCTION

Physical fitness is different from general health. Good health implies an absence of sickness; your general health may be pretty good. But your physical fitness may not be good enough to realize many of the goals you have established for yourself. That's why we offer this fitness program, to enable you to develop the cardiovascular and muscular strength to achieve your goals, many of which deal with sports. Other goals probably deal with community activities and coursework. Physical fitness will provide the energy and strength you need to engage successfully in a wide range of activities. It will also encourage you to develop the self-discipline you may need to improve your athletic performance as well as your success in class.

KEEP IN MIND

If you are a beginner: Don't push yourself too hard right away. You have lots of time to achieve the fitness levels you want. Excellent physical fitness doesn't occur overnight. You can't take a pill to get there in a day or two. Even if such a pill were available, you wouldn't want to take it anyway. The *process* of developing a physically fit body involves a lot of good times. The associations you develop with fellow students, teachers, and coaches will bring you a great deal of pleasure, and the hard work you experience will give you genuine feelings of accomplishment.

So don't look for an easy way. There isn't one, just a lot of enjoyable—and hard—work, but it will involve the kind of experience that will make you proud of who you are and who you are becoming.

ALSO REMEMBER

Work closely with your coach and fellow students. We will be emphasizing some very important safety pointers as we engage in running and lifting exercises. Pay careful attention to them. You don't want an unnecessary injury interfering with your training or performance in one or more areas. And remember that we all have different potential fitness levels. Don't develop the habit of comparing yourself with others. Stay with the program that is right for you. We will work closely with you to develop a program tailored specifically for you. Stick with it. The only person you're competing with is *you*. It's a competition you'll never lose if you work out with the right attitude.

Good luck with your program, and any time you have questions, be sure to contact your coach.

© 1995 by Michael D. Koehler

Why Physical Fitness?

The answer to this question becomes fairly obvious when athletes are introduced to conditioning activities in a particular sport. Mike's football coach at the University of Nebraska, Bob Devaney, created an unforgettable reality during the first day of every fall practice. Devaney required all the linemen to run a mile in full pads in under 6 minutes and 45 seconds, the backs in under 6 minutes. Anyone who staggered in late was "awarded" additional sprints after future practices and, if weight was the problem, put on a restricted diet at the training table.

Mike is quick to admit that jogging daily in the summer was the occupational equivalent of forced overtime, but, like overtime, it got the job done. Most players were in shape when they reported to practice in the fall, and Coach Devaney was able to refine player skills rather than work on conditioning. And the one or two of us who failed to heed Coach's warnings learned quickly that it was a whole lot easier to jog in the summer than sprint in the fall.

Poorly conditioned athletes are tired enough after a long preseason practice, but when they have the additional task of running wind sprints while their teammates are heading for lemonade, they learn a hard lesson. It's easier to maintain a car than buy a new one each year. Good fitness habits are mechanics that work for nothing. Just get them started, and they provide periodic tuneups to maintain peak performance—without the physical costs that come with unnecessary repairs and tuneups. To promote such habits in our athletes, we must provide the right process.

Considering the Entire Fitness Program

Whether junior or senior high or adult, anyone who engages in physical activity, particularly if it is strenuous, must experience three stages of development. As identified by R.M. Fitts, a prominent sports physiologist, some 30 years ago, the first stage is *cognitive*. Any athlete must first understand the skills needed to perform the activity. Such understanding is as critical for running and lifting weights as for throwing a baseball or shooting a basketball.

In one sense, this is a relatively easy part of total fitness. Much of it can involve videotapes, movies, demonstrations, anything to enhance the athlete's understanding of the why and how of exercise. Even the initial attempts to practice the skills are controlled and usually involve light weights or short sessions. Feedback from a coach or, later, a teammate is essential during this phase if young athletes are to develop correct habits. Without the understanding that results from this cognitive phase, young athletes experience more injuries and fewer benefits from their exercise programs.

Figure 1-2 explains this phase to young athletes and should be included in the booklet you eventually develop for them. It is written clearly and simply in order to accommodate the cognitive developmental levels of young junior high students. Once the athletes understand the why and how of exercise, they are prepared to experience the much longer *associative* phase. This phase is characterized by repeated practice and ongoing feedback from the coach. The coach's goal is to complement external evaluation with the athlete's self-evaluation in order to improve his or her own performance and to ultimately master the skill(s).

As the associative phase is completed, athletes find themselves thinking less and less about their performance. When they are capable of performing a skill at a high level of proficiency without giving it any thought, they are in the *autonomous* stage. All of us have reached the autonomous stage in one activity or another—when halfbacks take handoffs, basketball players dribble, shortstops field ground balls, and most adults drive cars.

Young athletes have achieved it when they automatically stretch before strenuous exercise, bend at the knees when lifting heavy weights from the floor, or steer clear of fast-food restaurants. The coach's job is to provide enough associative (practice) experiences to promote each athlete's autonomous growth—for our purposes, when performing fitness skills safely and effectively.

Providing Feedback

Feedback is very important throughout this process. When performing certain skills, athletes know immediately how they have done. The tennis player misses his or her first shot; the shortstop throws the ball over the first baseman's head; the basketball player misses the jump shot; and the young weightlifter is unable to lift the weight. Such feedback is called *intrinsic*; it is evident within the task.

Extrinsic feedback is necessary when the athlete sees that she has missed the jump shot or dropped the weight—but doesn't know why. At this point, a coach or knowledgeable teammate is needed to provide necessary information. This kind of feedback should be immediate. The sooner it is given, the sooner the athlete is motivated to attempt the skill the correct way and practice it again.

Extrinsic feedback takes different forms:

• *Feedback that corrects.* When the young athlete forgets to stretch before vigorous exercise or bends at the waist to lift heavy weights from the floor, he or she requires immediate corrective feedback. Early in the cognitive or associative periods, such feedback should come from the coach because of his or her authority. It should emphasize—sometimes vigorously—the correct way to perform the skill. Once the athletes understand the skills and can perform them correctly, corrective feedback can come from teammates, is required less often, and generally involves increasingly complex skills.

• *Feedback that praises.* Praise is important for two reasons; it helps motivate and it promotes conforming behaviors. Generic praise—"Way to go, Sue!" or "Great job, Tom!"—is not only reinforcing to Sue and Tom but encouraging to everyone else to try to imitate them. When Tom bends at the knees to lift the weight from the floor—"Excellent, Tom; you've been listening!"—everyone in earshot will try to do the same thing. This kind of praise, therefore, is effective when teaching your entire team the correct way to execute specific skills, when you want them all to conform to a correct behavior.

Remember, however, that praise is ineffective, sometimes even counterproductive, when used to reinforce one athlete for something others are unable to do. The

Figure 1-2

UNDERSTANDING PHYSICAL FITNESS

PAYING ATTENTION

Any good fitness program involves detailed explanations of exercises. If you want to get the maximum benefit from the exercise program you develop, be sure to pay careful attention to all the explanations. We probably will be using videotapes and demonstrations throughout the entire program, so listen carefully and ask questions whenever you don't understand something. Your failure to understand even one direction may result in injury or your inability to realize a fitness goal.

THE PROCESS

Every part of the fitness program begins with explanations. As indicated, your understanding of them is essential if you are to be successful in realizing your fitness goals. As important, however, you will be expected at some time in the future to help other students as they follow their programs. For example, you may "spot" for someone while he or she is bench-pressing. To be a good helper or "spotter," you will have to know correct technique and be able to provide specific advice or general suggestions. The actual practice of the exercises we will be using may take a long time, and we will need help from everyone. Be sure you understand as much as possible about each explanation; it will help you as well as that someone else you will be helping.

© 1995 by Michael D. Koehler

mature seventh grader who can bench-press 150 pounds 10 times deserves recognition for his hard work, but it is his hard work that should be rewarded, not the fact that he lifted 150 pounds. For him, specific praise is the answer—"Tom, your hard work is really paying off! The hours you've spent in this room haven't been wasted!" To praise him generically—"Tom, great job!"—may result in an unrealistic standard for the rest of the team, many of whom will be trying to lift 150 pounds once or twice instead of sticking with a lifting regimen that is more realistic and more effective for them.

• *Feedback that teaches a process.* Process feedback corrects an inappropriate action within the context of related skills. Corrective feedback addresses a specific action—"Mary, lower the weight as slowly as you lift it." Process feedback explains as well as corrects—"Mary, you might try less weight on that barbell. You're dropping it too fast. You might hurt yourself, and you're not getting the negative benefit from the exercise."

If Mary's face goes suddenly blank, you know immediately that more cognition is necessary. If Mary is a typical teenager, she probably missed out on some of the earlier explanation. Process feedback has revealed that now is the time to reexplain. Simple corrective feedback may not have uncovered Mary's lack of understanding. Remember, young athletes can know how to perform a skill but not understand it. We want them to understand every skill we expect of them, not just for them but for the rest of the team. In a short time we may want Mary to be able to explain the skill to a teammate.

How Good Does the Athlete Want to Be?

An athlete's commitment to any fitness program is usually a direct reflection of his or her personal and athletic goals. And let's admit it, on more than one occasion it may reflect the coach's ability to motivate athletes to do what "theyreallyoughtawanna." Good coaches not only inspire; they know how to create the conditions and circumstances that capitalize on whatever needs the athlete brings to the sport.

They also recognize, however, that the essential question is how good the *athlete* wants to be. How good the *coach* wants him or her to be is essential to the team's success, but it has less to do with the player's actual motivation. Motivation is dependent primarily on the athlete's needs, not the coach's. This is a critical consideration. As soon as you and I assume responsibility for player motivation, we start trying to create players in our own image and likeness. Leave that to the bible, not the playbook.

Consider this question. Where is the predisposition to grow, in the seed or the farmer? The farmer certainly wants it to grow; the seed's future is inseparable from his own. So he cultivates the soil, nourishes and waters it, clears out the weeds—does whatever he can to promote growth. He does these things because he realizes that the inclination to grow is in the *seed*. So it is with motivation. Coaches promote growth, but the inclination or the disinclination to grow is in the athlete.

How then do we promote growth in athletes? First, like the farmer, we find seeds of good quality and plant them in fertile soil. We find promising athletes and cultivate their talents by encouraging them and providing solid fitness programs. Then we promote their knowledge of physical fitness and associate it with their needs as young athletes. Be sure to coordinate the reproducible in figure 1-3 with others in the book; it is combined with those in other sections to make a complete booklet for each of your athletes (refer to the appendix).

Recognizing Player Limitations: How Good CAN the Athlete Be?

Family history is an important factor in the improvement of athletic performance. The media have us convinced that we are all genetically predetermined by our parents and grandparents. In fact, current research indicates that as many as 2,000 diseases or disorders have been linked to specific genetic predispositions. Such a statistic affects a significant percentage of the American population.

It is particularly significant regarding cardiovascular problems, particularly when we consider what we as coaches are asking our players to do each day. That physical fitness is relative, therefore, is an important consideration. Each of us may be genetically predisposed in certain directions, but other health factors are as important. Young athletes must understand that nutrition, muscular strength and endurance training, and cardiovascular conditioning all play important roles in athletic performance as well as lifelong health.

The reproducible in figure 1-3 clarifies much of this for your athletes. It is an important early page in the booklet because it assures the overweight youngster that he or she doesn't have to be overweight forever. Obesity does tend to run in families, but it is not inevitable. Proper exercise and nutrition can combat family predispositions.

The form also helps the slender athlete understand that proper nutrition and weight training can improve muscle tone and appearance. That members of the same family tend to resemble one another is seen at every parent-teacher night at school. Research shows, however, that genetics is not the sole determinant of physical appearance. Learned habits play an equally important role. The better the habits, the better the assurance that young athletes are not chained to genetic predispositions that are but one influence on their health and fitness potential.

Important Differences Between Junior and Senior High School Athletes

An initial caution: coaches and parents must remember that the average P.E. class in junior and senior high consists of competitive activities and a range of enjoyable activities that introduce students to lifelong recreational sports. They usually are not intended to provide for the general fitness needs of most youngsters. In fact, according to the President's Council on Physical Fitness, only 36 percent of the schools in the country require regular P.E. activities.

Athletic activities and conditioning programs, therefore, provide many youngsters with an important focus on general fitness and good health habits. The activities they provide need not be sport-specific. Junior high school athletes can improve aerobic

Figure 1-3

PHYSICAL FITNESS AND SPORTS

- Did you know that Michael Jordan was originally cut from his high school basketball team?

- Did you know that Wilma Rudolph, one of the greatest Olympic track athletes in history, was bedridden with a leg disease for two years as a child?

- Did you know that Jim Thorpe was only 5'4" and 115 pounds when he started the Carlisle Indian School at the age of 14?

- Did you know that Rockey Bleier was injured so severely in Vietnam that doctors told him he might never walk again? He went on to be the starting halfback for the World Champion Pittsburgh Steelers.

- Did you know that on April 2, 1931, baseball's greatest home run hitter, Babe Ruth, was struck out by Jackie Mitchell? Jackie Mitchell was professional baseball's first *woman* pitcher.

- Did you know that Ray Ewry, the man who won the most Olympic gold medals (10), was an invalid as a child?

The stories of such heroes and heroines in sport are endless. No one will ever really know the thousands of stories of young men and women who overcame tremendous adversity in their lives to achieve greatness as athletes. Nor will we ever know the thousands more stories of young people who overcame adversity just to walk or to be fourth-stringers on a high school track team. Their stories are unknown but every bit as significant, maybe even more dramatic because their efforts were unrecognized.

Most of us are very lucky. We don't have to overcome obstacles in our lives to play a sport. All we have to do is work hard to develop the skills and the necesssary strength to perform to the best of our ability. It really isn't important whether we win gold medals in the Olympics or become professional basketball's greatest players. It *is* important that we work hard and commit ourselves to our coaches, our teammates, and the practice needed to bring out whatever potential we have as athletes.

**OUR FITNESS PROGRAM IS A STEP IN THE RIGHT DIRECTION.
LET US WORK WITH YOU TO HELP YOU BECOME
THE BEST YOU CAN BE.**

© 1995 by Michael D. Koehler

conditioning by swimming, cycling, rowing, or hiking. Such activities satisfy their aerobic needs and promote an interest in exercise and lifelong fitness habits.

Section 5 suggests manual exercises (push-ups, sit-ups, chin-ups) instead of weight training exercises for junior high school athletes. The reasoning involves the physical development of junior high students and the potential for injury to their joints. Improper lifting techniques and unnecessarily heavy weights place undue strain on joints, often resulting in needless injury.

Certainly, some junior high school athletes can use weights, if the weights are not too heavy and the athletes' lifting techniques are correct. Generally speaking, however, younger athletes should be encouraged to perform manual movements that encourage a full range of motion but that lessen the potential for shocking the joints. More of this will be discussed in section 5.

The primary reason for physical fitness programs among junior high youngsters is the promotion of lifelong habits for good health. Secondary school students share this purpose but can realistically begin to focus on one or more sports for competition in high school and, perhaps later, in college. In both junior and senior high, the coach who promotes regular exercise for the nonathletic student has reflected a genuine interest in his or her work.

Getting Everyone Involved

Every child in school should be encouraged to participate in a good fitness program, particularly if much of it is conducted during the summer months. Too many schools emphasize fitness programs only for athletes. In fact, they tend to be sport-specific: summer football, summer baseball, summer basketball. Because some youngsters prefer four-part harmony to three-point stances, they are discouraged from joining such programs and improving their fitness levels.

Encouraging all students to engage in a summer fitness program offers at least two advantages. Students who are currently uninvolved in a sport discover (1) the value of physical fitness and (2) the enjoyment of a particular sport. The advantage for the coach is the effect he or she has on the lifelong fitness habits of a larger number of youngsters as well as the opportunity to interest more players in his or her sports program.

Any junior or senior high school athlete who has the potential and the desire to be an athlete should be involved in a challenging and well-supervised aerobic and strengthening program. Such students are easily motivated, so the coach need control only the pace and intensity of the program to ensure safety and to prevent burnout.

Those students who may be less active should be encouraged to find any exercise they like and stay with it. Most children are not athletically talented and tend to be self-conscious about involvement in physical activities. Because our society holds athletes in such high esteem, a word of encouragement or recognition from a coach goes a long way to engage inactive youngsters.

This same kind word teaches young athletes that physical activities, especially fitness programs, deemphasize competition and focus instead on an active and healthy lifestyle. Any aerobic or strength gain, even from the least talented athlete, can be applauded. Such gains may result from the coach's friendly push in the right direction but must never involve the emotional stress that accompanies fear of failure, the kind of fear that is associated so often with sports competition in our society. Sections 3, 8, and 9 will address competitive stress more fully.

Looking at Current Conditioning Levels

To understand current conditioning levels, coaches and athletes alike must have a general understanding of body fat. The percentage of one's body fat helps define general fitness. Some people jump on and off scales the way others run from one diet to another. Don't get us wrong; our society is loaded with folks who need to lose weight. Estimates indicate that 10 to 25 percent of all teenagers and 25 to 50 percent of all adults in the United States are obese. Obesity is excess body fat.

The problem is, scales and diets alone don't provide answers to questions involving body fat. We have seen 280-pound professional football players who have very low percentages of body fat. Conversely, we have worked with 140-pound high school athletes who have high percentages of body fat. Obviously, the weight scale alone won't tell us which of these athletes is in better condition.

The range of body fat for men is usually from 7 percent, which is very low, to 25 percent, which is high. Permissible levels of body fat for women are higher, from a low of 14 percent to a high of 31 percent. Any man or woman who tests higher than permissible levels is considered obese, and anyone who approaches the high end of the range needs to lose weight. Losing weight is not an issue, therefore, for the 230-pound fullback who has 9 percent body fat, nor for the 180-pound forward on the women's basketball team with 18 percent body fat.

Their aerobic capacity, strength, or flexibility levels may be an issue, but they don't need to lose weight. Any attempt to lose weight could, in fact, create a health risk for both of them. Very active people require a great deal of energy, the result of proper nutrition. Unnecessary or inappropriate dieting can result in improper nutrition, which in turn can affect emotions, the female menstrual cycle, and general health.

The fat cells are the fuel storage tanks of the body. When people take in more calories than they burn, their tanks store excess fat. Too much fat leads to obesity, which leads to a variety of health risks and the inability to perform complex athletic skills. At this point, proper nutrition and weight loss become factors. For specific information regarding each of these issues, refer to section 6.

Assessing Body Fat Percentage

• *Hydrostatic.* The "gold standard" for assessing body fat percentage is the hydrostatic method. Because it involves immersing the entire body in a large tank of water to measure water displacement, it is unrealistic for most junior and senior high school programs. Students who are either curious or concerned, however, about their body fat percentage and want an accurate assessment should make arrangements with their family doctors to have it measured hydrostatically. It is the most accurate method available.

• *Bioelectrical impedance.* This method promises a great deal of usefulness as well. Based on the belief that lean tissue conducts electric current better than fat tissue, this method involves transmitting a small current of electricity from one electrode to another on the same side of the body. The current is then measured according to established formulas.

• *Fatfold.* This is a much simpler method for assessing body fat percentage. It involves lifting or "pinching" the skin with a caliper and measuring the thickness of the skinfold. This method is also limited because it generally involves an accurate caliper and a trained assessor who will not apply too much pressure on the skinfold. Students interested in this method are encouraged to see qualified fitness trainers, physiologists, or their family doctors.

• *"Pinch an inch."* This method is the most simple and the least accurate, but it encourages young athletes to think about body fat percentages in relation to their conditioning levels. We use the reproducible in figure 1-4, therefore, to provide each athlete with a general explanation of body fat and to promote a preliminary focus on the relationship between nutrition and exercise.

Physical Fitness Is NOT the Impossible Dream

Every young athlete has a dream. It involves both appearance and performance, sometimes confuses fact with fantasy, but establishes an imaginary future that, with help from important adults, can result in realistic goals and a real commitment to hard work. It constitutes the essence of each player's motivation, however, and helps transform today's hard worker into tomorrow's blue chipper.

Our job as coaches is to keep the dream alive, to push young athletes within the framework of their physical capabilities but to manage the psychological pressures they often experience in sports. They must never feel they have failed. They may fall short of a strength gain or, in competition, lose a game, but they must never feel like failures. We all lose at one time or another in our lives. Michael Jordan was cut from his high school basketball team. But if we don't think of ourselves as *failures*, we sustain the will to continue striving for our goals. That's why we think the reproducible in figure 1-5 is so important.

Michael Jordan's successes are simply more notable than the equally dramatic accomplishments of "average" athletes. The gangling freshman girl who hopes one day to be a starter on the varsity basketball team and who lifts, eats, runs, and stretches her way toward her goal is as admirable in her own way as Michael Jordan. Her dream was as significant to her, as difficult to achieve—perhaps more so—and as dramatic in its attempt.

More dramatically, the fat little boy who gathers the courage to walk through the door of the weight room in order to realize a fitness dream and commits himself to his goal is to be encouraged and admired by everyone—especially his coach. Coaches should take interest in such youngsters and interact with them about their progress. Such students may never magically be transformed into All-Staters. They may never

Figure 1-4

YOU AND YOUR BODY FAT

Although "You and Your Body Fat" is a topic you'd rather avoid, it involves some serious thinking for all of us, especially young athletes. Excess body fat can cause problems with general health, appearance, and athletic performance. Because you have joined this fitness program to improve your appearance and performance, you'll want to know as much as possible about body fat and how to get rid of it.

First, you have to know what it is. When you take in more calories than you burn, your body stores the excess as body fat. Fat cells are the fuel storage tanks of the body. The only way to get rid of such fuel is to use it as a form of energy. That's why working out helps improve both strength and appearance. We will be discussing exercise and nutrition throughout the program in order to help you control body fat. You also have to know how to measure it in order to determine if you need to reduce your body fat. The *best* way to measure body fat is to see your family doctor to have the appropriate techniques used.

In the meantime, you can get an estimate of your body fat percentage by "Pinching an Inch"! It is the least accurate method, but it will give you a general idea of the possible percentage of body fat you are carrying around with you! Here's how you do it: pinch a fold of skin between your thumb and forefinger, then use the following tables to estimate your percentage of body fat. The best places on your body to "pinch an inch" are—for men—the chest, abdomen, and thigh and—for women—the upper hip, triceps, and thigh.

Fatfold Estimates	Men	Women
1/4"	5–9%	8–13%
1/2"	9–13%	13–18%
3/4"	13–18%	18–23%
1"	18–22%	23–28%
1 1/4"	22–27%	28–33%

Fat Level	Men	Women
Very low	7–10%	14–17%
Low	10–13%	17–20%
Average	13–17%	20–27%
High	17–25%	27–31%
Very high	over 25%	over 31%

Remember this: you may weigh a lot, but you may not have excessive body fat. Many athletes are well over 250 pounds but are carrying normal ranges of body fat. That's why it's important to see your family doctor if you think that weight loss is necessary. It may not be, or you may not have to lose as much as you think! Dieting for the sake of dieting can rob the body of necessary nutrients and actually harm you.

WHEN IN DOUBT, SEE YOUR DOCTOR.

© 1995 by Michael D. Koehler

Figure 1-5

A WORD ABOUT COMPETITION

Think about this: Competition has become a nasty word in some parts of our society. It has been blamed for the abuses that have happened and, unfortunately, continue to happen in college athletics. The *win-at-all-costs* mentality that motivates some college coaches has resulted in many students being used only for their athletic ability without any regard for their academic and career interests and needs.

To some extent these accusations are true. In fact, many coaches and young athletes seem unfamiliar with the philosophy of Vince Lombardi, who said: "Winning isn't everything. The *will* to win is everything." What Lombardi meant was this: The work we put into a contest, the desire that marks our effort, and our commitment to be everything we can be are much more important than winning a game or an event. Our *willingness* to practice and prepare for a contest is the ultimate victory, even if the contest itself is lost.

What does all this mean? It means simply that you can *never* be a failure. That's right. Whenever you commit yourself to a goal and work as hard as you can for that goal, even if you don't reach it, you are not a failure. Failures give up; they don't try. They accept falling short of their goals, so they no longer make an effort to reach them. Just think about it. Every time you work hard for something, you guarantee yourself that you will not be a failure. All it takes is the hard work.

And it means more: It means ultimately that you can't lose, especially as you find yourself involved in our fitness program! You will be competing only with yourself. The harder you work, the more you win. Remember, you are not competing with anyone else in the program. You will work on a program that fits your needs, and you will measure your improvement against your earlier performance.

Remember: Just the act of working hard means that you cannot be a failure! Follow all our safety procedures but work as hard as you can. *You can't help but be a winner!*

© 1995 by Michael D. Koehler

even become players, but they are models of commitment and ready examples of the real possibilities that inhere in the "impossible dream."

Fostering the Growth of Self-Discipline

The coach who feels that discipline is exclusively his or her responsibility had better reconsider the term. Certainly, we must establish expectations of behavior and reasonable and effective consequences for violators. This kind of external discipline is necessary for coaches and athletes alike to be able to focus on their primary goal which is the improvement of their individual and team performance, during practice and competition.

That's why we commit time early in the season for team discussions of rules regarding cutting practice, being late, swearing, criticizing teammates, fighting, even such specifics as sideline behavior and dress for away contests. "Setting the tone" is extremely important for any successful program, but the expectations and consequences that govern player behavior are just the first step in a process that results in *self*-governance.

Self-governance provides the internal discipline that characterizes great athletes and successful athletic programs. Ultimately, it is a term synonymous with other terms like commitment, class, and self-esteem. Self-esteem, for example, is not a gift from loving parents but a personal victory that is achieved only by overcoming obstacles like egotism and self-indulgence. Coaches promote the development of self-esteem when they help young athletes earn their dreams by working hard.

Dreams may be created in moments of leisure; they are realized, however, during hours of effort. Coaches teach this lesson when they develop conditioning programs that promote such effort and that lead to improved physical appearance and athletic performance. Nothing helps a young athlete make the connection between hard work and accomplishment like a good conditioning program.

When athletes realize the benefits of such hard work and commit to more of it, they are well on their way to self-discipline. It is the only kind of discipline that ever really works. Coaches who like to control and who rely on external discipline assume a mighty responsibility. Like lion tamers, they must be highly visible and must occasionally crack the whip to provoke the right behaviors in their athletes. Lions don't routinely jump on and off rolling barrels unless prompted, just as young athletes don't routinely spend an hour and a half in the weight room—unless they are self-disciplined.

Internal discipline is the core of commitment. It is the stimulus to action for those of us who don't depend upon, or require, others for direction. And it has little to do with external punishment. In fact, it is to external punishment what conscience is to a cattle prod. The more we develop it in our athletes, the less we have to ride herd on them.

Such development is not easily accomplished, and it is dependent on parental involvement, but a well-designed conditioning program can do wonders to teach young athletes the benefits of self-discipline. And once they see what it does for them, they learn to apply it in other areas of their lives. This book, then, provides the specifics of a conditioning program that develops young athletes in a variety of ways.

Training Smart for the Prevention of Injuries

In addition to developing them, it helps maintain conditioning levels and prevents injuries. The prevention of injuries is one of the strongest selling points to the athletes, as well as to parents and the school's administration. We were associated with a high school football program several years ago that lost a string of games one season due to critical injuries. Five key players separated or otherwise injured their shoulders.

The introduction next year of a comprehensive weight program strengthened every part of the players' bodies so that separated shoulders as well as twisted ankles and knees were virtually eliminated. This is not to say that someone didn't occasionally turn an ankle, but such injuries weren't epidemic. The team was able to win more games, but more important, the players maintained a level of physical conditioning that averted that rash of aches and pains that might have accompanied the onset of middle age.

Emphasizing the Need to "Slow Down Time"

As indicated earlier and recurrently throughout this book, "safety first" is a key principle in any conditioning program. One of the best ways to teach this principle is to relate it to other areas of athletic performance. Encourage your players to look at it this way. Great athletes slow down time. Many of them do it naturally, but some are taught to "see more" during the actual performance of their skills.

Great divers like Greg Louganis "see" exactly where they are in space during a dive. The world is not a blur to them as they twist and spin through space before hitting the water. Great ball carriers like Walter Payton "saw" blockers and tacklers in front of them as they ran through the line of scrimmage. And great hitters like Ted Williams "saw" the ball as it left the pitcher's hand. They all "slowed down time" during the actual performance of their athletic skills.

Certainly, such skills are, in large part, a perceptual gift from God, but they can be taught to the extent that young athletes can learn to focus on what they are doing at any given moment. Consider weightlifting. The youngster who "hoists" the weight and lets it fall to its original position probably does more harm than good to his or her muscles. Weights must be lifted slowly, deliberately, in order to maximize muscle contractions.

Flexibility exercises must be executed just as deliberately or else the athlete can damage muscles. In fact, young athletes must realize that gains in all areas of a conditioning program—flexibility, cardiovascular, and muscular—must be made progressively. Concentration and focus are key words for all of us, but especially for youngsters as they work to improve their performance as athletes.

Once they develop such concentration, they also learn to "slow down time" when confronted with unusual circumstances in life. Learning to avoid an automobile accident, an argument with a spouse, or a fight with one of life's losers starts with the ability to concentrate, to develop the self-control that is so essential to all of us. Some of it, at least, can be learned through athletic participation.

Let's Wrap It Up

The hazards of body fat are well documented; in fact, the media are beating it to death. For our purposes, however, let's be quick to acknowledge one important fact. If excessive, body fat detracts from personal appearance, is a health hazard, and inhibits athletic performance. It also negatively affects such "motor fitness" characteristics as speed, agility, and eye-hand and eye-foot coordination.

The fitness program outlined in this book, therefore, is designed to reduce body fat while it enhances cardiovascular and muscular strength. The total program addresses endurance and strength training, nutrition, and flexibility—the four essential components of effective fitness programs. It also promotes self-discipline in young athletes, the kind of discipline that carries over into schoolwork and personal behavior and results in a lifelong commitment to positive mental and physical health and to vigorous fitness habits.

Section Two

STRETCHING

FOR PERFECTION

First, a quick story. Back in the days before face masks, when a weight program for football meant push-ups during calisthenics and water on hot days was for sissies, stretching exercises were about as common as triple reverses. The result was a level of inflexibility that produced muscle tears and limited performance. Therapy (if we can call it that) was abstracted into the favorite saying of coaches at the time: "Wrap it up and run on it."

Because few high schools at the time provided comprehensive fitness programs for their athletes, many of us middle-agers are walking around today with torn hamstrings and serious cases of tendonitis. The pain may still be worth the memories, but occasional muscle inflammation is an avoidable reminder of the good old days.

Why Flexibility?

Torn hamstrings and tendonitis, as dramatic as they may be to all those ex-jocks out there, are only two of the many reasons to encourage young athletes to stretch out their muscles before vigorous exercise. The primary reason is to promote a full range of bodily motion throughout an activity. A well-stretched muscle has greater elasticity and helps throw a ball farther or cover a distance faster. The longer and quicker the stride of any athlete, the faster he or she runs.

The reproducible in figure 2-1, therefore, is important for young athletes, most of whom are too impatient to invest enough time in flexibility exercises. The twenty minutes it encourages will do wonders for their performance and help prevent unnecessary injuries. Illusions of immortality prevent most young athletes from thanking you

Figure 2-1

WHY FLEXIBILITY?

FLEXIBILITY AND TOTAL CONDITIONING

Cardiovascular and weight training are just two of the four components of a good conditioning program. They tend to be the most publicized, so most young athletes overlook the benefits of good nutrition and flexibility. A future section of your booklet explains the value of good nutrition. For now, let's look at the benefits of improved flexibility.

HOW GOOD DO YOU WANT TO BE?

Let's put it this way: you'll never even come close to your true athletic potential if you don't work hard to improve your flexibility. Your performance will be limited because your body won't enjoy a full range of motion, and you'll find yourself injured more often than your more flexible teammates. Flexible muscles have greater elasticity, more snap; they enable you to take longer, quicker strides, to jump further and higher. And they are able to withstand the punishment that athletic competition imposes on your body.

SOME MORE SPECIFICS

Vigorous exercise causes forceful contraction of muscles and tendons. Well-stretched muscles provide greater force in each movement, thereby improving agility and speed. In addition, because flexibility prevents muscles from tightening up quickly, it reduces the potential for injury.

SO WHAT DO YOU DO?

It's simple. Develop the habit of warming up your muscles and stretching them for 20 to 30 seconds *before, during,* and *after* competition. When you improve flexibility before and during vigorous exercise, you improve performance and reduce the possibility of injury to muscles and tendons. When you stretch after vigorous exercise, you help eliminate some of the chemicals in your muscles that make them sore the next day. Stretching, therefore, is a very important, if misunderstood, aspect of total conditioning. Great athletes have developed the habit of warming up and stretching their muscles.

If you want to be a great athlete, remember to do the same thing. And remember not to hurry the exercises. Do them slowly and steadily—deliberately—in order to get the most out of them. I'll help with a periodic reminder.

REMEMBER:
GOOD FLEXIBILITY BEFORE, DURING,
AND AFTER VIGOROUS EXERCISE

© 1995 by Michael D. Koehler

now, but years from now when middle-aged friends are battling trick knees, they just might remember you with renewed respect. The reproducible is one of the first pages in the booklet of exercises you will find in the appendix of the book.

The What and Why of Flexibility

Flexibility is accomplished in different ways, some of which are better than others. Obviously, the best exercises stretch muscles gradually without pain or the potential for injury. Following are four different approaches, the first three of which are the best:

• *Static stretching.* The static approach involves the gradual lengthening of a muscle until it extends beyond its normal length. The operational word is *gradual.* The impatience of young athletes and their superficial understanding of technique can result in serious problems if stretching exercises are done improperly. Coaches should help them understand that muscle(s) should be stretched to the point of discomfort, not pain. Then, the stretch should be held for 10 to 20 seconds, keeping in mind that the longer the stretch is maintained, the easier it is for the muscle to adapt to that length.

The static exercises in figure 2-2 provide a complete flexibility program for the young athlete who must perform stretching exercises alone. They are included with figure 2-1 in the booklet for distribution to each of your athletes. As with all exercises, the important principle is "Safety First." Any time an athlete feels pain, therefore, he or she should report to you. The pain may signal improper performance of the exercise or a damaged muscle.

• *Active stretching.* Active stretching exercises are performed without a partner. They involve the kinds of exercises provided in figure 2-2 and generally can be performed anywhere and any time the athlete wants to achieve greater flexibility.

• *Passive stretching.* This kind of stretching involves the use of a partner. It is appropriate for team sports and involves a range of exercises that can be done prior to practice or competition. Many teams incorporate passive stretching exercises into their daily calisthenics. They don't take long and provide the flexibility athletes need to avoid injury.

Use selected exercises from figure 2-2 to incorporate into your passive exercise program. Explain each carefully to your players. The "Safety First" principle is particularly important with these kinds of flexibility exercises. Horseplay in the locker room may be unavoidable, but it cannot be tolerated with passive stretching exercises. *A moment of carelessness could result in serious injury.* That's why the reproducible in figure 2-3 is included; it underscores the importance of safety and also provides documentation should an athlete be injured.

• *Ballistic stretching.* The ballistic approach involves a bouncing motion that forces a quicker and perhaps longer stretch of the muscle. It uses the same exercises as in static stretching but forces the muscle to lengthen more quickly. Because ballistic exercises of any kind carry a greater potential for injury, we recommend they be avoided at all times. When doing static or passive stretching, therefore, young athletes should be reminded to avoid a ballistic approach during the actual exercise.

Figure 2-2

FLEXIBILITY EXERCISES

DIRECTIONS:

The following 33 flexibility exercises are self-explanatory. Look carefully at each diagram and perform the exercise as illustrated. You may perform all or some of them, depending upon your coach's instructions. The important thing is that you increase the flexibility of the muscles you will be using during practice or competition. Talk to your coach about the exercises that he or she wants you to emphasize.

© 1995 by Michael D. Koehler

Figure 2-2 (cont.)

© 1995 by Michael D. Koehler

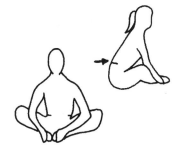

Figure 2-2 (cont.)

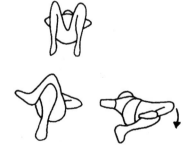

© 1995 by Michael D. Koehler

Figure 2-2 (cont.)

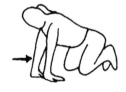

© 1995 by Michael D. Koehler

Figure 2-2 (cont.)

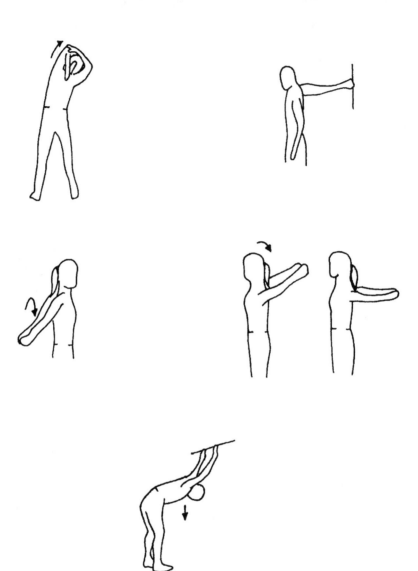

© 1995 by Michael D. Koehler

© 1995 by Michael D. Koehler

Figure 2-3

THE KEY WORD IS SAFETY

Flexibility is a significant part of our conditioning program because it promotes the full range of motion that results in improved performance and the reduced potential for injury. Unfortunately, if performed carelessly, flexibility exercises can cause injury. Our job is to make sure that doesn't happen.

Some Information

Following is an explanation of the different forms of flexibility exercises. Your understanding of each one will be the best first step in avoiding injury:

• *Active*. Active stretching involves the kinds of exercises you can peform alone. Study each of the stretching exercises in your booklet carefully before doing them. Your improved understanding of them will significantly reduce any possibility of injury.

• *Passive*. Passive exercises involve the use of a partner, someone who helps you stretch muscles by gradually applying pressure to different parts of your body. Passive exercises do a great job stretching muscles but can result in injury if your partner pushes too quickly or too hard. When we explain passive exercises, we will discuss this potential problem. Remember, *no horseplay* during passive stretching exercises!

• *Static*. Static exercises involve the gradual and deliberate stretching of a muscle or tendon for at least 20 to 30 seconds, sometimes more. The longer the muscle is stretched without pain, the more flexible it will become. *All* the stretching exercises you will be doing should be done statically.

• *Ballistic*. Ballistic exercises involve bouncing or forcing the muscle or tendon to stretch too quickly or severely. We already have emphasized the importance of a gradual and relaxed approach to stretching exercises. *None* of the exercises in your booklet, therefore, should be performed ballistically.

Some Advice

First of all, stretch before, during, and after vigorous exercise. Do it statically, *not* ballistically. And don't do any of these exercises carelessly, especially if you are stretching passively. If you have questions, talk to one of your coaches.

Warming Up to Increase Blood Flow

Because warming-up exercises increase the flow of blood to the muscles, they are essential preliminaries to any vigorous physical activity. Warming up enables muscles to contract faster and joints to enjoy a full range of motion, thereby reducing the potential for injury. The older the athlete, the more important the warming-up exercises; but younger athletes require similar activities, particularly during the early stages of competition or rigorous physical conditioning.

Mother Nature already has blessed them with a flexibility that is the envy of most middle-agers. Just watch any foursome of business execs wince in agonized admiration at the teenager who wraps herself around her driver after hitting the ball off the first tee. Even this young athlete loses flexibility, however, following strenuous activity, particularly the next morning after a rough contest or a vigorous workout. At this point, stretching exercises are especially important if he or she is to avoid pulled muscles.

Because most athletes are engaged in ongoing practice or competition, they must develop the habit of warming up before the activity itself. Many will forget to warm up because of nerves or lack of interest. It then becomes the coach's job to supervise the warm-up. The easiest way to assess an adequate warm-up is to determine if each athlete has broken a light sweat.

A light sweat guarantees that an athlete has increased the pulse rate, which provides a maximum oxygen supply to the body and helps to eliminate waste products from the muscles during strenuous exercise. The light sweat also indicates an increase in muscle temperature, which allows for more forceful contractions and improved performance. The colder it is, the longer athletes will have to warm up to increase the flow of blood to their muscles and tendons.

Generally, sports-specific exercises provide excellent warm-ups. They provide less vigorous rehearsals of the skills to be performed during competition. Tennis players, for example, can volley for ten to fifteen minutes; quarterbacks can throw and receivers can run patterns; sprinters can run at half speed for thirty- to forty-yard intervals. Following such warm-ups, athletes can then stretch their muscles to further increase the force of the contractions.

Warming Up the Well-Conditioned Athlete

The better the physical condition, the more vigorous the warm-up can be. Some sports require higher levels of physical conditioning than others. All athletes want to be in peak condition; some simply have to be in better condition than others. The top-notch wrestler, for example, probably requires a higher level of cardiovascular efficiency, both aerobic and anaerobic, than a defensive tackle in football. Golfers don't require the same conditioning levels as basketball players or boxers, nor do they require the same kinds of vigorous warm-up activities.

Boxers and wrestlers must often sweat heavily before a bout. The immediate intensity of their competition requires it. Golfers don't have to break such a sweat. Many of them do, particularly before a $25,000 putt, but they don't have to. Sprinters are often perspiring heavily before a race, particularly if it is outside on a cold day.

The brevity of their event and their levels of physical conditioning allow them to exercise vigorously before competition.

Bruce wrestled in college and discovered during his freshman year that he was starting out slowly during the first period of every match. He was finishing with plenty of strength but was placing himself at a disadvantage during the first period because it took him one to two minutes to get up to the pace of the match. Increasing the intensity of his prematch warm-up resulted in improved flexibility, quickness, and intensity.

Bruce's wife Carrie was a two-year state qualifier in high school track. She learned a lasting lesson during an early spring track meet sponsored by a school located along the North Shore of Lake Michigan. While her opponents were huddling under the stands to escape the occasional gust of wind off the lake, she was jogging the length of the football field ten to fifteen minutes before her event. By the end of the track meet, her opponents had forgotten how cold it was and were wondering why she was so much quicker out of the blocks than her opposition.

Experienced athletes, even young ones like Carrie and Bruce, know their bodies and their special needs for practice or competition. Inexperienced athletes usually don't understand or appreciate the effects of a good warm-up. Coaches must be available for constant reminders, particularly in sports like track, wrestling, and gymnastics. The immediate and continuous intensity of such sports, though usually short, requires a longer warm-up than sports like football and basketball.

Knowing When to Stretch

Because warming up and stretching don't in themselves strengthen muscles or cardiovascular levels, both are underappreciated by young athletes. That's why young athletes sometimes experience lower back problems, neck injuries, and, most commonly, hamstring, calf, and Achilles tendon pulls. Vigorous exercise invariably injures muscles. Rest permits healing and a shorter, tighter muscle. At this point, the muscle is even more susceptible to injury and requires a longer warm-up period and greater stretching.

Let's consider a couple of examples. Several years ago, the Pittsburgh Steelers were plagued with muscle pulls and strains. In fact, they were right up there with the league leaders in injuries. They decided to hire Paul Uram as a flexibility coach. After evaluating the players for muscle tightness, he integrated a series of stretching exercises into their conditioning program. The team went on to be relatively injury-free and to win two Super Bowls.

Less dramatically, a local high school football team made an interesting discovery about their conditioning program. The introduction of weight-training exercises reduced the incidence of shoulder and knee injuries significantly, but the players were missing games and practice because of muscle pulls. The coach took the team one day after school to work out with the school's Dance Club. The dance teacher taught them a range of warm-up and flexibility exercises and eventually helped them reduce their problems with pulled muscles and tendons.

Maybe the introduction of warm-up and flexibility exercises wasn't the exclusive reason for the Pittsburgh Steelers' two Super Bowls, but you'll never convince the players and the coaches that the prevention of unnecessary injuries didn't have something to do with their success. The same is true of most coaches and athletes who incorporate good flexibility exercises into their conditioning programs, both before and after competition.

Precompetition Flexibility

Warm-up and stretching exercises before competition should be controlled by the coach. The team should jog lightly or engage in sport-specific exercises at least a half hour prior to the actual contest. Basketball players can shoot around; football players can run pass routes; and tennis players can volley with an opponent or another player on the squad. Then the athletes should stretch their muscles in order to realize a full range of motion and follow the stretching with an increase in the intensity of the sport-specific warm-up.

Warming up and stretching exercises are equally important before and during weight training. The general warm-up should be followed by stretching, then a sport-specific warm-up that involves several different lifts but with light weights and high repetitions. This kind of warm-up will prepare the athlete's muscles for the greater intensity of heavier weights.

Encourage young athletes to remember the three primary causes for injury in the weight room:

1. Any attempt to lift too much weight and the failure to control the weight during the negative or eccentric part of the exercise
2. Failure to observe simple rules of safety, such as having a spotter, especially during a third repetition or any other time the muscles are becoming fatigued
3. Failure to warm up and stretch

Flexibility During Competition and Practice

This is an aspect of flexibility that is often overlooked by athletes and coaches. The heat of battle often results in disregard for anything but actual performance. Aches and pains are familiar to every athlete, particularly during competition. Dedicated athletes, no matter what their age or levels of experience, pride themselves on their ability to play through pain, to endure minor injuries in order to continue competing. As a result, they sometimes tend to ignore the warning signs that can lead to pulled muscles.

The inability of any muscle group to move through a full range of motion without pain is a sure sign of an impending problem. Tightness with or without minor pain is another sure sign. Running backs almost always fatigue their hamstrings and calves and are well advised to stretch them in the huddle or during a time out. Similarly, tennis players should stretch shoulder and neck muscles during breaks in order to maintain a full range of motion.

Athletes should be sensitive to tightness in muscle groups during weight training in order to maintain a full range of motion and prevent injury. We've already discussed the importance of warming up and stretching before vigorous exercise. It's also a good idea, however, to stretch for 20 to 30 seconds between sets to improve flexibility and promote a better range of motion. Certainly, stretching isn't required every time, but when tightness becomes apparent, the smart athlete postpones the next set until he or she can regain full flexibility.

The stretching exercises in figure 2-4 are categorized according to muscle group and can be performed any time the athlete has 20 or 30 seconds to devote to them. These kinds of exercises performed during competition can avert the kinds of muscle pulls and tears that often result in weeks of rehab and nonperformance. Athletes must constantly be encouraged to "slow down time" long enough during competition to be sensitive to the need for such exercises. Periodic reminders from the coach are a must.

Postcompetition Flexibility

Exercises that promote stretching and cooling down after competition or strenuous practice can prevent soreness by pumping fresh blood to the muscles. This supply of fresh blood helps rid muscles of lactic acid buildups that cause the soreness. Lactic acid is a byproduct of the breakdown of glycogen during strenuous exercise. Its buildup is inevitable every time an athlete seeks a maximum performance during practice or competition.

The anaerobic training of many athletes enables them to deal with the muscle fatigue that results from lactic acid buildups. We will discuss such training in a future section. Consistent with the purposes of this section, however, athletes should be encouraged to stretch and cool down after competition in order to avoid the soreness and potential injury that accompanies the sudden stop of strenuous activity. Figure 2-5 discusses this process for your athletes.

Ten Tips for Effective Stretching

The final section of the booklet you give each of your athletes should summarize the importance of warming up and stretching exercises. Figure 2-6 outlines each of the important factors for athletes to keep in mind. It serves as an excellent summary as well as an introduction for everyone involved in the program and should be used during preliminary meetings when safety factors are being discussed.

Coaches should encourage young athletes to heed all ten tips; coaches should pay particular attention to three or four of them. Perhaps one of the most important tips is to encourage athletes to engage in flexibility exercises for at least 15 to 20 minutes before competition or strenuous exercise. Time invariably is at a premium, even for the youngest among us. Young athletes have homework to complete, chores to do (if their parents are as good as we hope they are), friends to see, and phone calls to make.

Figure 2-4

MAINTAINING YOUR FLEXIBILITY

DIRECTIONS

Perform the following flexibility exercises whenever possible during practice or competition, particularly on hot days. Muscles tend to tighten up during vigorous exercise and can pull if athletes fail to maintain flexibility. The exercises are easy to perform and can be done during any lapse in the action. They are appropriate for all sports; their performance should become a habit for you.

THE EXERCISES

Each exercise is named and referred to by the number it was assigned in figure 2-2. Again, these are exercises that can be performed whenever possible during practice and competition.

Quadriceps Stretch (Exercise 10) - This exercise can be performed while using a teammate for stability. The quadriceps are pulled or strained easily on hot days, Perform this exercise at any time, but especially when you feel your quads tightening up.

Groin Stretch (Exercise 13) - Groin muscles also pull easily. This exercise will avoid that.

Hamstring and Achilles Tendon Stretch (Exercise 15) - These areas of the body are pulled more than any other in sport, especially on hot days. Use a teammate for support while you perform this exercise.

Neck Relaxer (Exercise 26) - This exercise helps prevent neck strains and is relaxing as well. Do it to loosen up your neck and shoulder muscles, especially whenever they feel tight or before you perform a complex skill such as shooting a free throw.

Shoulder Stretch (Exercise 27) - This, too, relaxes the muscles and relieves tension.

Lat Stretch (Exercise 29) - This exercise loosens up the latissimus dorsi, the shoulders, and the rib cage.

Others - You and your coach are advised to look through all the exercises in figure 2-2 to find more that will help during practice or competition. Remember: flexibility *before, during,* and *after* vigorous exercise!

© 1995 by Michael D. Koehler

Figure 2-5

THE COOL DOWN

Something to Think About:

By now, you are aware of the fact that cooling-down and stretching exercises performed *after* vigorous exercise help reduce muscle soreness. Strenuous exercise or competition pushes your muscles beyond their comfort levels by burning the chemicals that promote energy and by depriving them of sufficient oxygen. Any maximum physical effort depletes glycogen and oxygen reserves from the muscles and causes a buildup of lactic acid. The result is sore muscles, especially the next day after the muscles have been inactive.

So What Do You Do?

Cool down! Jog for fifteen to twenty minutes; break a sweat; stretch your muscles—slowly and deliberately. If you are unable to do these kinds of things immediately after exercise or competition, find some time to do them the next day. It's always wise to *ease* back into preparation for your next contest. Take the time to bring your muscles back to peak performance. The failure to heed the warning signs that they provide can result in injury, the kind of injury that may hold you out of competition for extended periods of time.

REMEMBER:
WARM UP BEFORE EXERCISE
AND
COOL DOWN AFTER EXERCISE!

© 1995 by Michael D. Koehler

Figure 2-6

TEN TIPS FOR EFFECTIVE STRETCHING

The following ten tips provide an excellent summary of the importance of warming-up and stretching exercises. They also provide important pointers. Read this information carefully.

1. Stretching should be preceded by a warm-up. Warming up increases blood flow and raises muscle temperature. Both are very important for muscle elasticity. Without a proper warm-up, stretching could result in sprains, strains, or muscle tears.

2. You should feel slight discomfort during stretching, but it should be mild and brief. If you feel pain—*stop immediately.*

3. Be sure to stretch at least 3 to 4 times a week.

4. Stretching sessions should last at least 15 to 20 minutes. You should hold each stretch for at least 30 seconds, making sure you build up slowly by the end of the 30 seconds.

5. Stretch major muscle groups first, then smaller. This ensures that the smaller groups have been slightly warmed up. Large muscle groups handle shock better than small muscle groups. Small muscles injure more frequently.

6. Stretch within one hour before strenuous exercise or competition to prevent injury and to prepare the muscles for maximum contraction and force.

7. *Don't bounce!* Stretching should be slow, steady, and relaxed.

8. Try to isolate muscles being stretched. You'll be able to feel it when a muscle has been properly isolated.

9. Stretch *during* and *after* vigorous exercise. This prevents muscles from tightening up and reduces the chance of soreness.

10. Don't give up because you are less flexible than others. Flexibility varies from person to person. You may not notice an improved range of motion immediately, but if you keep working at it—*you will!*

REMEMBER:
YOU HAVE TO STRETCH FOR PERFECTION!

© 1995 by Michael D. Koehler

They generally look at warming-up and stretching exercises much like driving the family car. They like to cruise up and down the main drag looking good, but they don't want to pay for the gas. They don't even want to warm up the engine before pulling out of the driveway. Our job is to make sure they don't put the "pedal to the metal" too early.

This leads to the next important point. Even if convinced that warming up and stretching exercises are important, many young athletes rush through them. They "bounce through" each exercise, risking potential injury and minimizing benefits. Coaches must be vigilant early in the conditioning program to remind each athlete to perform stretching exercises slowly and deliberately.

Finally, if you think it's tough getting young athletes to warm up and stretch before vigorous exercise, try afterward. We've had to corral entire teams to get them back into the weight room to cool down. Any parent, teacher, or coach realizes how difficult it can be to get youngsters to do what's in their best interests. Developing the habit of cooling down is in their best interests. It reduces lactic acid buildups and prevents much of the soreness that accompanies vigorous exercise.

So use the information in figure 2-6 to emphasize the importance of warming-up and stretching exercises. And remember to take the time to discuss the whole issue of flexibility. Young athletes have to do much more than read about flexibility in order to feel the need to perform the exercises outlined in this section. Once they sense such a need, they may even get into the habit of stretching when it isn't absolutely necessary.

Stretching Whenever You Feel Like It

Young athletes can stretch out hamstrings or quads when sitting in the classroom or studying at home. They can do the same with calf muscles and Achilles tendons. While standing around at practice during explanations or other down time, they can stretch back muscles, hamstrings, and quads. Once you see your athletes routinely stretching muscles and tendons, you can feel comfortable that they are developing the right habits.

These are the kinds of habits that are too weak to be felt until they are too strong to be broken. If coaches introduce them carefully and make routine reminders, they will become a habit. At that point they will become a part of each athlete's workout routine and will help maximize the total benefit of the conditioning program.

An Interview with Carol Myers

Carol Myers has coached gymnastics for fifteen years and has developed both All-Staters and All-Americans. Herself an all-round State Champion (USGF) and a two-year captain of the gymnastics team at Indiana University, Coach Myers has experienced both the joy and the trauma of athletic competition. Before completing her final two years at Indiana, she broke her arm in six places and required nine pins and six screws to hold it together. As a result, she learned—as few athletes do—the value and importance of good flexibility.

Always important to her, especially as a gymnast, good flexibility became a must for Coach Myers as she recovered from three surgeries and years of physical therapy, and she has communicated the same importance to all her athletes. During a recent interview, she shared many of her reasons.

Mike: "Talk to me briefly about the importance to a gymnast of good flexibility."

Coach Myers: "To become the best at any skill, you have to have flexibility. You can't do a split leap and not be in the splits. You can't do a front or back walkover and not have extreme back flexibility. It's one thing to perform the skill; it's another to perform it aesthetically. Only really good flexibility can guarantee that. Gymnasts, dancers, and divers go beyond the normal demands of flexibility because the skills otherwise don't look right."

Mike: "How much time would a gymnast or a dancer spend on flexibility before practice or a competition?"

Coach Myers: "A good 20 to 30 minutes between the stretching and getting the muscles warmed up. You know, a dancer spends all his or her life doing exercises two to three hours a day that are all designed to increase flexibility. The regimen of ballet, modern, and jazz dance demands it. They'll spend a good hour of their three hours of dance class working on flexibility."

Mike: "What is the relationship of such exercises to strength? Anyone who watches gymnastics competition has to admit that gymnasts are among the sports world's strongest athletes, yet they are among the most flexible."

Coach Myers: "Because they work at it! Because they recognize that you need to have all of it to be a good athlete: muscular strength, muscular endurance, cardiovascular strength, and flexibility. The kids who think they'll be better athletes if they improve their strength are probably right, but what if they pull one of those really strong muscles and miss competition for three or four weeks? Muscles pull when they're not capable of doing the work they're designed to do."

Mike: "In other words, one doesn't necessarily eliminate the other. The young athlete who wants to build up muscle strength doesn't necessarily have to become less flexible."

Coach Myers: "No, they have to work at it, though. If they just lift weights, they *will* decrease their flexibility. The muscles will really be tightening up. So once the weightlifting is done, they should be encouraged to spend time on flexibility exercises. It might even be fair to say that the more a young athlete lifts weights, the more he or she should concentrate on flexibility."

Mike: "Anything else?"

Coach Myers: "Yes, one thing. Every athlete is going to have an area in which he or she will be strong. Certain athletes are going to be stronger in their upper bodies; certain athletes will be better in their cardiovascular endurance; others will have stronger legs. But if they don't have everything in the package, they're not going to be the best athletes they can be. The best example to me is this: Most gymnasts are going to be pretty good athletes in other sports as well; the reverse is not necessarily true. I think that's because they do work so hard on muscle strength, endurance, *and* flexibility."

Let's Wrap It Up

Flexibility is the range of motion through which the body is able to move without undue pain or injury. As Coach Myers indicated, it increases agility and speed of performance and is an asset in all sports. Most important, it prevents injuries. When a muscle can be used through its full range of motion with control, it can withstand the ballistic movements of athletic competition. Flexibility also adds shape and suppleness to muscles, making them look better—a big plus for adolescent athletes!

In fact, this last reason can be one of the biggest selling points for flexibility exercises. Everyone can avoid bulging muscles and everyone can improve flexibility. Although body type, fat percentage, heredity, and previous injuries influence the body's flexibility, even the tightest person among us can improve flexibility with the right kind of approach.

Finally, young athletes should recognize the need to stretch before, during, and after vigorous exercise. Flexibility exercises may be the classroom equivalent of homework. Like homework, however, they are a necessary preliminary to any kind of test, whether it be in the weight room or on the court or field. Once athletes accept this reality, they will perform better during these tests and reduce the incidence of injury.

Section Three

THE COACH'S PLEDGE

First, a quick story. A prominent midwestern high school invited us one year to attend a luncheon meeting with all its head coaches, the school's athletic director, and a few counselors. The purpose of the meeting was to discuss the process for assisting their student athletes with college selection and recruiting. The meeting was prompted by extensive media attention given to the graduation rates of college athletes and the changes in NCAA legislation.

Most of the coaches in attendance agreed strongly that the school needed to do a better job of helping students find colleges that coordinated their athletic and academic interests. They were seeking a process that coalesced the efforts of coaches, counselors, parents, and the athletes themselves, whether or not the athletes were heavily recruited. They also agreed that the coalition should meet periodically to assure completion of its tasks.

A few coaches complained that the additional time required of such meetings was an imposition. They believed that they had already put in enough time in season. We weren't surprised by the reaction. Although it doesn't predominate across the country, it is representative of lots of coaches. What did surprise us was that so few of the uncomplaining coaches reacted to the complainers. A few looked askance at them, and several minutes later a couple made oblique references to "working for our athletes if they work for us." No one, however, contradicted them by asserting the need to extend their responsibilities beyond the season.

Maybe this is to be expected in a school where coaches want to respect each other's opinions and maintain working relationships. Many had been colleagues for ten to twenty years. Then again, maybe their silence was tacit agreement that expectations beyond the season are unreasonable, that they are paid barely enough now for all they do. Both sets of reasons are valid.

Valid or not, they both, however, obscure the involvement of the one person in the school who exercises the greatest influence on a student's athletic and, maybe, academic future—the coach. Coaches must reexamine their responsibilities to athletes, in and out of season. They must focus on what is important to youngsters and use their influence to help them develop positively. Many coaches may not understand that they experience a symbiotic relationship with their players. They need each other to enjoy their common love of sport and to assure a mutual sense of accomplishment.

Clarifying the Purposes of the Conditioning Program and the Coach's Role

It's necessary, therefore, for coaches to work closely with their athletes both in and out of season. Helping them with the transition from high school to college is just one postseason responsibility. Another involves using their influence to encourage players to focus on their educational responsibilities. A third, one with more immediate value for both coaches and players, involves their mutual investment in a weightlifting and conditioning program.

Figure 3-1 provides a reproducible that can be distributed early in the school year to athletes and their parents. You might want your athletes to take it home, or you might simply mail it. Just be sure that it gets into the hands of parents for its informational as well as public relations value. It sells you, the program, *and* the merits of physical conditioning for the enhancement of performance and the prevention of injuries.

Total body development makes the total athlete. Consistent total-body workouts, therefore, prevent muscular imbalance that may result from underdeveloped muscles that can tear, pull, or strain during competition or intense training. They treat each athlete's body as a total system with no weak parts. They improve strength, muscular endurance, flexibility, aerobic endurance, and agility.

The planned progression of the fitness program from manual movements to weight training allows the body to strengthen slowly, naturally, and completely. Safety procedures are easy to follow; they distinguish clearly between fatigue and pain. In fact, safety is one of the key elements of the program.

In essence, the coach's role is to get young athletes to do whatever is in their best interests. The coach is the promoter of good health habits, the facilitator of cardiovascular conditioning and strength training to enhance athletic performance and prevent injuries, and a focal person in each athlete's attempts to develop the kind of self-discipline that results in superior performance on the court or field, in the classroom, and at home or in the community.

Explaining the Relationship Between Training Rules and General Fitness

Fortunately, a clear and obvious relationship exists between the athletic program's training rules and good fitness and health habits. The media are making the relationship even more obvious each day as they publicize research findings that link drinking, smoking, and other drugs to an increased incidence of addiction among teens and

Figure 3-1

BEING A TOTAL ATHLETE

WHAT IS THE TOTAL ATHLETE?

The total athlete is any person, young or old, who works hard to improve and maintain a high level of physical fitness in order to improve athletic performance and prevent injury. Such a fitness program must be designed to improve cardiovascular efficiency, nutrition, and total body flexibility and muscular strength. To meet such needs completely, young athletes are encouraged to participate in well-organized physical fitness programs. Rarely can they meet their physical fitness needs by developing their own programs. We all need the helping hand as well as the experience and knowledge of trained personnel.

WHY BE A TOTAL ATHLETE?

The total athlete is careful to engage in a comprehensive workout that improves every aspect of his or her physical fitness. Some athletes, particularly inexperienced ones, create muscular imbalance by exercising only certain parts of their bodies and often fail to meet aerobic and flexibility needs. Although their self-created programs may improve appearance, they fail to enhance athletic performance and prevent a wide range of injuries. The total athlete meets *all* his or her fitness needs by engaging in a comprehensive program.

HOW TO BECOME A TOTAL ATHLETE

Fortunately, we have a comprehensive program that can meet the needs of every young athlete. All you have to do is join. But first, be sure to see your family doctor to receive his or her permission to engage in strenuous exercise. The permission forms and Athletic Code are available in the Athletic Department. Then, prepare yourself for a lot of hard work and good times. You'll find that the fitness room will become one of your favorite places. And once you become a "regular," you're going to like the way you look *and* feel.

And you'll enjoy not only your improved appearance and sense of self-esteem but your improved athletic performance and reduced number of injuries.

FOR MORE INFORMATION, BE SURE TO CONTACT OR CALL:
(INCLUDE APPROPRIATE NAMES AND NUMBERS IN THIS SPACE)

© 1995 by Michael D. Koehler

a variety of health problems. Frankly, some of them tend to be a little "preachy," a tendency to be avoided by coaches.

They are nonetheless accurate. Crack cocaine kills; poor nutrition is pathogenic; alcohol and its effects are killing hundreds of adolescents every day. On the flipside, exercise and proper nutrition promote good health, improved self-esteem, and a positive outlook on life. Whatever we as coaches can do to encourage such a lifestyle for our athletes will pay future dividends for each of them.

Young people much prefer explanations to exhortations, however, so figure 3-2 explains the *why* behind the school's training rules. We have observed over the years that such explanations do more than warnings to convince youngsters of their value. Again, be sure to share such handouts with parents. Often, the process for sharing such information can be as important as the infomation itself. Usually, an informational meeting in the beginning of the year is the best time.

Process Is the Thing

Such a meeting can be used for multiple purposes. Primary among them is the opportunity for parents and students to discuss with coaches and counselors not only the training rules but the realities of NCAA requirements, the importance of academics, and the availability of school personnel for additional information or help. If carefully planned, such meetings, some probably before school starts, can also be used by coaches to discuss their programs, to show protective equipment to apprehensive parents, and to sell their sports to potential players.

Some high schools provide such meetings first for freshmen and sophomores, then for juniors and seniors. Meetings focusing on two different age groups enable coaches and counselors to address different issues, some more immediately relevant to the athletes and their parents. Freshmen and their parents are interested in practice times and schedules, the impact of sports on classwork, and the specifics of the training rules; the upperclass students and their parents are interested in opportunities for pursuing a sport in college and such specifics as the NCAA Clearinghouse.

Junior high schools probably will use the meetings to focus on the value of athletic participation, its impact on studies, the nature of relationships with coaches, questions of safety, and competing on the high school level. Sometimes junior high parents are even anxious to discuss the NCAA and such specifics as Bylaw 14.3, the rule requiring high school athletes to maintain a certain grade point average, earn certain scores on the ACT and/or SAT, and maintain a core curriculum of 13 academic units in order to play a sport in college. Such discussions can be very profitable because they develop the kind of academic focus young athletes need when they enter high school.

Obviously, the process of providing such meetings should also involve other promotional ideas, such as newsletters from the AD's office, press releases to local newspapers, and periodic mailings. The point is, any time important information is provided, parents and students should have an opportunity to discuss it with appropriate school personnel, ideally in small-group meetings.

Psychologists have been telling us for a long time that the continued absence of information can cause anxiety in people, sometimes paranoia. Information run amok

© 1995 by Michael D. Koehler

Figure 3-2

SOME STRAIGHT TALK ABOUT TRAINING RULES

Do you know why so many states keep the drinking age over 21? They have learned from the medical community that our livers don't mature until we become young adults—at or beyond the age of 21! What that means is that teenagers have the potential to become alcoholics in a much shorter time than adults, in some instances, months for teenagers as compared to many years for adults. Our training rules also recognize similar problems. Smoking, drinking, and drug use can cause significant problems for all of us, but particularly for young people, who tend to be more affected by them.

Consider these additional facts:

1. Nicotine is a poisonous alkaloid. Just a small amount in your bloodstream can kill you in about an hour.
2. Smoking is as addictive as cocaine.
3. A recent university study found that adolescents who smoked marijuana ate irregularly and showed symptoms of nutritional deficiencies such as muscle weakness and fatigue.
4. Studies indicate that up to 10% of frequent marijuana smokers will become addicted.
5. Research also indicates that marijuana addiction leads to the use of stronger, more addictive drugs.
6. One of those stronger drugs is amphetamines, commonly called "speed." Recent research indicates that prolonged use can cause significant damage to brain cells, resulting in serious physical and cognitive problems.
7. Steroid use has been linked to heart and brain damage.
8. Alcohol use is directly linked to thousands of teenage deaths every year.
9. Alcohol addiction is passed on to family members. The sons of alcoholic fathers, for example, are four times more likely to become alcoholics than the sons of nonalcoholics.
10. When compared to the tissues of the lungs, a piece of tissue paper looks like a sheet of iron. That's why smoking and drug use are so dangerous to the lungs.

**THESE ARE JUST *SOME* OF THE REASONS
TO FOLLOW YOUR SCHOOL'S TRAINING RULES!
BE SMART—STAY HEALTHY!**

can do much the same thing. Inundating parents and young athletes with information without opportunities for discussion can be just as problematic, sometimes immobilizing the very people we're trying to inform. Coaches and counselors must be constantly vigilant, therefore, to the personal as well as the informational needs of parents and young athletes and provide a range of opportunities for them to discuss involvement in the school's programs.

The Athlete's Pledge

The Athlete's Pledge, provided in figure 3-3, is another example of information which should be discussed with athletes and parents. If presented thoughtfully by coaches and counselors, the experience of understanding and committing to such a Pledge could be among the most significant in the student-athlete's school career.

    The Pledge contains everything that coaches have valued since Spartacus told his gladiators to shape up. All of us realize that the positive student behaviors emphasized in the Pledge contribute not only to winning programs but to future successes and satisfying lives. The sports we represent and the conditioning programs we provide inevitably take a back seat to the much larger common bond we share as athletes and coaches. The Pledge provides the chance to begin forging that bond from the first moment coach meets player.

    Parents like it, too. Coaches represent to parents one of the school's most important resources, if they are seeking assistance with a "normally adjusting" teen—or for that matter—with any teenager! The Pledge, then, is much more than a set of expectations from the Athletic Department. It is one of the first important commitments a youngster will make, and it is a promise to parents that they have a partner as their children grow up.

The Coach's Pledge

The Coach's Pledge reaffirms that promise. It is the coach's statement of philosophy, a commitment to young athletes and their parents. As indicated in figure 3-4, the Coach's Pledge extends beyond the court or field and touches young athletes' lives in other ways. This is why the coach's job in any school is so significant. Our knowledge must reach beyond game strategy and motivational technique to an understanding of adolescent development and the interpersonal skills required to work effectively with young athletes, their parents, school personnel, and, in some instances, college coaches.

    Those of us who have been involved in coaching for a few years, therefore, understand that our jobs require a great deal of energy. Riding herd on so many psychic wild horses each day and handling phone calls and meetings with parents and with college and school personnel requires a special brand of energy—and that energy goes furthest when our activities are performed within a consistent and predictable conceptual framework, the kind that's provided in the Coach's Pledge.

Figure 3-3

THE ATHLETE'S PLEDGE

Individual and team success in sports results from commitment. The extent to which young athletes are able to make such commitments reflects their maturity as well as their dedication to family, friends, school, and team. Your coach already has made a similar kind of commitment. You will receive a copy of it. For these reasons, we ask you to read and agree to the following Pledge:

As an athlete in my school, I promise

1. To be a worthy representative of my teammates and coaches, abiding by school and community expectations and reflecting my team's values of commitment and hard work.
2. To maintain my health and fitness levels by following the training rules as prescribed by the Athletic Department.
3. To reflect the knowledge that a commitment to victory is nothing without the commitment to hard work in practice.
4. To attend every practice unless excused by my coach.
5. To understand that my future as a responsible adult relates more to my academic than my athletic activities.
6. To find the time to satisfy my family relationships and responsibilities.
7. To accept the responsibilities of team membership: cooperation, support of my teammates, shared responsibilities, positive interaction, and mutual respect.
8. To reflect good breeding by expressing my feelings and ideas intelligently and appropriately.
9. To reflect my belief that true strength involves gentleness and that even the toughest athlete is sensitive to others.

**I HAVE READ THE ABOVE STATEMENTS
AND PROMISE TO LIVE UP TO THEM.**

(Signature) _____

Date: _____

© 1995 by Michael D. Koehler

Figure 3-4

THE COACH'S PLEDGE

The Coach's Pledge extends beyond a knowledge of athletics and reaches into the life of each of his or her players. It is one of the most important responsibilities in the school and involves at least the same level of commitment that coaches expect of their players. Mutual respect and team membership are to be expected equally of player and coach and, for the coach, involve the following promises:

As a coach in my school, I promise

1. To be a model of appropriate language and behavior.
2. To respect and dignify each of my athletes as an individual.
3. To promote the safety of each athlete and to ask no more in practice or competition than each is capable of delivering.
4. To promote the conditions and circumstances that encourage each athlete to realize his or her full potential.
5. To impose time demands that acknowledge the primary importance of each athlete's academic and family responsibilities.
6. To promote among all athletes and coaches a solid sense of team membership.
7. To reflect in my coaching the best and most recent thinking and strategy in my sport.
8. To assist, whenever appropriate and mutually convenient, with the post-high school planning of my players as it relates to athletics.
9. To be available to parents at times that are mutually convenient.
10. To work, whenever appropriate, with other school personnel to guarantee the best interests of each of my student athletes.

© 1995 by Michael D. Koehler

The Pledge, therefore, is not only a promise to parents and young athletes but an interpretive map for the coach. Each of us needs a theoretical framework to guide our coaching behavior. The Pledge provides such a framework as well as the periodic reminder we sometimes need to do what *we* "reallyoughtawanna." In addition, the Pledge is a selling point for your program. It is your statement to young athletes and their parents that you are available to them, that your program is much more than strategy, and that you are committed to student athletes well beyond their conditioning and athletic performance levels.

Modeling the Right Way

Commitment is evidenced in other ways as well. As the kids are saying almost daily in the inner cities, "If you're gonna talk the talk, walk the walk." And as you and I say at least once a year: "Don't tell me; *show* me!" Well, when it comes to physical conditioning, especially if we want young athletes to develop lifelong fitness habits, we should make our commitment to physical fitness evident in *our* behavior and appearance.

Young athletes love to work out with their coaches. The well-conditioned coach, by his or her presence and work ethic alone, is a motivator to most kids; not only do they enjoy working out with such coaches, they are generally well-inclined to *listen* to them. When the coach who bench-presses 350 pounds explains the advantages and technique of the exercise, kids *listen;* conversely, when the pot-bellied wheezer tells kids to work aerobically and maintain a nutritional balance, kids laugh.

It's that simple. Don't try to trick them. The old saw, instructing children, "Don't do as I do, do as I say," doesn't work in the fitness room. It probably doesn't work anywhere else either, but especially not in the fitness room, where you and I have to "walk the walk." The professional athletes on TV who tell us that they are not role models are out of touch with reality. They may not want to *be* role models, but they are nonetheless. Role modeling isn't the only thing in life that requires something of us we may not want to do.

Every time we tell a young athlete, "Show me; don't just tell me," we invite them to expect a similar commitment from us. And if we don't evidence that commitment in our behavior and appearance, we're blowing in the wind when we try to exact that commitment from them. If we *really* believe that personal fitness and good health are lifelong habits, let's develop them now. This is another instance where a good habit, like a bad habit, is a chain that at first is too weak to be felt—until it becomes too strong to be broken.

Keeping the Parents Plugged In

It's important to recognize that any parent communication should be ongoing. Parents can be the most influential people in the whole process. They can sell their children on the fitness and athletic programs, and they can encourage the school's aministration to provide all the resources you need to purchase equipment and provide a suitable facility. Parents are not the enemy; they are a valuable resource that can make or break any athletic program.

Early notification

Perhaps the easiest way to keep parents informed initially about the benefits of the school's fitness program is to routinely mail copies of the coach's pledge with invitations for their children to join. Figure 3-5 provides a sample letter of invitation. Notice that it refers to the Coach's Pledge and emphasizes the value of injury prevention and safety, two obvious areas of concern to parents. Notice as well that it invites parents to visit the facility and to get to know the school personnel who will be working with their children. We have discovered over the years that these visits have done as much as anything else to sell the value of the program.

Ongoing notification

The best form of ongoing notification for parents is what we call the *Fitness-Gram*. A reproducible is provided in figure 3-6. It informs parents periodically of their child's strength and aerobic gains since the child first joined the program. The Fitness-Gram has a great deal of PR value and often is the subject of conversation in the community, especially after its first mailing. We have had parents tell us that the sudden awareness of their child's cardiovascular efficiency has prompted them to join the local fitness club, certainly to applaud the effectiveness of our program.

End-of-the-year notification

The end-of-the-year mailing (the reproducible in figure 3-7) reminds parents of the value of the program and provides such specifics as the limited number of injuries incurred by athletes in the course of the school year. It also provides specifics of some of the accomplishments of the school's athletes, from the personal and school records they have set in the fitness room to their performances on the field or court. In essence, the end-of-the-year mailing further justifies the fitness program and encourages parents to make sure their children join again the following year.

Any section of the end-of-the-year summary can be deleted if, for any reason, it is inappropriate for that particular year. If injuries, for some reason, have increased during one particular year, you may not want to mention that fact in the *Fitness-Gram*. You do, however, want to use the information to determine any adjustments needed for the fitness program for the following year. An increase in twisted ankles, for example, may signal a need for additional exercises specific to that part of the body.

Even the best school fitness program will realize only marginal success without the support of the parent community. The best way to secure their support is to share information with them about the program's advantages and successes. Effective public relations for any school fitness program is a four-step process.

1. Do something good.

Figure 3-5

SAMPLE LETTER OF INVITATION

(Date)

(Parents' Name
Address
City, State Zip)

Dear Parents:

It's the start of the school year and time to have your young athlete enroll in the school's fitness program. We extend this invitation for several reasons.

The fitness program

- Is fun. With the exception of actually participating in one or more sports, there is no better way to meet a wide range of positive and self-directed students.
- Promotes the development of fitness and health habits that have lifelong value for your young athlete.
- Develops the kinds of fitness levels that significantly reduce injuries during practice and competition.
- Establishes the muscular strength and cardiovascular endurance that improve athletic performance.
- Promotes total fitness: increased muscular strength, improved cardiovascular efficiency, flexibility, and sound nutritional habits.

Any young athlete, no matter how serious he or she may be about a particular sport, will benefit from involvement in our fitness program. All student athletes and their parents are encouraged to join. We also invite parents to visit the facility and to talk to the trainers and coaches who run the program.

Finally, please read the enclosed Coach's Pledge and be assured that our school is committed to your student athlete. Our fitness program is just one aspect of that comitment. If you have questions, feel free to call (Name) at (Number). Thanks for your time.

Sincerely,

Coach

© 1995 by Michael D. Koehler

Figure 3-6

FITNESS-GRAM

The following information provides an update of the progress your child has made improving his or her physical fitness. Only representative exercises are reported in this fitness-gram: push-ups, sit-ups, bench press, military press, curl, squats, 60-yard dash time, and quarter-mile time. As you read the information, you may have questions or require additional data. Your child can provide much of it, or you can feel free to call (Name) at (Number) for any additional explanations.

Entry-level Data	Current Data
Weight:	Weight:
Bench press:	Bench press:
Military press:	Military press:
Curl:	Curl:
Squat:	Squat:
60-yard dash time:	60-yard dash time:
Quarter-mile time:	Quarter-mile time:

The improvements, as listed above, are sure to improve athletic performance, reduce the incidence of injury, and promote lifelong health and fitness habits. Again, if you should have questions, feel free to give us a call at your convenience.

© 1995 by Michael D. Koehler

© 1995 by Michael D. Koehler

Figure 3-7

WHAT PHYSICAL FITNESS CAN ACCOMPLISH

We thought you might find the following information interesting. It details the individual and team accomplishments of the young athletes who have been involved in our school's fitness program.

Team accomplishments in interscholastic competition this year

Individual accomplishments in competition this year

Individual accomplishments/records in the fitness program this year

A summary of information about injuries

2. Tell the parents.

3. Tell the parents.

4. Tell the parents—and anyone else who will listen.

Maintaining Perspective

Interscholastic sports programs, like their intercollegiate counterparts, are extraordinarily influential in the lives of young athletes. They can sublimate their social, emotional, even intellectual development in an all-consuming love affair with athletics and the promises it offers. It promotes a narrow but powerful sense of personal identity, an elevated position in the school's pecking order, and even the promise of easy money.

It's not surprising that the world of sports prolongs the adolescence of athletes and opens the door to such a disturbing array of abuses in high school and college. Those of us who are committed to the nonmonetary richness it provides, therefore, must do what we can to encourage our athletes to maintain the proper perspective while involved in competitive athletics.

The "win-at-all-costs" mentality that is reported so widely in the media is teaching youngsters the wrong lessons and promoting athletics in schools and colleges for something other than its own sake. Fortunately, it is not widespread, but when it happens, sports run the risk of becoming a liability to young people and their parents.

The right perpsective, then, starts with each of us. As we associate with kids in the program, therefore, we must, first of all, have fun with them and spread lots of specific praise. We must also be sure to emphasize the message offered in figure 1-5, "A Word About Competition." The possibility of failure is immobilizing for many young athletes. The assurance that they *can't* fail if they keep trying and working is relatively new to them; once they accept the idea, it becomes a great motivator.

We help maintain the right perspective, then, when we focus on physical fitness as something inherently good, not just as a means to an end. Certainly, we can't diminish the value of improved performance and the prevention of injuries. These are critical considerations and are emphasized recurrently throughout this book, but we must never allow our athletes to lose sight of the simple pleasure of exercise for its own sake, just as we must always seek with them the *intrinsic* rewards of athletic competition, unencumbered by a fear of winning or losing.

An Interview with George Kelly, Coach of Four National Championship Football Teams at the Universities of Nebraska and Notre Dame

One of college football's classiest and most competent coaches, George Kelly has coached at Marquette University and the University of Nebraska—and he has been a fixture at Notre Dame for the last 26 years. During his entire career, which has spanned 42 years, he developed scores of All-Americans and pro football greats. Kelly worked with head coaching immortals Lyle Blackburn, Bob Devaney, Ara Parseghian, and Lou

Holtz. He has enjoyed four national championships, one at Nebraska and three at Notre Dame. Most important, he currently enjoys the regard of thousands of athletes and coaches as one of the genuine legends of college football.

No coach in college football is more qualified than George Kelly to discuss the Coach's Pledge to his or her athletes. Most everyone he has coached throughout his career has become not only a former player but a lifelong friend. Some coaches *talk* about their desire to work with young people; others *live* it—in everything they do. George Kelly's interest and commitment to young adults is genuine—as evidenced in the following interview:

Mike: "Over the past 42 years, you have established yourself as one of the premier college coaches in the country, partly because of the contributions you have made to so many championship programs and partly because of the friends you have made along the way. Helping maintain such winning programs and develop so many All-Americans involves a lot more than *Xs* and *Os*. What did you do to develop the relationships with your players that resulted in such a commitment from them?"

Coach Kelly: "Over the years, my technique as a coach changed, and it changed for the better. Years ago, coaches took great pride in being "macho" and demanding sacrifice from their players. As I grew as a coach, I realized that the more you care about them, the better they play. I learned that they don't care all that much about what you know about the game. They want to know how much you care about them, how concerned you are about them.

"Football is not a very natural game. It involves a lot of violent contact, so you have to be in a position to recognize those who are capable of playing it and to prepare your practices so they can be successful. And number two, you have to make sure the players are protected and be sure to avoid beating them up in practice."

Mike: "In essence, then, you want to be sure that you have assessed their capabilities so that they feel comfortable with the assignments you expect of them?"

Coach Kelly: "Exactly."

Mike: "Plus, the bottom line is—and I'm saying this because I know you—you're also saying that kids are more than players. They must have someone who is interested in them as people."

Coach Kelly: "Right. Let me give you an example. We had a freshman who came to me one year and realized that he would never beat out the current starter. He also knew that he wanted to play linebacker. He wanted to play badly and knew that he wasn't very tough. . . ."

Mike: "Excuse me—but he told you that he wasn't very tough?"

Coach Kelly: "Yes, but he found a way to play and played extremely well—to the point where he lasted five years in the pro league. Then, he went on to graduate from Harvard and became an attorney and is in charge of a large foundation now.

"And he wasn't a headhunter, but, doggone, could he play well on the outside and do the finesse things that had to be done out there."

Mike: "Initially in coming to you, obviously he felt a trust—to be able to be that honest with you, especially to admit that he didn't think he was that tough."

Coach Kelly: "Yes, very much so. And, you know, the kids at times would make light of him, but the longer he played, the more confidence he gained in himself, knowing that you didn't expect much more out of him than he was giving you because he was giving you all he had. It's then that you've made your point; inevitably, the athlete becomes a better player."

Mike: "To kind of wrap this up, is there one piece of information you would like to share with everyone out there who has the pleasure of coaching young athletes?"

Coach Kelly: "Yes, rather than establishing stature for yourself, you'd better be content making friends and creating close relationships with young people. Help them believe that you will not lead them astray and that you will not take advantage of them. And, as I said earlier, make sure they understand that you will not subject them to an environment that is something more than they can handle. You have to gain their confidence. Without that confidence, I don't think you can lead anyone to success. You don't motivate teams; you motivate individuals. The minute you try to motivate an entire team in the same fashion, you're going to lose 90 percent of them.

"You know, some kids are going to be very successful being third teamers."

Mike: "And make a great contribution to the team."

Coach Kelly: "Exactly. A player is not a failure because she or he is not a starter. That's what a team is all about. Everyone makes his or her contribution, and once a player understands that and trusts you, you're well on your way to developing that individual player as well as the team."

Let's Wrap It Up

Those of us who are sincere about our commitment to young athletes will find a solid philosophy in Coach Kelly's comments. Coaches like George Kelly are signs of hope in a media bombardment that shouts almost daily of child abuse, spousal abuse, parent abuse, teacher abuse, and athlete abuse. The reasons for such social problems are multifold, but one thing is certain. The abuse of athletes is inevitable when winning is the only purpose for competitive athletics.

A desire to win is characteristic of all of us; and, let's admit it, it's one of the ultimate purposes of any game. People don't deal cards, hit golf balls, or even throw darts to lose. But when winning becomes the *exclusive* purpose of any game, when broad opportunities for enjoyment and personal growth give way to a narrow focus on victory, especially victory at any cost, sports become a liability in schools, both high school and college.

Perhaps the Father of American Football said it best. In 1885, Walter Camp wrote these words in an article entitled "Athletic Extravagance": "Play not for gain but for sport. He who plays for more than he can lose with pleasure, stakes his heart." Many coaches and, unfortunately, some athletes have staked not only their hearts but their honesty, integrity, and decency and, along the way, have gained little more than the ephemeral recognition that accompanies victory. This is not true of coaches like George Kelly. His 42 years of coaching go well beyond games on Saturday.

The Coach's Pledge, therefore, involves much more than helping youngsters develop their athletic potential or even their lifelong fitness habits. As Coach Kelly indicated, it involves a recognition of the entire person. Only then will young athletes develop the character that sees them through adversity during competition and later in life, proud of *who they are* instead of just *what they have*.

Section Four

STRENGTHENING

THE HEART AND LUNGS

First, a quick story. It seems to many of us like only yesterday that the coach was having us sprint after practice and, late in each game, wondering why we were running out of gas. The more we slowed up on game day, the more we sprinted during and after practice. An obvious attempt to improve our conditioning levels, the wind sprints invariably seemed like punishment to us, unending and only partially effective.

In fact, that is the worst part of the experience for a lot of athletes; it seems a never-ending cycle: run out of wind late in the game—run wind sprints the next day in practice. It's no wonder that recent research indicates that youngsters are passing up athletics in favor of activities that seem to be more "fun." How much fun can *anyone* have struggling through a conditioning exercise that seems punishing and isn't meeting his or her complete conditioning needs?

Many middle-agers are walking around today with torn hamstrings because no one told them as young athletes to improve flexibility and to mix aerobic with anaerobic conditioning exercises. Certainly, the terms *aerobic* and *anaerobic* are foreign to your players, so spare them the unnecessary confusion. Just be sure to provide them with opportunities to improve their oxygen uptake (aerobic) while they increase their tolerance for muscle fatigue (anaerobic). Both elements are important to athletes, no matter what the sport.

HOW IMPORTANT IS CARDIOVASCULAR EFFICIENCY?

Look at it this way: Any strenuous activity that continues for 15 to 20 minutes or more generally requires good cardiovascular efficiency. Even short-burst activities like foot-

55

ball require strong aerobic capacity. Each player's muscles, especially late in the game, require oxygen to release maximum energy. They also, however, require anaerobic capacity to tolerate fatigue, a subject we will discuss later in this section.

Let's define the terms first. *Aerobic* literally means "with oxygen." It is oxygen in the blood that helps release energy to the muscles and that helps burn the excess fat that can inhibit athletic performance. *Anaerobic* means "without oxygen" and characterizes intense activities such as sprinting, short-burst speed skating, fast-break basketball, and sprint swimming. In anaerobic exercise, the body uses oxygen and depletes energy sources faster than the cardiovascular system can replace them, so such activities usually last no more than 30 to 40 seconds.

Anaerobic activities burn glycogens, the sugars provided by simple and complex carbohydrates, such as candy (simple carbohydrates) and pasta and cereal (complex carbohydrates). Because aerobic exercises burn glycogens *and* fat, which is oxygen-dependent, let's discuss them first. They are the kinds of activities that promote improved cardiovascular efficiency as well as improved appearance and athletic performance.

Athletes who practice hard aerobically may not have the body mass that less fit players have, but they tend to have greater endurance and quickness. Consider this example. A few years ago, a former college coach of Mike's was preparing his team for an Orange Bowl game. During a phone conversation, Mike asked the coach how he expected his team to do in the game. The answer was unequivocal: "We're going to get hammered."

Mike thought he was kidding. The team had one of the biggest lines in college football, was steeped in decades of tradition, and entered the game undefeated. After expressing his surprise, he was told, "They have a bunch of 270- and 280-pounders boiled down to 230 and 240. We haven't played a team this year with their quickness and strength."

The coach was right. His team lost 40–0 and limped back home wondering what had happened. A 280-pound lineman, no matter how powerful he may be in the weight room, is a pushover late in the game when he runs out of oxygen. Muscles without an adequate supply of energy lose strength, and players don't perform as well. It's that simple. The biggest, strongest player on the team must also be in good cardiovascular condition if he or she doesn't want to get "hammered."

Here's another, very convincing way to discuss the importance of cardiovascular efficiency with young athletes (adults, too). Tell them that the heart is a pump that, with exercise, circulates more blood with each beat, thereby reducing the number of times it has to beat in a minute. O.K., this may come as no startling revelation to anyone. Include mention of the following statistics, however, and you'll open even the sleepiest eye.

A normal heart rate ranges from 55 to 75 beats per minute (bpm). A well-conditioned athlete's heart may beat around 50 beats per minute, sometimes 40. In essence, the athlete's heart will pump as much blood because of the volume and force of each stroke, accomplishing the same amount of blood flow with less effort. The primary advantage of fewer beats per minute is startling.

In just one day, the athlete's heart beats 36,000 fewer times than the normal heart, which translates to 13 million fewer beats each year. It doesn't take a math whiz to conclude that the poorly conditioned heart, which may work at a minimum rate of 100 bpm, may have to beat 20 million times more often each year because *someone* is unwilling to get off the couch. Like a well-tuned automobile engine, the well-conditioned heart works less, rests more, and generally lasts longer.

It is also better at fighting off illness. Improved blood flow brings more nutrient-rich blood to cells and increases the immune system's resistance to sickness, usually resulting in fewer colds each year for the well-conditioned person and shorter battles with the symptoms. A solid program of aerobic exercise even increases bone mass, making the bones less susceptible to breaking.

The psychological benefits are equally striking. Aerobic training reduces stress, aggression, and hostility and improves self-esteem by developing self-discipline and an increased sensitivity to personal needs. People not only feel better when they improve their cardiovascular efficiency; they feel better about themselves because of the personal accomplishments they experience.

Professional players like Ronnie Lott in football, Martina Navratilova in tennis, and Nolan Ryan in baseball are excellent examples of athletes who have endured the relative abuse of their sports by maintaining aggressive conditioning programs. All three can be found exercising after games in order to refine their skills and to work off the lactic acid that makes muscles stiff and resistant to exercise the next day. They are committed to their sports and, more important, to their own physical well-being.

A Word About Proper Equipment

The most important piece of equipment for any athlete is the shoe. With proper fitting shoes that prevent jolts to the tendons and joints, young athletes have all they need to improve their cardiovascular efficiency. Treadmills, aerobic bicycles, and rowing machines certainly have their advantages. They are inviting to adults and introduce an element of convenience for any workout, but Jim Thorpe, Jesse Owens, and Babe Zakarias managed without them, and so can the vast majority of young athletes.

Give a youngster a jump rope, a good pair of shoes, and a safe place to run, be sure to provide the proper encouragement, then get out of the way while he or she improves cardiovascular efficiency. Add the manual movements outlined in section 5, and you are well on your way to developing a well-conditioned athlete. Certainly, weight rooms and fitness centers contain valuable training aids, but their absence should never become an excuse for inadequate conditioning.

The Specifics of Aerobic Training

All players, therefore, in every sport, must develop total fitness by strengthening their muscles, improving their flexibility, and developing their cardiovascular systems. Weight training strengthens muscles in the fitness room; a well-conditioned cardiovascular system strengthens them during competition. Good athletes require both.

Let's dispel a misconception before we go any further. Oxygen itself does not supply energy to muscles. Simple and complex carbohydrates, transformed into glycogens, are primary suppliers of energy, but the muscles can't use either until they are transformed into adenosine trisphosphate (ATP) by a series of biochemical reactions in the body. Fat is also a major source of energy—in fact, it is the primary source during extended aerobic activity. It is oxygen—again—that generates the ATP and releases the fat as energy.

It stands to reason that the more efficient the flow of oxygen, the more effective the supply of energy to muscles during exercise or competition. This is particularly true of aerobic activities such as jogging, distance swimming, slow volleys in tennis, and bringing the ball up court in basketball. During such activities, the cardiovascular system is able to supply and replenish the energy needs of the body as the activity continues.

Food provides the energy source. The body stores glycogen (chains of glucose molecules) primarily in the muscle cells and the liver. Fatty acids are stored in cell membranes all over the body. Because fat is oxygen-dependent, it is released only during aerobic activity: mildly strenuous exercises such as jogging, walking fast, or bicycling at a moderate speed. Perhaps the best way to determine if an exercise is aerobic is to try to talk while performing it. If the athlete can't talk because he or she is gasping for breath, the activity probably is anaerobic and should be modified.

Fat, therefore, is not a "bad guy" in any athletic activity. Obviously, like anything else in life, it can be harmful if excessive, but if maintained appropriately, it plays a vital role in athletic performance. Look at it this way. One pound of fat can "energize" 30 to 40 miles of jogging. We experience problems when our bodies store *too much* fat. Because none of us plans a 1400-mile jog before breakfast, we probably don't need 40 pounds of *excess* fat. We must remember, however, that to burn it off, we must exercise aerobically.

Some fat is essential to our health; for example, we don't want to achieve a zero body fat percentage. Not only does fat provide for our aerobic energy needs, it also lines the membranes in our body cells, including those in the brain! It may be true, therefore, that some of us have more "fat in our heads" than others, but that may not be all bad. So the next time someone calls you a fathead after losing a game, thank that person!

Also keep in mind that excess body fat is eliminated from the body generally. Fat can't be reduced only in specific parts of the body. Tests on tennis players, for example, reveal that, although one arm is used to swing the racket, both arms retain similar amounts of fat. The steady reduction of fat from the body is accomplished through moderate, deliberate, and extended exercise. After approximately 20 minutes of such exercise, fatty acids become the primary sources of fuel for the body, and the fat cells begin to shrink.

Such continuous, low-intensity activities provide several valuable benefits for athletes and nonathletes alike—including the improvement of oxygen intake and the elimination of body fat. General fitness is a lifelong proposition, but it falls short of the physical demands of competitive training. This is an important distinction, one that deserves further discussion.

Distinguishing Between General Fitness and Competitive Training

Most of us grew up with the "no pain, no gain" theory of athletic training. The middle-agers among us who competed athletically as young adults probably still use it as a prescription for our continuing fitness needs. That's a problem. The general fitness needs of a 45-year-old coach are considerably different from the competitive training needs of a world-class sprinter, or even those of a junior high middle-distance runner.

If adults are to sustain fitness programs, they have to find an element of pleasure in them. In essence, they have to perform activities that are well within their maximal aerobic ranges and that can be performed almost daily without pain or soreness. They are involved in such exercises to lose weight or simply feel better. In addition, their activities are not highly specialized but can be performed by anyone who wants only to improve or maintain good fitness habits.

Conversely, young athletes train primarily to realize performance goals, to excel in sports for themselves and their teammates. They often like the side effects of feeling good during the day and looking good on the beach, but their cardiovascular training regimens focus on energy production and utilization as each contributes to highly specialized activities. In essence, athletes can expect some pain in order to realize the kinds of athletic gains they seek.

We as coaches, therefore, must help young athletes realize that they seek other kinds of rewards for their involvement in competitive sports. They are much less interested in the development of lifelong fitness habits, although their involvement in sports certainly creates such an interest. They are primarily interested in training activities—no matter how painful—that promote improved athletic performance in order to experience the internal and external satisfactions that come from winning.

We want to avoid excessive pain and the imposition of exercises that are potentially dangerous, but we want to push our athletes within the framework of their potential in order to increase their chances to win. When asked once why he worked his players so hard, Joe Paterno said that he didn't want players coming back to him years later claiming that they could have won a national championship if Paterno had pushed them just a little harder.

It makes sense. No matter how hard we try to softsell athletic competition, the ultimate purpose is still victory, certainly not at the expense of honor and integrity but clearly within the framework of decency and hard work. Otherwise, what value does it have? Paterno understood that. Perhaps that's one reason why he developed so many winning programs and decent young athletes, each of whom was willing to pay the price for victory on the field and for success in later life.

Figure 4-1, therefore, should be distributed to each athlete in the school, probably during the team's first meeting. It distinguishes between general fitness and athletic training and sets the stage for the youngster who may be unprepared to make the physical commitment required for success in sports. It also addresses the misguided notion that everything we do in practice or competition should be "fun." In sports, fun is the byproduct of hard work. The committed athlete realizes a deep sense of personal satisfaction and a level of self-esteem that transcend "fun."

RELATING AEROBIC TO ANAEROBIC CONDITIONING

That brings us to anaerobic conditioning. Here's where the pain comes in and the "fun" gets postponed until the benefits of hard work are realized. The degree of the athlete's pain is dependent upon the needs of the individual sport. Anaerobic conditioning is athletic training at its purest. It is the kind of training that pushes athletes

Figure 4-1

FITNESS TRAINING

FOR WHAT PURPOSE?

Let's take a look at fitness training and discuss what it means for different people. When most adults join fitness clubs, they usually are interested in losing weight and/or improving their general health and appearance. They want to look good—and have fun. They wear colorful jogging outfits, break a sweat on the treadmill or the bike, watch their diets, and even lift weights. In essence, they do everything athletes do—but less vigorously. They want their workouts to be fun, a total experience that makes them look good and feel good about themselves. When their workouts stop being fun, they don't want to do them any more.

Athletes are involved in fitness training for other reasons. We have gotten involved in our respective sports because we enjoy them; we have fun playing them. But we recognize that the goals we have developed for ourselves in these sports require a kind of training that goes well beyond colorful jogging outfits and 20 minutes on the treadmill. Fitness training for athletic participation is much more demanding than fitness training for general conditioning. We realize that the kind of training we do often is *not* fun; it's hard work. It pushes us beyond our physical limits and often leaves us sore and stiff.

We also realize, however, that, without it, we will never realize our athletic goals. As athletes, we know that "fun" is the byproduct of hard work. We know that when we start running around looking for fun for its own sake, especially if we don't have to earn it, it rarely makes us genuinely happy. Our happiest times provide a deep sense of personal satisfaction and improved self-esteem—and that comes from hard work. That's the way it is with sports now, and that's the way it will be with everything we do later in life.

So for now let's call that hard work a

Full and total commitment to
Useful and vigorous exercise that brings us the
Needed strength to realize our athletic goals.

REMEMBER:
GOOD ATHLETES SEEK OUT HARD WORK;
THEY KNOW THAT THE FUN WILL FOLLOW.

© 1995 by Michael D. Koehler

beyond their limits, that introduces them to new heights of endurance and, ultimately, performance.

In the process, however, it can cause each athlete to question his or her sanity. Whenever athletes approach their anaerobic thresholds, which are usually 60 to 70 percent of their energy and physical potential, they can expect to experience mild to excessive exertion. And as they continue to exercise anaerobically, they can expect buildups of lactic acid, which cause fatigue and pain in the muscle.

During this kind of intense exercise, the heart and lungs are unable to keep up with the body's energy demands. Muscles then depend on their glucose stores, which can be converted into energy without oxygen—anaerobically. If intense exercise continues and the body burns glucose without oxygen, the glycogen stores in the muscles and liver will run out. At that point, the athlete is exercising without energy and "hits the wall," that is, becomes physically unable to sustain the activity.

That's why athletes, depending on their individual sports, must train both aerobically and anaerobically. Aerobic training improves the athlete's ability to take in oxygen and use it more efficiently, which has implications for the supply of energy to the muscles as well as weight loss. In essence, it eliminates waste products from the muscles and metabolizes fat faster. Aerobic training, therefore, is the main contributor to appearance as well as performance.

On the other hand, anaerobic training is associated almost exclusively with athletic performance. Most sports are performed anaerobically, particularly those that involve short, all-out bursts of speed that leave athletes breathless. Fast-break basketball, 100-meter sprints, long touchdown runs, and inside-the-park home runs normally involve an all-out effort that requires time to rest in order to take in more oxygen.

Athletes require this kind of training in order to build up the muscle's tolerance for this kind of fatigue. The downside of anaerobic training is that the muscle burns glucose faster and builds up lactic acid, which can result in the shutdown of the muscle. The upside is that anaerobic training teaches muscles to remove waste products faster, produce less lactic acid, and strengthen the heart. This section provides materials for both aerobic and anaerobic training.

A Reminder About Warming Up

Warming up the muscles and tendons before any kind of exercise is critical, especially before high-intensity activity. Most anaerobic activities are high intensity and high impact. That is, they involve a maximum effort and, often, some kind of jolt to the muscles, tendons, and ligaments. As indicated in an earlier section of the book, athletes should warm up before such activities in order to assure a full range of motion. Anything short of a full range of motion increases the potential for injury.

Cool-down activities are similarly important. They provide the transition from vigorous activity to inactivity and help the body return to normal metabolic levels. They are the same kinds of exercises performed during the warm-up phase and help prevent stiffness following high-intensity, high-impact activity. Following a 10-minute cool down, the athlete should be fully recovered. If still exhausted or fatigued, the athlete probably was working too hard.

Physically fit people recover faster than those less fit. Evander Holyfield, for example, can recover from his maximum attainable heart rate in about 30 seconds. That's asking a bit much of young athletes, especially after vigorous competition, but we can expect it of them after most practices—if they perform the appropriate cool-down exercises each day.

AEROBIC ACTIVITY FOR WEIGHT REDUCTION

Moderate aerobic activity—even jogging or fast walking performed well below the anaerobic threshold—if done for 30 minutes or more, can result in stiffness the next day. Warming-up and cooling-down exercises, therefore, are very important for persons of all ages. They avoid shock to the system before and after even moderate activity.

Aerobic exercise is essential for weight loss. Only with moderate but extended exercise and nutritional restraint can people lose weight correctly. A wide range of diets have proven to be popular but ineffective approaches to weight loss. They are both expensive and convincing; many overweight people accept their promise because they fail to understand the relatively simple relationship between weight loss and aerobic exercise.

This fact is especially bothersome for those of us working with overweight and poorly conditioned youngsters who dream of athletic success but awaken each morning to another day of inactivity and nutritional indifference. That's why we make the reproducible in figure 4-2 available to all students early in the year. We *never* volunteer it for particular students; their weight is probably very sensitive to them. We do, however, make it available in the gym and athletic areas to pique their curiosity.

Such students should exercise aerobically at least three times a week. The very poorly conditioned youngster may start his or her program walking, then progress to jogging and weightlifting. Initially, any amount of exercise will improve cardiovascular efficiency and produce some weight loss if the youngster complements exercise with improved eating habits. We all know how easy it is to rationalize after vigorous exercise; the endorphins kick in and we feel so good about ourselves that we stop on the way home for a couple of cheeseburgers and a vanilla shake.

Young people are no different. The good they do with exercise is easily compromised by the bad they do at the fast-food counter. Most youngsters are active enough to burn off occasional dietary excesses. Less active students, however, require prompting from someone they respect, often a coach, to change their life styles. Even a minor change, if started early enough, can pay dividends later in life.

Such youngsters also discover in themselves the potential for athletics. This is not to suggest that your intervention will transform every couch potato in school into a blue chipper, but many will begin to enjoy exercise to the point of developing the physical stamina and self-confidence to shun the potato chips after school and try a sport. At this point, you've helped your program and, more important, encouraged a youngster who may be on the road to lifelong fitness.

As expressed in figure 4-2, everyone in the fitness program must understand the relationship between moderate exercise and weight loss. The overweight youngster

Figure 4-2

IS WEIGHT LOSS YOUR GOAL?

EXERCISE! EXERCISE! EXERCISE! Exercise and a nutritionally balanced diet are the only sure-fire ways to lose weight. You will hear about a range of very appealing diets advertised on radio and TV; some may even work temporarily. You won't consistently lose weight and keep it off, however, until you maintain a balanced program of exercise and diet. But first, think about your goal.

The obvious first question is, "Do you really need to lose weight?" Sometimes appearances are more important than reality in our society. Don't become the victim of someone else's perceptions of proper appearance. Think about it this way. Losing weight may be exactly what you need to do if your percentage of body fat is high. If it's low, you may not have to lose as much weight as you think you do.

First things first: See your family doctor or a qualified trainer to determine your percentage of body fat. Then compare it with these numbers:

Men: low body fat = 7 percent or lower
high body fat = 25 percent or higher

Women: low body fat = 14 percent or lower
high body fat = 30 percent or higher

If, for example, you're a 5'10" female who weighs 150 pounds with a body fat percentage of 21 percent, you probably don't need to lose weight, certainly not as much as you think you do. If, as a male, you're 6'4" and weigh 235 pounds with a body fat percentage of 13 percent, you're in pretty good shape. If your body fat percentage is higher than it should be, you do need to lose weight, but be sure to do it properly and safely.

Next Steps: See your family doctor for the best kind of diet for you, then engage in a regular program of aerobic activity. Aerobic activity involves extended but *moderate* exercise: jogging, bicycling, walking, swimming—any activity that makes you breathe harder and perspire mildly. If you exercise too vigorously, that is, if you are unable to talk while exercising or you have to stop after a while to catch your breath, you are not exercising aerobically and will lose very little weight!

SEE A COACH FOR THE SPECIFICS OF A PROGRAM JUST FOR YOU!

© 1995 by Michael D. Koehler

who pushes herself too hard for five minutes may benefit from the running but not nearly as much as when she learns to run more slowly for longer periods of time. The longer the exercise, the more fat she will burn.

Good things happen when we exercise. Our bodies process oxygen more efficiently. We burn fat if we run aerobically for extended periods of time. If we exercise two hours before eating, we curb our appetites, and we even slow down the physiological effects of aging! That fact may not sell the program to youngsters, most of whom are anticipating immortality anyway, but it will do wonders for those adults in the building who need to shed a pound or two.

Students may show little concern for the physiological effects of aging, but some of them will be grateful for the rest of their lives if you help them deal with the psychological effects of being overweight in a weight-conscious world. Figure 4-3 provides the kind of information such students require to find the right kinds of exercises for themselves. You might attach this reproducible to figure 4-2 or provide it separately, perhaps introducing it to the students with a brief explanation.

Recognize that the caloric expenditures are only averages. Each is dependent not only on the activity but the intensity of the exercise. Individual differences should be expected; the purpose of the chart, therefore, is to provide only general indications of the relative caloric expenditures to be anticipated. Any loss of weight obviously depends on the intensity, duration, and frequency of the exercise and the eating habits of the athlete.

The caloric expenditures may be a little shocking to inexperienced athletes! The numbers will seem surprisingly low in comparison to the work they just did. The same thing happens to adults who run for half an hour and suddenly realize they have burned off the equivalent of a glass of milk. In addition to discouraging them from that piece of chocolate cake after dinner, such a sudden realization makes their commitment to running seem silly.

It's important, therefore, for coaches to help young athletes understand that aerobic exercise and improved physical fitness have other effects on metabolism and caloric expenditure. First of all, fit people have more energy; they do more during the day, are more active, burn off more calories performing their daily routines. Second, the body has to work hard to restore its glycogen levels after exercise, a process that in itself requires more energy and a subsequent expenditure of calories.

Finally, vigorous exercise, even if performed aerobically, causes small tears in the muscles (sometimes big ones!) that require repair. This repair process also requires energy, which results in the additional expenditure of calories. Weightlifting, then, also burns calories, especially after a specific focus on one or two muscle groups. That's another reason why serious lifters exercise muscle groups on alternate days, to provide time for muscles to repair themselves before additional exercise.

The relationship of nutrition to physical fitness and weight loss will be discussed in a future section. The relationships among the three are extremely important, particularly when young athletes seek to either gain or lose weight to enhance their performance in certain sports. In fact, weight loss and weight gain are often seriously misunderstood aspects of athletic preparation and performance.

Figure 4-3

BURNING OFF THE CALORIES

Interested in weight loss? First of all, are you absolutely sure you need to lose weight? If so, how much? If you're not sure of the answers to these questions, you might think about seeing your family doctor to get an assessment of your percentage of body fat. An average range for men is from about 10 to 22 percent, for women 16 to 28 percent. If you fall in that range, you may not have to lose as much as you think; in fact, you may not have to lose any!

If you do have to shed a few pounds, consider the following exercises. They are only approximations but they'll give you a good idea of caloric expenditures. They should be performed *moderately*! That is, you should be able to talk while performing them. You probably will break a sweat, but you shouldn't push yourself too hard. If you do, you won't lose any weight! Fat is dependent on oxygen to burn, so you must perform *aerobic* exercises—the kind on the chart.

Do them about 3 to 4 times a week, and see me if you need more information. Be sure to see your family doctor for the body fat assessment and to get his or her permission to engage in these kinds of activities. You'll have to have a doctor's release on file in the Athletic Department.

Good luck!

	10 minutes	30 minutes
Aerobic Dance	90	270
Baseball	40	120
Basketball	95	285
Calisthenics	45	135
Canoeing	50	150
Cycling 7 mph	44	132
Cycling 9.5 mph	68	204
Cycling 12 mph	115	345
Dancing fast	90	270
Digging	90	270
Field hockey	91	273
Football	90	270
Gymnastics	45	135
Hill climbing	82	246
Hockey	70	210
Judo	120	360
Jumping rope (70 jumps per minute)	110	330
Lacrosse	68	204
Racquetball	74	222
Running 12-minute mile	92	276
Running 8-minute mile	132	396
Running 6-minute mile	171	513
Stair-climbing walking	98	294
Stair-climbing jog (stairmaster)	110	330
Squash	74	222
Skating (ice and roller)	50	150
Soccer	70	210
Swimming fast crawl	87	261
Tennis singles	75	225
Walking 20-minute mile	45	135
Walking 15-minute mile	65	195
Weight training	75	225
Wrestling	140	420

© 1995 by Michael D. Koehler

Avoiding Dramatic Weight Changes

Before anyone considers a dramatic change of weight for any reason, particularly if it involves vigorous athletic competition, he or she should first consider the relationship of body fat to body weight and visit the family doctor. A quick review of figure 4-2 indicates that the average body fat percentage for men ranges from a low of 7 percent to a high of 25 percent and for women a low of 14 percent to a high of 30 percent, depending upon age. Young athletes should be aware of these percentages in order to avoid possible problems with excessive weight gains or losses.

For example, the 6'1" center on the girls' basketball team who weighs 160 pounds and has 22 percent body fat doesn't really have to lose weight to improve either her appearance or her performance on the court. When social pressure begins to compare her with less athletic and smaller classmates, she may conclude that she needs to lose weight. This kind of reasoning is especially true of adolescent girls who are also tall. Because many of them already are self-conscious about their height, they conclude that the only factor they can control is their weight, so they go on unnecessary and potentially harmful diets.

Fortunately, as most adolescents grow older, they realize that attractive men and women come in all shapes and sizes, that "attractiveness" is a function not so much of how good we look but of how good we feel about ourselves. Physical fitness, therefore, no matter how big or small we are, provides not only the appearance but the self-confidence and vitality that make us attractive.

Young athletes try to lose weight for other reasons as well, some of which are causes of concern to adults. Unfortunately, some wrestling coaches aren't as concerned as they should be when they encourage young athletes to lose two pounds in 24 hours to make weight before a match, but their parents should be. Starving off weight before a match can be both debilitating and discouraging.

In the first place, most of the weight loss is nothing but water, which will be replenished soon after the match. The weight will have to be lost again. Such dramatic weight loss also results in the loss of lean muscle tissue, normally from large muscles, which can affect strength during the match. A more desirable alternative for wrestlers, especially young wrestlers, is to compete at a weight that is consistent with body composition and to maintain body weight through self-disciplined exercise and eating habits.

On the other end of the continuum is the youngster who seeks a dramatic weight *gain* in order to be the starting tackle on the varsity football team. Again, coaches often contribute to this kind of problem, in this instance by telling players they'll have to "bulk up" in order to play the position. Gaining a few pounds or putting on a lot of weight is appropriate over time, but pressure to do so on a short-term basis can cause health problems as well as increase the likelihood that young athletes will use steroids to realize their goals.

Certainly, most coaches apply such pressure unintentionally, but the result is the same. A much better alternative for the football coach is to suggest a position on the football team that is more in line with the athlete's body composition. The small tackle might be an excellent tight end, pulling guard, fullback, or noseguard on defense. This topic will be discussed more fully in Section 6.

TRAINING AEROBICALLY

Simply stated, aerobic training involves the large muscles of the body in continuous and, often, strenuous movement for an average of 15 to 20 minutes at a time, sometimes longer. The bigger the muscle involved in the exercise, the more energy expended, fat being the primary source in extended aerobic activity. Weightlifting, for example, is not an aerobic activity. It benefits appearance and athletic performance, but it doesn't burn fat or do much to improve cardiovascular efficiency. Doing biceps curls for a minute and a half burns only the glycogen stores in the muscles and doesn't begin to use fat as an energy source.

The body's big muscles provide most of the power and use most of the energy stored as fat. Activating these muscles for moderate but extended periods of time draws upon the body's energy supplies and burns off the fat. It doesn't burn off selectively; our fat supplies are drained off generally, hence the need for extended exercise.

The body's big muscles—the gluteals, quadriceps, and abductors—are the prime movers for aerobic exercise, use the most energy, and require a steady flow of oxygen. That's why the exercises listed in figure 4-3 are so important for young athletes. They engage young athletes in the kinds of moderate activities that burn fat and improve the body's use of oxygen. Running is perhaps the most prominent because it doesn't require special equipment and can be done almost anywhere.

Aerobic Training and the Total Athlete

All coaches, no matter what the sport, must emphasize the importance of aerobic activity with their athletes and provide time during the week to improve cardiovascular strength. Whoops! We can hear them now, those frazzled many out there who don't have enough time now to get everything done in practice. How will they accommodate the added imposition of 15- to 20-minute blocks of time for aerobic running? They make a good point.

Skill development and refined strategies are the critical components in preparation for upcoming games or meets and require the greatest amount of time. We will not argue that point. On the other hand, aerobic training can be performed only one day a week, if that is all you have time for—probably the day after a game, to burn off lactic acid and to eliminate the muscle fatigue that interferes with a fresh start for the next series of practices.

In addition, coaches must emphasize the importance of aerobic training during the off-season, so that athletes are well conditioned when the season starts and require only periodic aerobic activity to burn off lactic acid and maintain cardiovascular strength. A couple of laps after practice can accomplish that. They restore oxygen to the muscles, reduce muscle fatigue for the next day of practice, and provide the cool down athletes require to maintain peak performance.

By contrast, consider the coach who assigns wind sprints after every practice. He or she is involving athletes in anaerobic activity, which builds up more lactic acid, and promotes muscle fatigue that evening at home. Other coaches who alternate wind sprints with 15 minutes of jogging *after* practice improve the overall conditioning of their athletes. They also have discovered ways *during* practice to provide for the anaerobic needs of their athletes. Scrimmages and short-burst activities that promote skill development are all anaerobic and improve muscle tolerance for lactic acid buildups.

Both aerobic and anaerobic exercise are important to your athletes. The coach who says that her sport is exclusively anaerobic and trains her athletes accordingly may well run into problems late in each contest when her kids start to run out of gas. Just watch a couple of those 300-pound NFL linemen lead a running play around right end late in the fourth quarter. On a sustained drive, they need both aerobic and anaerobic strength to maintain performance. So do junior and senior high school athletes.

Interval Training

Exercise physiologists are promoting interval training as an excellent way to boost fitness and performance levels. It consists chiefly of brief periods of anaerobic activity (sprinting) followed by longer periods of aerobic activity (jogging). The "interval" of anaerobic activity should approximate the length of maximal output in the individual athlete's sport. Short but intense anaerobic exercises, 10 to 15 seconds long, should have a 3:1 ratio of jogging to sprinting. Football players, for example, might sprint for 10-second intervals and jog for 30 seconds.

Sports that require longer anaerobic outputs will have ratios of 2:1 or 1:1. Wrestlers, for example, might push themselves for two to three minutes, then jog for an equal amount of time, being sure to check their heart rates to determine a return to normal before resuming anaerobic activity. Every athlete must assure appropriate recovery before resuming the anaerobic interval. This is a key factor because interval training is grueling.

It is also very effective. Consider these studies—one conducted at the University of Massachusetts, the other at the University of Miami. Each studied a control group and an experimental group of exercisers. The experimental group was involved in interval training, the other in uninterrupted aerobic activity. Their findings indicated that the athletes involved in interval training experienced at least a 10-percent increase in their cardiovascular endurance.

According to the researchers, two factors accounted for the improvement: (1) Those involved in interval training conditioned their bodies to use energy sources more efficiently. (2) They delayed the time when their bodies had to use the energy source. These are two significant advantages of interval training. The first indicates that physically fit people make the best use of their energy systems, the second that they don't need them as quickly as those who are less fit.

Interval training, therefore, is useful for any athlete. Although it is possible in season, it is most appropriate during the off-season, when athletes have the time to improve their conditioning levels. Track coaches use it frequently during in-season practice sessions, but most coaches in other sports don't have the half hour or so required to do it justice.

Because the length of intervals is dependent upon the unique demands of the sport, the intervals will vary for different athletes. The reproducible in figure 4-4, how-

Figure 4-4

INTERVAL TRAINING

IMPORTANT: The following program is very demanding and should not be attempted if you haven't discussed it with your coach. Be sure to talk to your coach before engaging in interval training to be sure that the program is right for you.

A General Program

If your coach has given you permission to engage in interval training, read the following program and perform *all* of it very carefully:

1. *STRETCH* yourself completely to guarantee that you don't pull any muscles. Stretch for at least 10 to 15 minutes, maybe more, depending upon how tight you are from previous exercise. Use the stretching and flexibility exercises in your booklet or get some from your coach.

2. *WARM UP* for at least 5 to 10 minutes. It should be a vigorous warm-up, not exhausting. Do it at approximately 60 percent of your maximum heart rate. Again, refer to your booklet or see your coach for specific warm-up exercises.

3. *SPRINT* for 30 to 90 seconds, depending on your particular sport (see your coach for specifics), at 80 percent to 90 percent of your maximum heart rate.

4. *Jog* for 90 to 180 seconds, depending upon the length of your sprint. During this time, be sure your heart rate drops to 70 percent of its maximum. Be sure not to do any more repetitions until your heart rate drops to this level.

5. *Do 4 to 6 more repetitions* of the above program.

6. *Walk very slowly* until your heart rate drops to at least 60 percent of its maximum.

7. *Do another 4 to 6 repetitions* of the entire program.

8. *Cool down* for at least 5 to 10 minutes, using the cool-down activities in your booklet or those suggested by your coach. All cool-down exercises should be done at no more than 60 percent of your maximum heart rate.

REMEMBER:
THIS IS A VERY CHALLENGING PROGRAM.
SEE YOUR COACH BEFORE STARTING IT—
YOUR FAMILY DOCTOR, TOO, IF YOU OR YOUR PARENTS HAVE QUESTIONS!

© 1995 by Michael D. Koehler

ever, is general enough to accommodate any sport. Just remember when assigning the length of the jog and the sprint to provide a 3:1 ratio for short sprints and a 2:1 or 1:1 ratio for longer sprints. Again, football and basketball players will sprint for 10 to 15 seconds with up to 45 seconds of jogging, while wrestlers and middle-distance runners will sprint for longer periods of time, perhaps 90 seconds with 90 to 180 seconds of jogging.

Interval training may not be appropriate for all athletes. Many younger athletes don't have the stamina for this kind of strenuous activity, nor do they need such training. Interval training is for the very serious-minded athlete who has already proven his or her physical skills. Notice as well the importance of warm-up and cool-down activities. Finally, instruct athletes who are capable of interval training to engage in it no more than three times a week and to make sure they have a doctor's permission.

Staying Fit Aerobically

Aerobic training may be most appropriate during the off-season, when time is not the enemy. For young athletes, off-season for one sport may be in-season for another. Most youngsters have primary interest in one or two sports but probably should be encouraged to participate in more; exposure to other sports may lead to greater commitment to total fitness. Sometimes athletes even discover that they are better suited to their "secondary" sports.

Second, involvement in other sports helps to maintain both aerobic and anaerobic conditioning levels. The exposure to another coach and to a different team's expectations can often provide the motivation a young athlete needs to sustain levels of performance. It also provides opportunities to develop additional, complementary skills, thereby improving the athlete's total performance.

Athletes who are committed to one sport, however, and those who are not involved in summer activities require exercise programs to see them through the off-season. The programs provided in figures 4-5 through 4-8 meet the aerobic needs of most young athletes. They are maximal programs and should be adjusted to meet the unique needs of certain athletes. They may be too strenuous for some junior high schoolers and not strenuous enough for some high school seniors.

Notice that they include anaerobic exercises as well. The mix of aerobic and anaerobic exercises meets the total off-season conditioning needs of all athletes. Notice as well that room is provided at the bottom of the form for sport-specific exercises. Although the form provides some anaerobic exercises, you may want to include others that are more appropriate for your sport or for particular positions on your team.

Football players, for example, will perform different exercises based on position. Linemen may practice their pulling techniques or simply sprint downfield for 5 to 10 yards to practice getting off the ball faster. Defensive backs may practice their back peddle for 15- to 20-yard bursts in order to work on pass coverage. Offensive backs may run 20-yard sprints to practice hitting the line and exploding into the secondary.

Basketball, soccer, and field hockey players, on the other hand, run between 8 and 10 miles each game. Most of this running involves anaerobic bursts, interspersed with periods of aerobic jogging. On this basis, interval or dash training is most appro-

Figure 4-5

OFF-SEASON WORKOUT
SOCCER, FOOTBALL, FIELD HOCKEY

INTRODUCTION

The following activities are designed to accommodate your aerobic and anaerobic needs during the off-season. You will be following a 5-day program. It probably is a good idea to have days one and two on Monday and Tuesday and days three, four, and five on Thursday, Friday, and Saturday. Take Wednesdays and Sundays off to rest your muscles. Remember, these exercises are for your cardiovascular system; they are *not* to replace your weight workout.

See me or your coach for specific examples of skill-related exercises. They will vary according to your sport. Your coach may also have some isolated skills he or she wants you to work on during the off-season. Be sure to write them down and incorporate them into your total workout. If you have any questions, be sure to see me.

YOUR WORKOUT

DAY ONE: 3-mile jog. Remember to take your time; jog within your aerobic range.

DAY TWO: 2-mile jog, followed by 10 to 15 minutes of jumping rope.

DAY THREE: Ten minutes of skill-related activity. This should provide a good warm-up for the next two exercises. Next, run a fast mile; don't sprint it but stride it as strongly as you can. Finally, cycle for 20 minutes.

DAY FOUR: 4-mile jog. Again, run it slowly in order to stay well within your aerobic range.

DAY FIVE: 10 minutes of rope jumping, followed by 10 minutes of skill-related activity. Conclude the workout with 10 minutes of swimming. Swim for 10 minutes. This is a good cool-down for your workout.

MY SKILL-RELATED EXERCISES ARE:

**TAKE SOME TIME TO RELAX YOUR MUSCLES,
THEN DO YOUR WEIGHT WORKOUT. REMEMBER:**

SAFETY FIRST

**IF YOU FEEL TIRED, BE SURE TO REST UP
BEFORE STARTING YOUR WEIGHT WORKOUT.**

© 1995 by Michael D. Koehler

Figure 4-6

OFF-SEASON WORKOUT
BASKETBALL, VOLLEYBALL, BADMINTON, AND TRACK

INTRODUCTION

The following activities are designed to accommodate your aerobic and anaerobic needs during the off-season. You will be following a 5-day program. It probably is a good idea to have days one and two on Monday and Tuesday and days three, four, and five on Thursday, Friday, and Saturday. Take Wednesdays and Sundays off to rest your muscles. Remember, these exercises are for your cardiovascular system; they are *not* to replace your weight workout.

See me or your coach for specific examples of skill-related exercises; then write them on the bottom of the page. They will vary according to your sport. Your coach may have some isolated skills he or she wants you to work on during the off-season. Be sure to write them down and incorporate them into your total workout. If you have any questions, be sure to see me.

YOUR WORKOUT

DAY ONE: 3-mile jog. Remember to stay well within your aerobic range. Conclude with 20 minutes of sport-related skills.

DAY TWO: 2-mile jog. Again, stay within your aerobic range. Then, climb stairs for 10 minutes, followed by 10 minutes of rope jumping.

DAY THREE: 5-mile jog. Yes, you can do it; just stay within your aerobic range.

DAY FOUR: 1-mile jog, primarily as a warm-up activity. If you are a basketball, volleyball, or badminton player, find some teammates and play a 30-minute game. If a track athlete, practice your starts by taking 10-yard sprints. Do this at least 15 times, then jog another mile.

DAY FIVE: 4-mile jog, followed by 10 minutes of sport-related skill practice. Conclude with a 10-minute swim.

MY SKILL-RELATED EXERCISES ARE:

**TAKE SOME TIME TO RELAX YOUR MUSCLES, THEN
DO YOUR WEIGHT WORKOUT. REMEMBER:**

SAFETY FIRST

**IF YOU FEEL TIRED, BE SURE TO REST UP
BEFORE STARTING YOUR WEIGHT WORKOUT.**

© 1995 by Michael D. Koehler

Figure 4-7

OFF-SEASON WORKOUT
BASEBALL, SOFTBALL, FIELD EVENTS

INTRODUCTION

The following activities are designed to accommodate your aerobic and anaerobic needs during the off-season. You will be following a 5-day program. It probably is a good idea to have days one and two on Monday and Tuesday and days three, four, and five on Thursday, Friday, and Saturday. Take Wednesdays and Sundays off to rest your muscles. Remember, these exercises are for your cardiovascular system; they are *not* to replace your weight workout.

See me or your coach for specific examples of skill-related exercises. They will vary according to your sport. Your coach may also have some isolated skills he or she wants you to work on during the off-season. Be sure to write them down and incorporate them into your total workout. If you have any questions, be sure to see me.

YOUR WORKOUT

DAY ONE: 2-mile jog. Take your time and run well within your aerobic range. Follow this with 20 minutes of sport-related skill practice.

DAY TWO: 1-mile jog. Take your time; this is a good warm-up activity. Follow it with 10 minutes of stairclimbing, then 10 minutes of jumping rope.

DAY THREE: 3-mile jog. Again, stay well within your aerobic range.

DAY FOUR: 1-mile jog, followed by 20 minutes of sport-related skill practice.

DAY FIVE: 2-mile jog, followed by 10 minutes of stairclimbing or jumping rope. Conclude with a 10-minute swim.

MY SKILL-RELATED EXERCISES ARE:

TAKE SOME TIME TO RELAX YOUR MUSCLES, THEN DO YOUR WEIGHT WORKOUT. REMEMBER:

SAFETY FIRST

IF YOU FEEL TIRED, BE SURE TO REST UP BEFORE STARTING YOUR WEIGHT WORKOUT.

© 1995 by Michael D. Koehler

Figure 4-8

OFF-SEASON WORKOUT
WRESTLING, GYMNASTICS, AND SWIMMING

INTRODUCTION

The following activities are designed to accommodate your aerobic and anaerobic needs during the off-season. You will be following a 5-day program. It probably is a good idea to have days one and two on Monday and Tuesday and days three, four, and five on Thursday, Friday, and Saturday. Take Wednesdays and Sundays off to rest your muscles. Remember, these exercises are for your cardiovascular system; they are *not* to replace your weight workout.

See me or your coach for specific examples of skill-related exercises. They will vary according to your sport. Your coach may have some isolated skills he or she wants you to work on during the off-season. Be sure to write them down and incorporate them into your total workout. If you have any questions, be sure to see me.

YOUR WORKOUT

DAY ONE: 3-mile jog. Remember to stay well within your aerobic range. This exercise is designed to improve your cardiovascular strength.

DAY TWO: 2-mile jog. Again, jog easily. Follow this with 10 minutes of jumping rope.

DAY THREE: 4-mile jog. Yes, you can do it. Just stay within your aerobic range, no matter how long it takes.

DAY FOUR: 1-mile jog, followed by 10 minutes of stairclimbing. Conclude with 10 minutes of rope jumping.

DAY FIVE: 2-mile jog, followed by 10 minutes of jumping rope. Conclude with 15 minutes of sport-related activity, followed by a 10-minute swim.

MY SKILL-RELATED EXERCISES ARE:

**TAKE SOME TIME TO RELAX YOUR MUSCLES, THEN
DO YOUR WEIGHT WORKOUT. REMEMBER:**

SAFETY FIRST

**IF YOU FEEL TIRED, BE SURE TO REST UP
BEFORE STARTING YOUR WEIGHT WORKOUT.**

© 1995 by Michael D. Koehler

priate for them. It meets their aerobic and anaerobic needs and sustains the levels of conditioning they require to start practice each year prepared to work on skills and strategy. Off-season conditioning schedules may also involve short sprints from the "ready position," quick shuffling activities to improve foot speed and defensive skills, and plyometric or jumping exercises that improve vertical jump and quickness.

Baseball and softball players also require good aerobic and anaerobic conditioning. The aerobic component helps maintain appropriate weight levels and sustains good physical fitness, and the anaerobic enhances sport-specific skills, such as sprinting the bases and chasing down a fly ball. Volleyball and badminton players have similar conditioning needs but require plyometric and other anaerobic exercises to complement their performance. Examples of these kinds of exercises are provided in figure 4-9. Mix and match as you see fit.

Tennis players, swimmers, and cross country runners require high levels of aerobic conditioning. Depending on their individual events, all may also require anaerobic conditioning. Short bursts are required in each sport, and all the athletes must have the ability to fight off muscle fatigue, particularly late in each event.

Wrestlers must be in excellent physical condition to be consistently successful. Those who rely on their strength and skill levels and disregard their cardiovascular conditioning often find themselves on their backs. Wrestlers who "hit the wall" in the third period might as well forewarn their coaches to throw in the towel because they're going home early. Off-season conditioning programs for wrestlers, therefore, involve a lot of rigorous interval training, not the kind of program for the faint of heart.

Coaches are well advised to consider the strength and conditioning levels of their athletes before requiring certain off-season programs. Athletes involved in interval training during the off-season should be mature enough to handle the demands of such programs. The competitive conditioning levels of our athletes must always take a back seat to their developmental levels and health and safety needs.

Replacing Body Fluids

The replacement of body fluids is, perhaps, one of their most important health and safety needs. Water constitutes approximately 60 percent of the average person's body weight. A loss of only 5 percent of the body's water content can lead to headaches, weakness, and rapid pulse, all of which are symptoms of heat exhaustion. It also can lead to diminished mental capacity.

A 10 percent loss is very dangerous and can lead to heatstroke. The belief, therefore, that water consumption during strenuous exercise is to be avoided is potentially very dangerous. Young athletes must be encouraged to drink water frequently during vigorous exercise for all the reasons mentioned in figure 4-10. Loss of water results in a depletion of blood cells, the buildup of toxins in the body because of decreased urination, less oxygen to the muscles because of reduced blood volume, and reduced perspiration, in effect, the loss of the body's natural cooling mechanism.

Humid weather is particularly troublesome, as is the idea of accelerating weight loss by wearing plastic suits. Both inhibit the body's natural cooling system by preventing perspiration from evaporating. The result is heat buildup. Coaches—particu-

Figure 4-9

COMPLEMENTARY EXERCISES FOR BOTH IN- AND OFF-SEASON WORKOUTS

SOMETHING TO THINK ABOUT

All athletes require speed and jumping ability. The following exercises are designed to improve both. You may not be able to do all of them. Do the ones you can, making the appropriate adjustments for each. Be sure to talk to your coach to develop a workout program that is just right for you, and ask him or her for demonstrations of all these exercises as needed.

WARM-UP EXERCISES

Perform these exercises deliberately. If you are outside and it is cold, do more of them. If it is warm, do them less frequently.

Walking Toe Up - Walk for approximately 20 yards on your heels, keeping your toes pointing up.

Skipping - Skip for approximately 20 yards, emphasizing the motion. Exaggerate it as much as possible.

Side-stepping - Move as quickly as possible sideways. Don't crossover step but exaggerate the movement of your arms.

Backward Run - Run backwards as fast as you can, bringing your heel up to your buttocks and extending your foot backward as you run.

JUMPING EXERCISES

Don't do all these exercises consecutively; do only those that you can do well. See your coach for the specific exercises for you. If you can't perform them successfully, you won't get much out of them. The purpose of these exercises is to put force into the ground and then get it out of the ground as you perform the jump. Do all these exercises on a relatively soft surface, something that will be easy on your joints. Do *not* do them on concrete or any other hard surface. All these exercises will improve your jumping ability and your speed.

Ankle jump - Keeping your legs straight and your feet together, spring off the balls of your feet, using only your ankles to jump off the ground. Do these for a distance of 10 yards, then come back 10 yards.

Jump-Ups - With your hands on your hips and your feet together, bounce up onto a box that is about a foot high. Be sure it is stable and covered with something soft, like a rug. Do this 10 to 15 times, stepping back down to the ground after each jump.

Backward Jump-Ups - Do the same bouncing motion, only do it backward. Be sure to keep your feet together and step back to the ground after each jump.

Standing Long Jump - Do 10 standing long jumps, pausing after each jump to gather yourself. Jump as far as you can on each jump.

© 1995 by Michael D. Koehler

Frog Jumps - These are like standing long jumps, only you will squat down and gather yourself like a frog before jumping again. These jumps are to be done consecutively with little pausing between each one.

Off and On Box - Stand on the box and jump off backward. Use the force of your landing on the ground to jump back on the box immediately. Emphasize the bouncing motion and do this exercise 10 times consecutively.

Hurdle Jumps - With your feet approximately together, jump over a series of hurdles or another obstacle at an appropriate height for you. Emphasize the bouncing motion. Don't jump and stop to gather yourself. You should bounce over each obstacle. Do this approximately 7 or 8 times.

Puddle Jumping - Take 15 to 20 long, bounding strides, as if jumping over a series of puddles on the ground. Emphasize the motion of each long stride.

Again, talk to your coach to determine which of these exercises is best for you and the number of repetitions you should do. If a box is not available, find something that is stable and approximately 12" off the ground. If 12" is too high, lower the height until you can perform the exercise comfortably. The important thing is to use proper form in order to maximize your benefit from the exercise.

RUNNING

Conclude each jumping session with three to five 40-yard runs. Perform each run this way: Get in the starting position that is appropriate for your sport, an upright "ready" position if you play volleyball, basketball, or tennis, a stance if you play football or track. Explode out of the position and sprint hard for 20 yards. After the first 20 yards, stride hard for the remaining 20 yards, running as *relaxed* as possible. Don't run with fists or any strain on your face. Run as relaxed as possible. This final exercise will condition you to run easily and stride out, making you that much faster.

Again, see your coach for explanations of any of these exercises, and be sure to perform only those that you can do properly and comfortably. As always, *safety first* is our slogan. We want you to improve your fitness levels, not injure yourself.

© 1995 by Michael D. Koehler

Figure 4-10

YOUR NEED FOR WATER

Drink Water During and After Practice

Not too many years ago, adults used to tell youngsters not to drink too much water during or immediately after exercise. They reasoned that it might upset their stomachs. WRONG! Young athletes need a constant supply of water during any kind of vigorous exercise. In fact, some people now say that you need at least a half cup of water for every 10 to 15 minutes you exercise. Replacing body fluids maintains energy levels and prevents such things as cramping and extreme fatigue.

C.U.B.S.

Remember the word "Cubs" every time you practice. Here's what it stands for:

C - *C*ells. The body's cells require a lot of water to do their job.

U - *U*rination. Water consumption stimulates the urination that eliminates toxic and harmful materials from the body.

B - *B*lood. Water increases the volume of blood in the body, which carries more oxygen to the brain and muscles.

S - *S*weat. Water consumption stimulates perspiration, which is the body's cooling mechanism.

Water, Water Everywhere

To paraphrase a poet you'll bump into in English literature, we have water, water everywhere, so drink a lot of it. Drink it at home, too, especially after a particularly vigorous or hot workout and/or on hot and humid days. Remember, the loss of body fluids can be potentially harmful to you, and it can result in the loss of mental capacity! As an athlete, you don't want to lose anything, so drink water—lots of it!

© 1995 by Michael D. Koehler

larly those involved in football, softball, field hockey, or any sport that practices or competes in hot weather—should be aware that jerseys saturated with perspiration have the same effect on athletes. It is wise, therefore, to take them off—propriety permitting—or change them periodically.

Coaches should also ensure that their athletes drink water before they become thirsty. They should drink at least 8 ounces of water for every 10 minutes of vigorous exercise. Coaches need not schedule water breaks every 10 minutes, simply provide ample supplies of water, particularly on hot days, and allow athletes to take a drink whenever they want one.

The old notion of avoiding water during vigorous exercise is about as accurate as giving kids a lean piece of meat before a game. Both are nutritionally shortsighted. The piece of meat will bring blood to the stomach instead of the muscles, where the athlete needs it; and the absence of water will cut down on the volume of blood, further reducing the supply of oxygen to the muscles. Players lose on both counts.

This bit of advice is particularly important for wrestlers who believe that they can cut weight by staying away from water. As indicated already, they will lose weight, but they will discover that the weight loss is temporary. More important, they will discover that the absence of water causes slight heat exhaustion, which results in lassitude, headaches, and nausea—three conditions a young wrestler would just as soon avoid.

And what about those sport drinks we hear so much about? They're probably helpful, but simple sugar water accomplishes much the same thing. Immediately after exercise, the muscles work hard to replace glycogens. Because the heart is the primary muscle in the body, it absorbs sugars first, before the other muscles in the body have a chance to replenish them. Once it has an adequate supply, it gives the other muscles the go-ahead to take in their share.

This replacement of sugars is accomplished best by simple carbohydrates, candy and sugar cubes. We need not worry about well-conditioned athletes suffering the ill effects of eating candy after vigorous exercise. Their bodies will absorb it so quickly that it will provide much more benefit than potential harm. A candy bar and a quart of water, that's the best bet after strenuous exercise. And keep the water handy *during* exercise; it is one of the best safety precautions a coach can provide for her athletes.

A Reminder to the Junior High Coach

Much of what has been discussed in this section may be too extreme for the average junior high school athlete. This is not to say that the programs and exercises are inappropriate, just that they may be too strenuous for some, even most, junior high school youngsters. Coaches are well advised, then, to modify them in order to accommodate the developmental levels of their athletes.

It might even be advisable to train aerobically and lift weights on alternate days. Such a program has two advantages. It provides an appropriate workout, and it prevents young athletes from burning out due to unreasonable demands on their bodies.

As with weight training, the primary principle for cardiovascular exercise for young athletes is a gradual progression of intensity in a well-supervised program.

Let's Wrap It Up

Most young athletes are so active that intense programs of cardiovascular activity are unnecessary. If coaches spent just one day mirroring the activities of their young athletes, assuming they survived the experience, they would worry less about the athletes' needs for cardiovascular endurance. This is not to say that we should abandon the focus of this section; it's just that we need not emphasize it too rigorously, particularly for the younger players.

As discussed in section 5, the joints of young athletes are immature and are subject to injury if they engage too rigorously in high-impact aerobics, activities like running and raquetball. Bicycling and swimming may provide the same aerobic benefits without risking damage to young tendons and ligaments.

Any athlete, young or not so young, must realize that training for competitive sports is a demanding proposition. Winning in sports is the result much more of hard work than of natural talent. Good athletes expect exhaustion and pain when they prepare for intense competition. The younger the athlete, however, the faster he or she loses interest in sports when the training demands exceed the pleasures of winning.

Most youngsters engage in sports because of an idealized vision they have of competition. We must do our best as coaches to keep that vision alive and not introduce them too quickly to the demanding realities of competitive sports. Commitment to hard work, as desirable as it may be for youngsters, should never obscure their simple love of participation. As with every other relationship in their lives, once love is nurtured, the commitment will follow.

Section Five

STRENGTH TRAINING:

EXPLANATIONS AND PROGRAMS

Introduction

Young people lift weights for a variety of reasons. Some just want to look good. Most often, their motivation has a lot to do with the opposite sex. Others want to improve their athletic performance. These motives can also relate to the opposite sex. Still others have been conditioned by their coaches to believe that strength training can prevent serious injuries. This reason has little to do with the opposite sex. It is purely selfish—smart, too.

Consider a recent article in the *International Journal of Sports Medicine* that indicated that exercise, specifically weight training, is an excellent way to prevent broken bones. A professor from Arizona State University emphasized that repeated stress on bones, such as in rigorous weightlifting, increases their density, which improves their durability under tension. Weight training, therefore, involves a whole lot more than looking good.

In fact, its potential to prevent injury is often overlooked by coaches and players alike. Strength training has been associated with improved performance for so long that its effects on reduced injury have been ignored, especially by athletes. We know of a high school tackle who is a perfect but unfortunate example of emphasizing performance over reduced injury.

Tom was about 6'5" and weighed well over 300 pounds. After his sophomore year in high school, he was being looked at by at least 50 major colleges across the country. Obviously, he had the size, but Tom also had strength and quickness. Because of his promise as a college athlete, his dad put him on a weight program to improve his upper body strength. The program worked well. By the start of his senior year, he was bench-pressing 380 pounds and was expected to be one of the best high school prospects in the nation.

But Tom ran into a problem during the second game of the season. He damaged cartilage in one knee, sat out two games, returned to action, and damaged the other knee. Two knee operations later, Tom missed his senior year in football and suddenly found himself recruited by fewer and fewer colleges. Only after the knee operations did Tom start strengthening his legs.

By then it was too late. The damage had been done. Tom and his dad apparently had forgotten that weight training should strengthen every part of the body, particularly the legs. The most serious athletic injuries happen to the legs. Achilles tendons are ruptured; ankles are twisted; and knee ligaments are torn. Often such injuries end playing careers. A major element in such tragedies is that many of these injuries can be prevented.

Coaches can prevent them by involving their athletes in comprehensive strength-training programs. In the process, they will improve individual and team performance. This section provides several reproducibles for young players that will help them benefit from such programs. You'll notice that all the programs emphasize weight training for every part of the body. Let's start, however, with a word to the coach.

Muscles Play a Big Role

There are 600 muscle groups in the human body comprising approximately 40 percent of body weight. The percentage varies with the individual's body type and level of conditioning. No matter how well-conditioned these muscles, however, they play an important role in appearance, general health, and even digestion and self-esteem. They support the skeletal system; they help heat the body; they protect internal organs; they even play a major role in digestion (peristalsis). They also control movement of the body.

This latter function may seem to be the focus of this book. All the factors, however, must be considered when engaging young athletes in strength training programs. Good health is a lifelong proposition; the right habits must start early in a child's life. Through a series of muscular contractions, we can do amazing things with our bodies, from standing confidently to shake someone's hand before a job interview to doing back flips on a balance beam. Each of these movements requires training.

When we isolate a movement and concentrate it, we have an exercise. When we add resistance to that movement, we have strength training. Such training strengthens not only the body but the athlete's self-esteem and confidence. These two characteristics affect his or her performance every bit as much as physical strength. The remainder of this section, then, focuses on performance enhancement and injury prevention. But first, a word of precaution.

Always Warm Up

Persons reading this book must realize that the most important factor in a strength-training program is safety. Numerous studies have proven that warming up maximizes the benefits of exercise; it also minimizes injuries. This one principle has obvious implications for coaches and athletes alike. When warming-up exercises become a regular part of the athlete's strength-training regimen, he or she gets stronger, and the coach has not only better-conditioned athletes but a program that meets the safety needs of kids. Parents like that; so does our legal system.

Encourage young athletes to recognize, first of all, that stretching and warming up are not the same. A warm-up is designed to increase blood supply to the muscles, raising their temperature and making them more pliable and resistant to injury. Recent experiments, for example, affirm that low muscle temperatures decrease reaction time, muscle excitability, and peak contraction force. Without such warming up, premature stretching can cause tears in tendons and ligaments and weaken joints.

In addition, recent evidence indicates that warm-up exercises prepare the heart for increased output without shocking it. One study had 44 men run on a treadmill for 10 seconds at 9 miles per hour without a warm-up. Thirty of the subjects showed abnormal changes in their heart rate and blood pressure. The same men, given a 15-minute warm-up before the same exercise, eliminated or reduced the abnormal changes, proving that the increased blood flow resulting from a warm-up eases instead of shocks the heart into vigorous exercise.

It's wise, therefore, to distribute passouts such as those in figure 5-1 to all the athletes in the program. You might incorporate them, along with others in this section, into a booklet for each athlete. Because your athletes have achieved or been blessed with different strength levels, no single warm-up is appropriate for everyone. What may be a warm-up for one may be maximal effort for another. The passouts, therefore, discuss warming up generally but provide the specific principles that underlie its importance. You'll notice that the exercises are appropriate for students involved in the manual movements as well as the actual weightlifting.

The What and Why of Belts

Coaches must impress on young athletes that belts are as important to strength training as the weights themselves. They are important for several reasons. The lighter elastic belt helps heat the lower back and increases the blood flow to the area, thereby further reducing the incidence of injury. It also compresses the midsection and provides additional support. The other, more common type of belt is the leather or hard nylon belt which prevents the back from hyperextending or hyperflexing beyond the spine's normal range of motion.

The lower back is a common area of discomfort for any athlete who trains hard. It is an area covered with very small, deep muscles, all of which are affected in one way or another by the upper back's larger muscles, the latissimus dorsi, and the lower back's larger muscles, the gluteus maximus. Our experience has taught us that using belts and proper form for all exercises strengthens the lower back and prevents injury from delaying workouts and strength increases. Use the reproducible in figure 5-2 to emphasize the importance of the proper belt.

Let's Cut Down on Injuries

Each of the previous topics and all the following information emphasize one basic principle: IF IT HURTS, STOP. Young athletes must understand the difference between muscular fatigue and pain. Jimmy Taylor, the Pro Football Hall of Fame fullback for

Figure 5-1

A WARM-UP REMINDER

As indicated already in the flexibility section, a good warm-up is essential before vigorous exercise. Without it, athletes risk injury to muscles, tendons, and joints. Read the following information—and FOLLOW IT. Our total conditioning program is designed to eliminate injury and improve your performance, not harm it. As usual, if you have any questions, be sure to grab me or one of the other coaches.

ANOTHER LOOK AT THE "WHY" OF WARMING UP

A good warm-up

1. Increases the rate and strength of muscular contractions.
2. Prevents injury.
3. Increases coordination and ease of movement.
4. Gives you a "second wind" faster.
5. Avoids sudden shock to the heart.

THE "HOW" OF WARMING UP

1. A good warm-up should be intense enough to increase body temperature and cause mild perspiration, but not fatigue.
2. Warm-ups should include large muscle groups. This will increase body temperature faster.
3. Warm-ups are mentally as well as physically beneficial if they involve movements that are consistent with the movements you normally perform during competition. See me for examples.
4. A good warm-up should take fifteen to twenty minutes.

FOLLOW THESE RULES

WARM UP,
    THEN STRETCH,
        THEN LIFT OR EXERCISE,
            THEN COOL DOWN,
                THEN STRETCH AGAIN.

© 1995 by Michael D. Koehler

Figure 5-1 (cont.)

WARMING-UP ACTIVITIES

Following is a list of activities that will provide a good warm-up for most weightlifting and other athletic activities. They are complements, not replacements for the sport-specific exercises mentioned in the flexibility section of your booklet. Be sure to start each activity slowly, gradually increase the intensity to about 50% of your maximum heart rate or to a point where you break a sweat, then slow down during the last minute or two in order to cool down.

ACTIVITY	TIME	COOL DOWN TIME
Walking	20 mins.	none
Jogging	10 mins.	2 min.
Stationary bike	12 mins.	1-3 mins.
Rowing	10 mins.	2 mins.
Stairclimbing	10 mins.	2 mins.
Jumping rope	10 mins.	2 mins.
Basketball	12 mins.	2 mins.
Handball	12 mins.	2 mins.
Swimming	14 mins.	1 min.
Tennis	14 mins.	1 min.
Baseball drills	15 mins.	none
Skating	15 mins.	none
Calisthenics	12 mins.	none
Ski machine	10 mins.	2 mins.
Soccer	15 mins.	none
Football pregame	15 mins.	none

Cold weather may require a few minutes more for each warm-up activity, warm weather fewer minutes. Just remember to start out slowly and gradually increase the level of intensity until you break a sweat, then slow down to restore your heart rate. If you perform these activities just before competition, don't cool down completely, or you'll tighten up again, especially if it's cold outside. And remember to stretch after the warm-up. Refer also to the information you have on proper stretching exercises.

© 1995 by Michael D. Koehler

Figure 5-2

USE A BELT!!

Reasons

Belts aid in support of the lower back when lifting weights. They also restrict movement, in essence, to be a constant reminder of proper form when you are doing strenuous exercises.

When to Wear a Belt

Many lifters feel that belts are necessary when lifting heavy weights and doing overhead exercises. Because it takes only 15 seconds to put on, we feel that a belt should be worn *at all times*! It provides the safety insurance you need to prevent unnecessary injury.

In Addition:

Remember to do the proper abdominal exercises to strengthen your stomach even more. Then wear the belt, too. It will provide even that much more support.

Remember:

**ALWAYS
WEAR
A BELT !!!**

© 1995 by Michael D. Koehler

the Green Bay Packers, used to work so hard that he broke blood vessels in his head. At one time, Taylor was the prototype for all young fullbacks. Kids can find much to emulate in Taylor's commitment to the game, to his teammates, and to his family. Breaking blood vessels in your head, however, is something we discourage.

As we discussed in section 4, athletes increase their cardiovascular efficiency by engaging in less intense training programs. The athlete who hopes to improve heart and lung efficiency by running consecutive 100-yard sprints may improve form and *an*aerobic capacity, but will be in for a big surprise when she or he begins gasping for air late in the game. The same is true of strength training, especially for young athletes. Seeking only a maximum effort each time he or she lifts, the young athlete strengthens muscles only marginally *and* risks debilitating injury.

Distinguishing between muscular fatigue and pain may be relatively easy for the veteran athlete, but it is very difficult for the beginner. Figure 5-3 provides answers to the three important questions that must be asked each time a young athlete experiences pain. You might keep the reproducible for your own reference, or you might provide a copy in the booklet for each of your students.

1. Is the pain asymmetrical? Is it restricted to a single part of the body? Is it found, for example, in one biceps and not the other, one hamstring and not the other?
2. Does the discomfort occur immediately with a particular exercise?
3. Does the pain continue through the rest period? Muscular fatigue should gradually disappear during rest and should not recur immediately when the exercise resumes.

Because all of us have different tolerances for pain, coaches must get to know their athletes and watch them for signs of pain. A pain that provokes an outcry from one athlete may involve only a body twitch from another. Coaches have to be sensitive to these individual signs. They also have to be aware of any hereditary predispositions that athletes bring to the training program.

Figure 5-4 provides a reproducible that you can modify and give to each of your athletes before the first strength-training session. It covers athletic participation as well and requires a doctor's approval. The second page covers emergency situations. The third page is especially helpful because of the specific information it provides. Requiring the use of this form is much more than a legal safeguard for the school. It also gives the coach valuable information about the tolerance levels of each of his or her athletes. Pushing a young athlete who simply can't do it isn't in the best interest of the athlete, your relationship with him or her, or the morale of the rest of the players.

An effective strength-training program is a *safety first* program. Any athlete with a preexisting injury or a predisposition to injury is a special case and must have a specialized program with periodic input from a doctor or a physical therapist. In the absence of such input and information, if the coach or teacher is unsure of the appropriateness of an exercise, the first rule of safety applies: IF IT HURTS, STOP!

We helped a coach one year who wanted to increase a young sprinter's time in the 100-meter dash by improving her upper body strength. She was blessed with nat-

Figure 5-3

PAIN VS. FATIGUE

During a vigorous exercise program, every athlete will experience muscle fatigue. The harder you work your muscles, the more they hurt. The pain that results from fatigue is good for you; the pain that results from injury is a sure sign that you should stop exercising immediately. How do you tell the difference? Here are some suggestions:

1. Asymmetrical pain

If you are involved in an exercise that involves both arms or both legs and pain occurs in only one of them, you probably (not necessarily, but probably) have injured a muscle, tendon, or joint in that area of your body. At that point, STOP EXERCISING IMMEDIATELY and see me or one of the other adults in the area.

2. Immediate pain

If a pain hits you immediately in a specific spot, stop exercising and see me. If the pain hits when you start a particular exercise the next day, STOP EXERCISING IMMEDI-ATELY and see me. You may have injured a muscle, tendon, or joint during the previous day's exercise, and it may be more obvious the next time you exercise.

3. If the pain doesn't go away

As indicated already, muscle fatigue resembles pain that can result from injury. So remember that muscle fatigue will go away during a rest period. If after a rest period, therefore, you still feel a pain in one specific part of your body, DON'T RESUME EXER-CISING. See me immediately.

REMEMBER:

We're not exercising to get hurt. We're exercising to PREVENT injury and to improve our appearance and athletic performance. So if you observe any of the above characteristics or are uncertain about a specific pain, see me. Let's not take any chances.

© 1995 by Michael D. Koehler

Figure 5-4

ATHLETIC PERMIT CARD

ID #_____

List: Fall Sport _____ Season #_____
Winter Sport _____ Season #_____
Spring Sport _____ Season #_____

Name_____Date _____
     (last)   (first)   (middle)

Address_____City _____Zip _____

Phone _____Counselor _____(Circle class for) FR SO JR SR

Father's Name _____Work #_____Mother's Name _____Work #_____

Date of Birth _____Place of Birth_____
       (mo/day/yr)   (city)   (county)   (state)

Physician_____Dr. phone number _____

In Emergency Call _____
         (name-relationship)   (phone number)

Athletic Agreement

_____ believes that it is the function of the athletic department to provide sports that are interesting, wholesome, stimulating, and enjoyable for all students. The overall objectives are to develop physical fitness sports habits and skills, sports understanding, sportsmanship, and a spirit of competitiveness in each boy and girl. All parents and athletes are asked to read and discuss the implications of participation in the high school athletic program before signing this form. THIS FORM MUST BE FILED ANNUALLY IN THE ATHLETIC OFFICE BY THE FIRST DAY OF PRACTICE FOR THE ATHLETE'S SPECIFIC SPORT SEASON.

An athlete in _____ will be subject to athletic code disciplinary action if he or she commits any of the following violations:
1. Falsification of information on this form.
2. Theft or vandalism of any school property.
3. Repeated acts of unsportsmanlike conduct.
4. Use, sale, distribution, or possession of tobacco (all forms), alcohol, marijuana, look-alikes, any other illegal drugs or related paraphernalia, or the abuse of prescription/nonprescription drugs.,

Each Athlete and Parent(s) must attend an athletic code meeting once every two years.

We advise all athletes to be adequately covered by hospitalization insurance. Your signature indicates that you will accept financial responsibility in case of injury to your child sustained in connection with these activities. Please indicate your insurance preference.

_____ We plan to insure our child in the school insurance program.

_____ We do not wish to purchase the school insurance. We believe that our present accident insurance provides adequate coverage.

Our son/daughter has our permission to practice and compete in the interscholastic athletic program. We realize that such activity involves the potential for injury which is inherent in all sport, and on rare occasions a severe injury, including permanent paralysis or death, may occur.

Each athlete is responsible for any uniform and/or equipment issued to him/her. Any article lost or damaged, other than ordinary wear and tear, must be paid for by the athlete.

Date_____Parent Permission _____
I agree to conduct myself in accordance with the athletic agreement. Failure to do so may result in disciplinary action.

Date_____Athlete's Signature _____

Doctor's Permit

(Freshman school physical form will be used to meet this requirement.)
Physical must be current within one calendar year.
I have examined this student on this date and find him/her to be physically fit for athletic participation.

_____MD _____
(Doctor's stamp *required*, a signature only *will not* be accepted)   Date of Examination

© 1995 by Michael D. Koehler

Figure 5-4 (cont.)

ATHLETIC MEDICAL EMERGENCY CARD

Name _____

              (last)   (first)   (middle)

Class _____Phone_____Age _____Sport(s) _____

Home Address _____City _____Zip_____

Physician _____Phone _____Hospital _____

In case of emergency, attempt to contact a parent at home. If we cannot be reached, attempt to contact the alternate listed below:

Alternate Name _____Phone _____

Relationship _____

Please list any medication your son or daughter is now taking on a regular basis.

_____

Please list any medications your son or daughter is allergic to.

_____

Please list any impaired organs your son or daughter might have.

_____

Please list any type of insect bite to which your son or daughter is allergic. Please list the medication to be taken.

_____

- -

    Permission is hereby granted to the attending physician to proceed with any medical or minor surgical treatment, X-ray examination, and immunizations for the above-named student. In the event of an emergency arising out of serious illness, the need for major surgery, or significant accidental injury, I understand that an attempt will be make by the attending physician to contact me in the most expeditious way possible. If said physician is not able to contact me, the treatment necessary for the best interest of the above-named student may be given.

    Permission is also granted to the athletic trainer to provide the needed emergency treatment prior to the student's admission to medical facilities.

_____   _____

Father's Signature   Date   Mother's Signature   Date

Work Phone_____   Work Phone _____

Comments or added directions:

_____

_____

_____

© 1995 by Michael D. Koehler

Figure 5-4 (cont.)

MEDICAL HISTORY

Please describe any past or current musculosketetal conditions you have incurred (i.e., muscle pulls, sprains, fractures, surgery, back pain, or any general discomfort).

Head/Neck_____

Shoulder/Clavicle _____

Arm/Elbow/Wrist/Hand _____

Back _____

Hip/Pelvis_____

Thigh/Knee _____

Lower Leg/Ankle/Foot _____

© 1995 by Michael D. Koehler

ural speed and a never-say-die attitude. Having received the necessary forms, we started her program one Saturday afternoon. Everything was going well until we introduced her to bench presses. She indicated immediate pain in her right shoulder.
Following a short diagnosis, we sent her home to make a doctor's appointment.

Realizing that most teenage girls like the doctor's office about as much as a weekend grounding, we called the home to explain her condition to her parents. They
thanked us, made the appointment, and discovered a congenital weakness in the girl's
shoulder. Fortunately, the problem didn't require surgery, just an adjustment in her
training program. She went on to set school records during her junior and senior years
and to qualify for the state championships twice.

We were happy to help her. We also enjoyed having one of our basic principles
of safety reaffirmed. Had someone pushed our young sprinter and told her to "get
tough" during those bench presses, she might have experienced irreparable damage to
her shoulder, or at the least been forced into surgery. *Safety first* is always the most
important component of any strength-training program.

Proper Form Creates Substance

Safety first applies as well to our emphasis on proper form. Young athletes who don't
bend at the knees when they lift weights from the floor ultimately damage their backs
and may expect in middle age to be moaning and wincing every time they get out of
a chair. Similarly, athletes, young or old, who bench-press free weights without a spotter (someone to grab the bar if the exerciser can no longer lift it) risk having the bar
fall on their faces or necks, breaking noses, knocking out teeth, or, worse, suffocating
them.

It's amazing how quickly these accidents occur in a gym. Because few young athletes enjoy the luxury of having a personal trainer, the coach must guarantee that the
athletes exercise in teams of two throughout the entire workout, regardless of the exercise. Taking turns while lifting weights provides the necessary rest time between each
repetition, and it guarantees a spotter—sometimes a cheerleader, too—during each
exercise. A helping hand, whether it's catching a bar or providing a little applause,
sometimes goes a long way.

Proper Form to Increase Strength

Proper form has other advantages as well. It also allows the athlete to isolate muscles properly to make the appropriate strength increases. Such increases occur when
muscles are contracted both with and against gravity. The popular notion of weight*lifting* involves motion against gravity, or what is termed *positive* or *concentric* action. It
occurs when muscle tension is great enough to overcome a resistance and move a
weight against gravity. In essence, the weighted resistance is lifted *up*, whether the
exercise itself is an arm curl or a bench press.

Eccentric contraction operates *with* gravity. It occurs when the muscle slowly
returns from a contraction to its resting length. This is also called working the muscle

negatively; it stretches the muscle completely *and* it exercises an antagonistic muscle group. Arm curls, for example, involve an erect stance, both arms straight, the palms of the hands facing forward holding the barbell as it rests on the upper thighs. The weight is then lifted (concentric/positive action) toward the chest, then slowly lowered (eccentric/negative action) to the original straight-armed position. Slowly lowering the barbell to its original positon on the upper thighs stretches the biceps to their maximum range and works the triceps, the *antagonistic* muscle group on the back of the upper arm.

To maximize their strength increases, therefore, athletes must learn to *lower* weights as well as *lift* them. They must be lowered slowly to provide full range of motion. Lowering them quickly (ballistic action) fails to work the muscle properly and often results in serious injury to the athlete because of the stress it places on cartilage, tendons, and ligaments.

The same is true of manual movements such as chin-ups. The student who does 12 chin-ups but comes only halfway down after each one is cheating herself or himself by eliminating a full range of motion. A youngster's desire to do a lot of chin-ups is getting in the way of the need to increase strength. His or her counterpart, who does only 6 chin-ups but slowly lowers his or her body to a straight-arm position after each one will strengthen the biceps and back muscles and make faster strength gains. In fact, the second athlete will soon be doing 20 chin-ups correctly while the first one is still doing only 12—incorrectly.

One of the keys for the coach is to help kids set aside their egos in order to perform weight-training exercises correctly. That's why it's important for the coach to model each exercise or have someone else model it, using proper form. Having the students paired off helps in this regard. They can spot for each other as well as remind each other of proper execution. No young athlete likes to slack off while a friend is watching!

In addition, you'll notice when you see the exercises provided in this section that each exercise involves one or more safety hints—pointers that prevent injury. During your discussions with the team or individual athletes, it is always wise to emphasize those pointers, not just to avoid legal problems, but to do what is in the best interests of your athletes.

A Word About Breathing

The advice is simple: Inhale during the eccentric or negative action of the exercise; exhale during the concentric action, when the bar is being lifted. In fact, the more weight being lifted, the harder the athlete should exhale. The reasons are twofold. First, athletes are more explosive when they exhale forcefully. Forced exhalation contracts more muscles, increasing the strength of the movement. Consider the football player or the sprinter coming out of his or her stance. Football players are great at grunting during their first six or seven steps. Most obviously, watch a shot putter or a discus thrower at the moment of release. Each will scream to exaggerate the release of air.

Second, excessive pressure on the vascular system is potentially very dangerous. This kind of pressure occurs when athletes don't breathe during the concentric phase of a lift. Many believe that holding their breath gives them more power. We strongly advise our athletes not to do this. In fact, we tell them to blow the pressure out. The harder the exercise, the deeper the exhale. Such breathing provides oxygen to the muscles, fueling them for a maximum workout.

The rule is "Inhale as the weight is lowered; exhale as the weight is lifted." Or as we put it so often: "Blow through the strain."

Considering Needs of Junior High Students

Coaches must be careful to consider the ages and developmental needs of young athletes before involving them in a program of weight training. The growth plates (epiphyseal) of junior high students are composed of cartilage to allow for continued growth. Because they have not ossified yet, they are particularly prone to injury. Weight training for such students is often more a problem than a benefit.

In addition, the low testosterone production of junior high boys inhibits muscle repair as well as muscle gain. It's wise, therefore, for coaches and teachers to emphasize manual movements for young athletes to ensure safety and to allow their bodies to adapt naturally. As you will see, the manual movements provide everything any athlete needs to increase his or her strength. In fact, many of them are too difficult for female athletes and require adjustments. Coaches should work closely with each athlete to develop a program that meets his or her individual needs.

Strength Training Without Weights: Manual Movements

Manual movements may not fit the popular image of bodybuilding, but they provide the same strength increases, reduce the incidence of injury, and can be performed anywhere. In fact, many of the students will discover that this is an extremely challenging program. With slight variations in execution, manual movements also provide for isolation of certain muscles and involve similar positive and negative contraction. Push-ups with the hands close together, for example, exercise the arms, particularly the triceps. With the hands wide apart, push-ups provide an excellent workout for both the arms and the chest, especially the pectorals.

Chin-ups with an open grip (the palms of the hands facing the athlete), provide a strong workout for the biceps. With a closed grip (the palms of the hands facing away from the athlete), they exercise the biceps differently and exercise the forearms, too. If the athlete uses the same grip and raises her or his body so that the bar touches the back of the head instead of the chin, she or he provides an excellent workout for the back and shoulder muscles.

All the manual movements and their variations for junior high and other young athletes are detailed in the several reproducibles provided in figures 5-5 and 5-6. The material is provided as a set of reproducibles. Again, make a loose-leaf notebook for each player. The younger the athlete, the more important this information. We work

Figure 5-5

EXERCISES FOR THE ABDOMINALS

Read this program carefully before starting the exercises. All the exercises in this section are designed to strengthen your abdominal muscles. They range from relatively easy to difficult and are designed to bring you to a high level of fitness. Don't do all of them during your exercise session, just two or three, depending on your abdominal strength. Start with exercise 1 and do 3 sets of 25 sit-ups. Then do the same with exercise 2. STOP. If these two exercises were easy for you, do exercises 2 and 3 the next time you work out, then exercises 3 and 4, and so on until you can do exercises 9 and 10. In other words, you should work on two of these exercises at least three times a week to strengthen this area of your body. And remember: Always start your workout with these exercises. Anyone who wants to be a good athlete or just be physically fit must have a strong center of gravity. That's why these exercises are so important. Depending upon your age, body type, and strength levels, you may not be able to do 3 sets of 25 of exercises 9 and 10. Don't worry about that. The important thing is that you improve your current strength levels. These exercises will help.

Exercise One

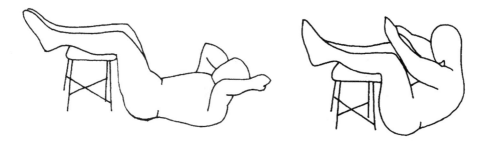

NAME - Elevated Leg Sit-ups (3 sets of 25)

PROCEDURE - Place legs on stool, chair, or bench and sit up, raising your chin to your knees. Do 3 sets of 25 sit-ups.

ADJUSTMENTS - If these are too difficult, place your legs on the ground with a slight bend at the knees and do 3 sets of 25 sit-ups. If these are too difficult, elevate your legs again on the chair or bench and do "crunchies." Simply raise your head so that your chin touches your chest and reach your hands to the sky. Do 3 sets of these 25 times, each time making sure you feel contractions in your abdominal muscles.

SAFETY HINT- Don't lock your hands behind your head. During periods of exertion, you may pull your head too far forward and damage your spine.

Another hint: If after doing the 3 sets of 25 crunchies, you find that you can't do exercise 2, *don't do it*. Keep doing the crunchies 3 times a week until you can do the elevated leg sit-ups. Then do them until you can do exercises 1 and 2 without back pain or exhaustion. In addition, with any of these exercises, if you should feel back pain, stop the exercise and talk to me immediately.

© 1995 by Michael D. Koehler

Exercise Two

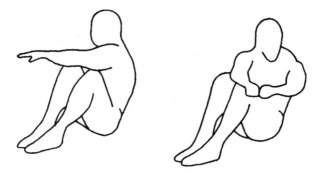

NAME - Seated Bent Knee Sit-up (3 sets of 25)

PROCEDURE - Lie on the floor with your knees bent. Sit up, placing your arms straight out—again, not to hurt your neck—and bring your chest to your knees. A reminder: Once you feel comfortable doing these first two exercises, start your workout with exercise 2 and combine it with exercise 3.

SAFETY HINT- Again, be aware of back pain. In fact, be aware of any pain. These exercises will dramatically improve your strength if you perform them regularly. You need not strain yourself to the point of exhaustion.

Exercise Three

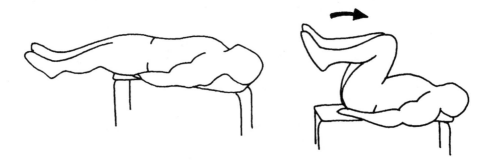

NAME - Flat Knee-ins (3 sets of 25)

PROCEDURE - Lie flat on bench or floor. If on a bench, be sure to let your legs hang down, feet touching the floor. Place your hands under your buttocks for back support and raise your knees until your thighs are at a right angle with the rest of your body.

SAFETY HINT- Be sure to place your hands underneath you. The lower back support is very important to prevent aggravation to your back.

© 1995 by Michael D. Koehler

Exercise Four

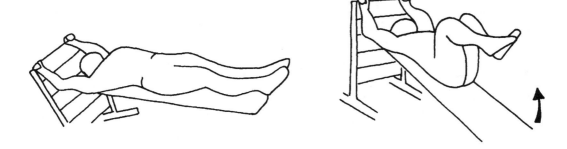

NAME - Slant Board Knee-ins (3 sets of 25)

PROCEDURE - Starting on the lowest incline of the slant board, hang fully extended and bring your knees to your chest until they reach a right angle with the rest of your body.

ADJUSTMENTS - Increase the intensity of the exercise by elevating the slant board. Once you can perform the exercise on the highest incline of the slant board, move on to the next exercise.

SAFETY HINTS - As always, don't push yourself beyond your current strength levels. Don't *start* this exercise at the highest incline of the slant board. Start within your target range; make progress at your own pace.

Exercise Five

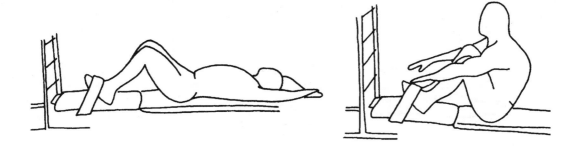

NAME - Slant Board Sit-ups (3 sets of 25)

PROCEDURE - Place your feet under the stabilizer, knees bent, with the slant board at its lowest incline. Keeping your arms straight in front of you, sit up, touching your fingers to your toes. Don't lower yourself to a resting position on the board. Your shoulders should not touch the board, just your back. This procedure will keep constant tension on the abdominals. They should be contracted throughout the entire 25 sit-ups.

ADJUSTMENTS - Again, adjust the elevation on the slant board until you can do 3 sets of 25 at the highest level of elevation.

SAFETY HINTS - Don't keep your hands behind your head. As with all sit-ups, such technique can be potentially damaging to your neck.

© 1995 by Michael D. Koehler

Exercise Six

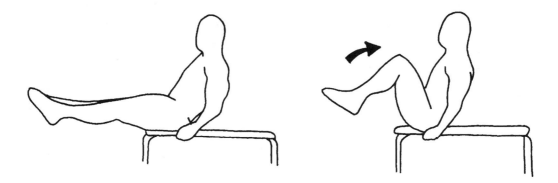

NAME - Bench V Sits (3 sets of 25)

PROCEDURE - Sit on the edge of a bench with your legs extended. Place your hands behind you for support, as in the picture, and grasp the sides of the bench. Bring your legs to a right angle and *slowly* push them back to the extended position. It is important that you bring them up slowly and return them to the extended position slowly.

SAFETY HINT - Grasp the sides of the bench very tightly. The support you provide is very important to prevent back pain.

Exercise Seven

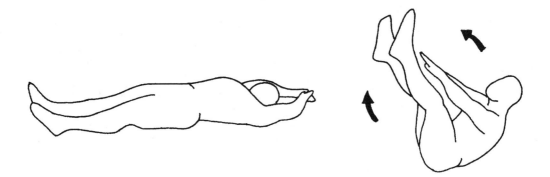

© 1995 by Michael D. Koehler

NAME - Lying Flat V Sits (3 sets of 25)

PROCEDURE - At this point, the V stands for Victory. You're making really good progress to have come this far. Keep up the good work. Lie flat on the floor with your arms extended overhead, then bend at the waist, simultaneously raising your arms and your legs. Touch your toes, making a V with your body, then lower back to the prone position.

SAFETY HINT - Perform this exercise slowly in order to prevent a jerky motion that could injure your back. You'll notice that a slow motion will also provide additional control.

Exercise Eight

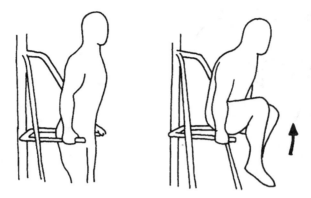

NAME - Straight-arm Vertical Leg Raise (3 sets of 25)

PROCEDURE - Using the dip stand, grip the handles on the end of each bar and raise yourself to an extended position. Raise your legs slowly to a right angle. Slowly lower your legs to their original extended position.

SAFETY HINT - Do not drop from the dip stand; use the pegs to step down or slowly lower yourself to the ground to prevent shock to the spine.

Exercise Nine

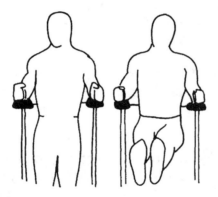

NAME - Vertical Knee-in (3 sets of 25)

PROCEDURE - Again using dip stand, place your arms on the pads and your hands on the grips and push your body against the back pad. Slowly raise your straightened legs to a right angle with your body and slowly lower them to the extended position.

SAFETY HINT - Again, be careful not to drop from the dip stand.

© 1995 by Michael D. Koehler

Exercise Ten

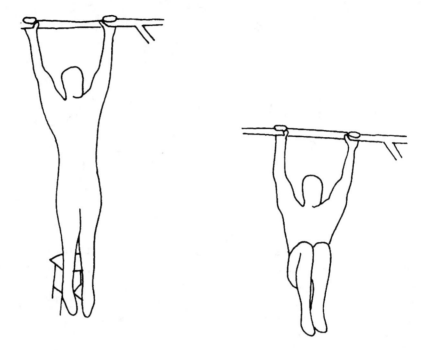

NAME - Hanging from Chin Bar Knee-ups (3 sets of 25)

PROCEDURE - Grasp the bar at shoulder width or a little wider. Be sure you're comfortable. Fully extend your body and raise your knees until they form a right angle. Be sure to raise and lower your legs slowly in order to realize maximum benefit from the exercise.

SAFETY HINT - Be sure to use a chair or a stool to get down from the bar. Unnecessary jumping from the bar, especially if you're tired, may injure your back.

REMINDERS

These exercises are designed to provide a natural progression from easy to difficult. Don't force yourself to do the more advanced exercises until you're ready for them. You probably will start with the first and second exercises but may progress quickly to a combination of 3 and 4 or 4 and 5. Ultimately, you will want to be doing exercises 9 and 10 and, if you progress beyond them, exercises 9 and 10 followed by another set of any one of the other eight. Recognize as well that you may never get to exercises 9 and 10. Such a progression is especially difficult for junior high school students.

If you are interested in improving your appearance or athletic performance, however, you will work hard at each of these exercises and *will* realize definite strength increases. It's unimportant which of the sets you are doing; it is important that you benefit from the experience.

© 1995 by Michael D. Koehler

Figure 5-6

YOUR COMPLETE WORKOUT

Like the abdominal exercises, these exercises involve a progression from easy to difficult and will meet all your strength needs without using weights. In fact, this is a very difficult program and may require as much as three months work for you to master it. You may never master it because of your age, but if you stay with it, you will improve your strength and appearance considerably. Again, stay within your own range. Goals for girls will be different from those for boys. For some girls, 3 sets of 25 will always be too difficult. Don't worry about that. Just work to accomplish your own goals by focusing on the adjustments contained within each exercise. The important thing is not that you master the program but that you improve your strength, appearance, and/or athletic performance. This program will do all of them for you. It's important that you determine your goals and stick with them. And, remember, you don't have to do every exercise in this program every day, or even every other day. Make the right combination to guarantee the program that's best for you. I will help you.

Exercise One

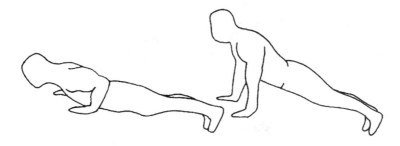

NAME - Push-ups

PROCEDURE - Position your body parallel to the ground with your weight on your toes and the palms of your hands as illustrated in the drawing. For the first part of the exercise, position your hands approximately shoulder width. Keep your body as straight as possible throughout the exercise. Slowly lower yourself until your chest touches the floor, inhaling as you go down. Then slowly raise yourself as you exhale. Repeat the process for 3 sets of 25 or as many as possible.

ADJUSTMENTS - The goal is 3 sets of 25. You may not be able to do this many. If you can't do many at first, adjust your original position so that your knees are on the ground and do everything else the same way. Also, keep your hands close together if you want to emphasize work on your triceps (the muscles in the back of your upper arm), relatively far apart (wider than your shoulders) to work your pectorals (your chest muscles).

SAFETY HINT - Report shoulder or elbow pain to me immediately, and when you complete the exercise, lower yourself slowly; don't just drop to the floor!

© 1995 by Michael D. Koehler

Exercise Two

NAME - Free Squat

PROCEDURE - Stand erect with both arms crossed over your chest. Keep your head and back straight and your feet planted about shoulder width. Inhale as you squat down. When your thighs are approximately parallel to the floor, stop. Your head and knees should remain straight throughout the entire exercise. Exhale as you push yourself back to an erect position. Repeat the process until you complete 3 sets of 25 or whatever goals you have set for yourself.

SAFETY HINT - Do not squat beyond the point where your thighs are parallel to the ground. If you go beyond the parallel, you may stress your knees. Also, as with all exercises, do not push through knee pain. If you experience pain, see me immediately.

Exercise Three

NAME - Dips

PROCEDURE - Using a dip stand, grip the ends of the bar and position yourself straight-armed. While you inhale, slowly lower yourself by bending at the elbows, keeping them as close to your body as possible. Try to touch your biceps to your forearms to get the maximum benefit from the exercise. Then exhale as you slowly raise yourself back to an erect position.

ADJUSTMENTS - If you are unable to lower yourself to the point where your biceps touch your forearms, go down as far as you can. Remember, work within your own range. Girls may want to bend the elbows only slightly and then return to the original position.

© 1995 by Michael D. Koehler

SAFETY HINTS - Call me over the first time you do this exercise or have a teacher or another coach watch you. We will want to check the proper form and make sure you are experiencing no pain. Again, establish your own personal goals regarding the number of times you do this exercise.

Exercise Four

NAME - Ballet Squat

PROCEDURE - Stand erect with your head and back straight, your arms crossed over your chest, with a wide stance, maybe 4 to 5 inches wider than your shoulders. Turn your feet out and slowly bend at the knees until your thighs are parallel to the floor, your knees over your toes. While exhaling, push up to your original starting position. Try to work up to 3 sets of 25.

SAFETY HINT - Do not bend beyond the parallel position, or you will risk damage to the knees. If you have pain the next time you try this exercise, see me immediately.

Exercise Five

NAME - Declining Push-ups

PROCEDURE - Place your feet on a bench or chair and assume the same position as in exercise 1. While inhaling, lower your body slowly until you touch your chest to the floor. Exhaling, slowly push yourself back to the original position.

ADJUSTMENTS - If you do not want to do this exercise, at least at first, simply focus on exercise 1 and progress to this exercise as it becomes possible.

SAFETY HINT - Keep your head and back straight in order to get the full benefit from the exercise and to reduce lower back strain.

© 1995 by Michael D. Koehler

Exercise Six

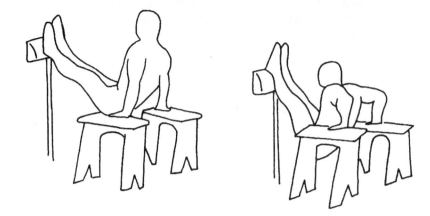

NAME - Triceps Push-ups

PROCEDURE - Place your feet on a chair or other support that elevates them at least parallel to the floor. Position yourself straight-armed between two benches or chairs and slowly lower your body, keeping your elbows together. Exhale as you push up. Again, the ultimate goal is 3 sets of 25. Go at your own pace and do only as many as you can.

ADJUSTMENTS - A simple adjustment is to sit on the ground, your hands placed approximately a foot behind you. Lean back so that your arms are bent at the elbows. Then do the push-ups by straightening your arms. Progress to the more difficult exercise outlined above by placing your hands on the benches or chairs but by keeping your feet on the ground instead of elevating them.

SAFETY HINT - Be sure the benches or the chairs are stable. You might have someone hold them for you.

Exercise Seven

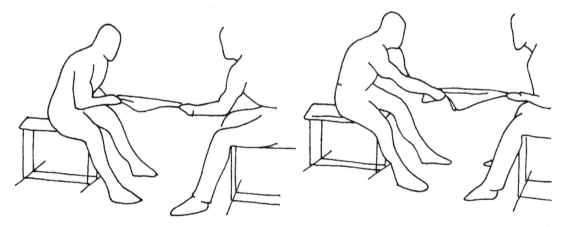

NAME - Seated Lat Pull

PROCEDURE - Sit on a bench, your partner seated opposite you. Each holding one end of a towel or rope, slowly pull it back and forth, not with the attempt to pull your partner off the bench but to offer enough resistance to exercise the back muscles.

© 1995 by Michael D. Koehler

© 1995 by Michael D. Koehler

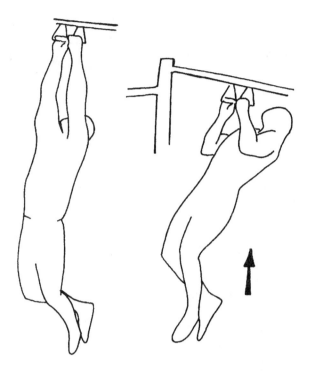

NAME - V Bar Chin-ups

PROCEDURE - Attach a V bar to the chin-up bar. The V bar should be positioned higher than your extended reach. Use a stool or a chair to reach it and pull yourself slowly to a position where your chin touches the chin-up bar. Inhale as you lower yourself to a hanging position and repeat the process, exhaling as you lift yourself.

ADJUSTMENTS - If a V bar is unavailable, grasp the chin-up bar with both hands, one in front of the other, and pull yourself up the same way. You may not be able to pull yourself up high enough to touch your chin on the bar. If need be, simply flex your arms and hold that position for 10 to 15 seconds. Try for as many 10-second intervals as possible.

SAFETY HINT - Don't fall to your original starting position; lower yourself slowly. Falling can damage your shoulders or elbows. In addition, use the stool or chair to get off the chin-up bar. Dropping from the bar can damage your back.

Exercise Nine

NAME - Front Chin-ups

PROCEDURE - Use a stool or chair to raise yourself to a chin-up bar. Grasp the bar with a closed grip (palms facing down), hands about 18 to 20 inches apart. Inhale then exhale as you pull yourself to a point where your chin touches the bar. Slowly lower yourself to your original hanging position. Don't swing; execute the exercise slowly and deliberately to keep your body steady, and don't kick your feet. Let your legs hang straight down during the entire motion.

ADJUSTMENTS - As with the V bar chin-ups, you may want to start by doing flexed arm hangs instead of chin-ups. If this is the case, try to find a chin-up bar that is low enough to grasp from the ground. Grip the bar, flex your arms, and hang for as many 10-second intervals as possible.

SAFETY HINT - As already mentioned, don't drop from the bar. Use a stool or chair to step down, making sure the stool is stable.

Exercise Ten

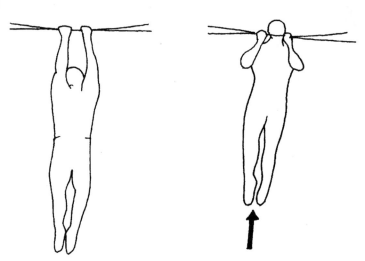

NAME - Reverse Grip Chin-up

© 1995 by Michael D. Koehler

PROCEDURE - Same as front chin-ups but with hands in an open grip (palms facing up). Execute the exercise in the same way and observe the same safety hint. Make the same adjustments as with the other chin-ups if this exercise is too difficult.

REMINDER

This program involves some very difficult exercises. You probably won't want to do all of them during each exercise session. And you probably won't be able to do 3 sets of 25, at least initially. In fact, you probably will have to make many of the adjustments suggested in each exercise. But that's OK. When you develop your goal sheet, establish an initial program that you can perform and set target goals that will mark your improvement. I will help you with this. Let's also be sure to incorporate an aerobic workout, flexibility exercises, and the proper diet. I will help you with this, too.

© 1995 by Michael D. Koehler

with several coaches who require each of their young athletes to master each of these programs before being allowed to work with weights. One of them summed it up best when she said: "If one of my girls can't do one push-up, why in the world would I have her work on bench presses?"

Her reasoning makes sense, but free weights may still have a place in the life of young athletes. The young man who can't do a chin-up and is physically weak in all other regards probably *should* work with very light weights to increase his arm strength. Light weights, sometimes just the bar, provide optimal resistance for young, underdeveloped athletes. The boy or girl who is unable to do a push-up or a chin-up may require a very light weight to start working on arm strength.

A young athlete may use a spotter to help lift him or her to do chin-ups (weight reduction may also be in order!), but once he or she can do chin-ups, they should be continued until there is sufficient strength to work with weights effectively. Encourage your athlete to work the muscles negatively as well as positively while doing the chin-ups. Remember that falling ballistically after the chin-up can damage shoulder and elbow joints.

Such warnings, as well as descriptions and explanations of the manual exercises, are provided in the reproducibles. Coaches can distribute them in meetings at appropriate times during the year. You may want to seriously consider making them prerequisites to the weightlifting segment of your strength-training program. They provide realistic assessments that make goal setting so much easier for players. The difficulty of the program also impresses upon young athletes just how much work is required to become a standout performer.

The entire program is very challenging. For this reason, coaches should meet with students to help them organize a workout program that is reasonably demanding. Athletes need not follow these workout programs from exercises one through ten; for most of them, it is advisable to mix and match the individual exercises. In addition, they should be encouraged to make whatever adjustments are needed in each exercise to develop a program that satisfies their individual strength needs.

Where You Are and Where You Want to Be

More about goal setting: If, like us, you practice with every club in your bag to master your golf swing, you've discovered that the swing is one thing, accuracy another. The same is true of passing a football, shooting a basketball, or throwing a softball. The proper motion is important, but so is hitting the target. Weightlifting has its targets, too. Disregarding them can result in a lot of wasted motion for young athletes.

It's important, therefore, for coaches to have their players determine exactly what they want to accomplish before starting their weight programs as well as the program of manual movements. Coaches know the strength requirements of their respective sports. The development of goals, therefore, should involve both the player and the coach. The form in figure 5-7 promotes such mutual planning.

Obviously, goals regarding specific strength increases will change as the athlete progresses; the target goal, however, will remain the same. It will continue to serve,

Figure 5-7

WHERE DO YOU WANT TO BE?

This form is designed to help you realize your athletic and/or personal goals. As you'll see, it asks for specific targets and then helps organize a total conditioning program to reach them. You probably will need your coach's help with some of the specifics. It would be a good idea to meet with him or her to talk about this form.

Primary Goal: Identify what you hope to accomplish athletically or personally with this total conditioning program. (Examples: "I want to be the starting left tackle next year," "I want to lose fifteen pounds," or "I want to make the varsity field hockey team."):

Related Goals: List the related goals, as needed, that must be accomplished to realize the primary goal. (Examples: "I have to improve my pass blocking skills"; "I need to improve my speed in order to lead block for the running backs"; "I have to improve my leg strength in order to move my opponent out of the hole"; "I need more arm strength to control the stick.") If your goals are nonathletic, don't worry about this section. If athletic, list at least three related goals and get your coach's input with them:

1.

2.

3.

4.

5.

Conditioning goals: Finally, list the specific weightlifting or other conditioning activities you must engage in to reach your related goals. Your coach will be helpful here, too. (Examples: "I'll have to improve my upper body strength"; "I'll have to reduce my speed in the forty by half a second"; "I'll have to work on my leg strength": "My arms wil have to get stronger.")

List at least three specific conditioning goals:

1.

2.

3.

4.

5.

Specific Program: Now, with your coach, list the specific program you must follow to reach your conditioning goals. Remember to increase the specific exercises in intensity during the workout and on a weekly basis. The program should include, as needed, cardiovascular, flexibility, and diet considerations as well as a weightlifting program. Use your computer program, if one is available. Attach the program to this sheet, so your coach can keep it on file.

© 1995 by Michael D. Koehler

therefore, as the primary motivation for the athlete to improve his or her performance. Even the performance goals may change as other muscle groups require strengthening, but the target goal will continue to be the reminder the coach needs to reaffirm the good intentions of players!

What Are Aerobic and Maximal Muscle Strength?

An understanding of maximal muscle strength must involve a discussion of slow- and fast-twitch muscle fibers. It's a topic that can get pretty complicated, but for our purposes, let's just say that fast-twitch fibers respond quickly to stimuli but, due to a relatively low supply of blood, fatigue quickly. Fast-twitch fibers are the prime movers during short, intense activities (generally 90 seconds or less), such as throwing a discus, running with a football, or running the 400-meter dash. Such activities quickly burn glucose and glycogen stores in your body and are anaerobic (without oxygen). As you will see in a future section, they are only marginally effective for weight-loss training, but they are essential for the athlete who is involved in a sport that requires explosive strength.

Slow-twitch fibers, on the other hand, do the work during activities that last longer than two minutes, such as during a basketball game or a cross country competition. They involve aerobic (with oxygen) activity and are generally classified as endurance training activities.

An important characteristic of slow- and fast-twitch muscle fibers is their genetic predisposition. Some athletes are more explosive than their teammates; others have the ability to last longer in activities requiring endurance. The young athlete who is predisposed to fast-twitch muscle fibers generally will experience more success as a halfback, a basketball guard, or a sprinter. Those with slow-twitch muscle fibers may be more successful playing in the line or running endurance races.

Equally important, even those of us who are genetically predisposed can maximize our potential in each area. Those with predominately fast-twitch fibers can increase their endurance; and those with slow-twitch fibers can gain explosiveness. In essence, that is the purpose of this book, to engage young athletes in conditioning programs that provide everything they need: strength, speed, and endurance.

Determining Maximums

The first step in the weightlifting program is to give each athlete a maximum strength test in order to develop or select the right program. Such tests are appropriate only if the coach knows the athlete's history and capabilities and feels absolutely comfortable that there will be no risks involved. The tests determine the maximum amount the athlete or student can lift *with perfect form.*

Start at a moderate weight and do one repetition; add weight until the athlete can lift it only once. That weight will constitute his or her maximum strength. Be careful not to overdo the first test. Don't allow the lifter to strain too hard or to use anything other than perfect form, making sure that he or she exhales fully through the exercise.

These tests are relatively important because, as you'll see, the exercise programs require repetitions at 60 to 70 percent of maximum capacity. If a bench press, for example, requires 3 sets of 10 repetitions at 60 percent of maximum strength and the athlete can lift a maximum of 100 pounds, then he or she will lift 60 pounds for 3 sets of 10 lifts.

When athletes or students progress well into the program, they can test their maximum strength daily, although this kind of frequency really isn't necessary. It is recommended that they test maximum strength at least every six weeks, unless each is following a computerized program and the increases are predetermined for them.

Weight Training for Improved Performance

Improved strength is a function not only of weightlifting but of appropriate manual movements, increased flexibility, cardiovascular efficiency, and proper diet. Let's not lose sight of that as we discuss our weightlifting program. If *we* lose sight of it, so will our athletes, and their need for *total* conditioning will suffer.

As we keep total conditioning in mind, we can then emphasize the value of weightlifting. The youngsters' commitment to physical conditioning and athletics has definite carry-over value in other areas of their lives. We probably wouldn't be involved in athletics if we didn't believe that. So do what you can to secure their commitment to the weightlifting programs in figure 5-8. Again, organize them in the form of a booklet and give one to each of your athletes. That way, they can review them at home, too. The booklet will also emphasize the importance of each program, both to enhance performance and to reduce injury.

Notice that the programs begin with abdominal exercises. That area of the body involves the prime definers of body strength and ability. The abdominals are involved in every athletic movement. If you have embarked upon the wonders of middle age, you have discovered that as the abdominals go, so goes the back. Much back pain in later life—and many injuries to athletes—result from weak stomach muscles. As indicated in the section on manual movements, the abdominal exercises should be intensified as athletes are able to do 3 sets of 25 repetitions of any single exercise.

The weightlifting programs are divided into four levels of intensity. We have not referred to them as freshman, sophomore, junior, and senior or as 9, 10, 11, or 12 because most high school seniors don't like the idea of being unable to perform at a sophomore level. So we simply refer to them as Programs A, B, C, and D. Sooner or later, the kids will figure out the designations; you can offset their disappointment, however, by constantly praising their individual work. They will learn, as you have, that making individual progress and working hard are their own rewards.

In addition, each of the programs has been divided into three phases. The divisions are designed to provide gradually increased intensity and variety for each workout. Will some athletes move through programs A and B quickly? Of course. Each program is excellent for a P.E. class but may not provide the intensity a well-conditioned athlete requires, even if that athlete is only a freshman in high school. The variations, therefore, are endless; coaches must revise them carefully, however, in order to avoid injury to young athletes. Descriptions of the actual exercises follow.

Figure 5-8

WEIGHTLIFTING PROGRAMS

Level A

Sequence 1
This first sequence should be followed three times a week and should take roughly 40 to 45 minutes to complete. Do 3 sets of each exercise with 10 repetitions at 60% of your maximum strength (3 x 10 x 60%).

Maximum Strength x .60 = *Weight Used*

Two Abdominal Exercises
Bench Press
Military Press
Triceps Extensions
Chin-ups
Barbell Curl
Leg Extension
Leg Curl

Sequence 2
Do 4 sets of these exercises with 10 repetitions at 70% of your maximum strength (4 x 10 x 70%).

Maximum Strength x .70 = *Weight Used*

Two Abdominal Exercises
Bench Press
Upright Row
Triceps Kickback
Barbell Curls
Leg Press
Leg Curl

Sequence 3
Do 3 sets of these exercises with 10 repetitions at 70% of your maximum strength. This sequence may take an hour or longer (3 x 10 x 70%).

Maximum Strength x .70 = *Weight Used*

Two Abdominals
Bench Press
Inclined Bench Press
Military Press
Upright Row
French Curl
Triceps Extension
Barbell Curls
Dumbbell Curls
Chin-ups
Squats
Leg Curls

REMEMBER: SAFETY FIRST

© 1995 by Michael D. Koehler

Level B

This program is more aggressive than the previous one. Be certain that you use proper form, wear a belt, and follow all our rules of safety. Remember: Safety First! All these exercises should consist of 4 sets of 10 repetitions at 70% of maximum strength.

Sequence 1

Maximum Strength x .70 = Weight Used

Two Abdominal Exercises
Bench Press
Behind Neck Press
Bent-over Row
French Curl
Barbell Curl
Squat
Leg Curl

Sequence 2

Maximum Strength x .70 = Weight Used

Two Abdominal Exercises
Bench Press
Inclined Bench Press
Behind Neck Press
Upright Row
Bent-over Row
Barbell Curl
Dips
Squat
Leg Extension
Leg Curls

Sequence 3

Maximum Strength x .70 = Weight Used

Two Abdominal Exercises
Bench Press
Inclined Bench Press
Military Press
Behind the Neck Press
Lateral Raise
French Curl
Triceps Extensions
Chin-ups
Bent-over Row
Barbell Curls
Dumbbell Curls
Lunge
Leg Curls

REMEMBER: SAFETY FIRST

© 1995 by Michael D. Koehler

Level C

These exercises will work your muscles to and through fatigue, so be sure to work with a partner. Watch each other closely. This is a very strenuous program. Do not perform these exercises on the day *before* or *of* a contest.

Sequence 1 (3 x 10 x 70%)

Monday and Thursday	*Tuesday and Friday*
Two Abdominals	Two Abdominals
Chin-ups to 30 or Max	Bench Press
Bent-over Rowing	Inclined Bench Press
Triceps Kickbacks	Military Press
Barbell Curl	Upright Rowing
Dumbbell Curl	French Curl
Squats	Triceps Kickbacks
Straight Leg Dead Lift	Dips

Sequence 2 (3 x 10 x 70%)

Monday and Thursday	*Tuesday and Friday*
Bench Press	Maximum chin-ups (try for 30)
Inclined Bench Press	Bent-over Rowing
Dumbbell Flies	T-Bar Rowing
Military Press	Barbell Curls
Behind the Neck Press	Dumbbell Curls
Upright Rowing	Preacher Curls
French Curl	Squat
Triceps Extensions	Lunge
Triceps Kickbacks	Straight Leg Dead Lifts

Sequence 3 (3 x 10 x 70%)

Mon./Wed./Friday	*Tuesday/Thur./Sat.*
Two Abdominals	Two Abdominals
Bench Press	Squat
Inclined Bench Press	Lunge
Military Press	Straight Leg Dead Lift
Upright Rowing	Leg Curl
French Curl	Bent-over Row
Triceps Extensions	Barbell Curl
Dips	Dumbbell Curl

Level D

This is the toughest program in the booklet. Once you master it (and it won't be easy!), get one of the coaches to make adjustments to increase the intensity. Each sequence is done with 3 sets of 10 repetitions at 70% of your maximum strength. Do not perform these exercises on the day *before* or *of* a contest.

© 1995 by Michael D. Koehler

Sequence 1

Mon./Wed./Friday	Tues./Thurs./Sat.
Two Abdominals	Two Abdominals
Bench Press	Max. Chin-ups to 30
Inclined Bench Press	Dead Lift
Behind the Neck Press	Barbell Curls
Dumbbell Press	Dumbbell Curls
Lateral Raises	Preacher Curls
French Curls	Squat
Triceps Extensions	Leg Press
Triceps Kickbacks	Leg Curl
Dips	

Sequence 2

Mon./Wed./Friday	Tues./Thurs./Sat.
Two Abdominals	Two Abdominals
Bench Press	Chin-ups to 30
Inclined Bench Press	Dead Lift
Dumbbell Flies	Barbell Curls
Upright Row	Preacher Curls
Lateral Raise	Military Press
French Curls	Squat
Triceps Extensions	Lunge
Triceps Kickbacks	Leg Curls
Dips	

Sequence 3

Mon./Wed./Friday	Tues./Thurs./Sat.
Two Abdominals	Two Abdominals
Bench Press	Chin-ups to 30
Inclined Bench Press	Cleans
Military Press	Barbell Curls
Upright Row	Dumbbell Curls
Behind the Neck Press	Squat
French Curls	Lunge
Triceps Extensions	Straight Leg Dead Lift
Triceps Kickbacks	

© 1995 by Michael D. Koehler

REMEMBER: SAFETY FIRST

Regarding the Programs

Level A

This is a base program. For athletes who are unable to work at even the 60 percent level, coaches are advised to reduce the amount of weight by requiring a lesser percentage. For athletes who are capable of a tougher base program, coaches can talk with colleagues or training professionals to intensify the program or to add sport-specific exercises, such as neck exercises for wrestlers and dead lifts and shoulder shrugs for football players. Sport-specific exercises are discussed in section 6.

Encourage athletes to sit during as many of the Level A exercises as possible because of the support it provides the back. In the case of barbell curls, have the lifter bend slightly at the knees to improve the tilt on the pelvis and relieve pressure on the lumbar spine. If young athletes cannot bend at the knees and perform the exercise correctly, have them sit and use dumbbells. And always keep the principle of interaction in mind: *Listen and talk* to your athletes to get an understanding of how their bodies are responding to the workout, then make appropriate adjustments.

Level B

This level is as strenuous as most young athletes can handle. It is still a baseline program for well-conditioned athletes, but some athletes may have a tough time keeping up. Modify the program accordingly. Girls, for example, may have trouble with bent-over rowing. You might simply take it out of their programs and substitute a head-supported barbell rowing or a lat pull-up while lying on a bench. Finally, this level is more aggressive than Level A. Coaches must watch, therefore, for belt use, correct form, and proper breathing throughout each exercise.

Level C

Research has indicated that muscles are aerobically and maximally stronger when worked *to* and *through* fatigue. Because the program prefatigues muscle groups, spotters and coaches must watch lifters carefully. This is a rigorous program, designed only for well-conditioned athletes who want to improve speed and strength and who already possess the physical development and the knowledge of proper form needed to handle the exercises safely. Students or athletes who don't use the proper form must be instructed not to do these exercises.

Level D

The time and effort required for this program demand that it be performed by serious-minded and experienced athletes. Notice, for example, that it requires additional work on Saturdays. It is exceptionally aggressive for athletes and students who want to train hard. For example, the dead lift has been included for a couple of reasons. First, it is an important exercise for top-notch athletes. And second, the first three programs have made the back strong enough to handle the rigors of this exercise.

If some of your better athletes can handle this program with relative ease, then vary the levels of intensity. Maintain the order, however. Each program has been designed to work large muscle groups first, smaller muscles second. This is an important part of the program. It is also important not to perform any of these exercises on the day *before* or *of* a contest, especially Levels C and D.

Let's Wrap It Up

This section has provided the programs that will satisfy the strength needs of most junior and senior high school athletes. In fact, even the basic program may be too intense for some of your beginners. In that case, it is wise to reemphasize the value of the manual movements explained and diagrammed earlier in this section. Some few of your players, however, may require more intensity in their programs.

Before considering any of the following alternatives be sure that the athletes are ready for increased intensity. *Wanting* to impress teammates with variations in intensity isn't quite the same as *requiring* the variations. Coaches must make such assessments themselves. But if the athlete is ready for increased intensity, here are a few ways to do it:

- Increase the amount of weight lifted. Raise the maximum percentage from 60 percent or 70 percent to 75 percent.
- Increase the pace. The rest time between sets should be approximately 45 seconds. To increase intensity, watch the clock and allow only 30 seconds or less between sets, using the same program.
- Do "Super Sets." Move immediately from one set to another, emphasizing the same muscle group. Go from a bench press, for example, to a military press or from barbell curls to preacher curls with only a marginal break between the two exercises.
- Spotters. A lifting partner aids in spotting, checking form, and motivating. When one partner has completed the exercise, the other begins—with little time between exercises. The combination of reduced time between exercises and "cheerleading" from the partner generally results in increased pace.
- Engage in circuit training with aerobics. Athletes might do bench presses, triceps extensions, and bent-over rowing, followed by five minutes of jumping rope.

There are endless variations possible to increase the intensity of a workout. Regardless of the variation used, coaches should be careful to determine if athletes actually require the variations. These are very challenging programs in their own right and generally will satisfy the strength requirements of most junior high and secondary school athletes. The next section explains the specific exercises.

Section Six

STRENGTH TRAINING:

FOCUSING ON

THE ACTUAL EXERCISES

Coaches want to guarantee that the programs outlined in section 5 provide sport-specific exercises that use muscles in fundamentally the same way they will be used in competition. They may want sprinters, for example, to do barbell work to emphasize upper body strength, shotputters to emphasize squats, and football linemen to do a lot of bench presses. This section provides additional information about sport-specific exercises.

This section also emphasizes to athletes that during the off-season, the activity itself provides an excellent cool down after the weight workout. Football players can play catch, for example; basketball players can scrimmage for ten to fifteen minutes. These cool-down exercises become excellent complements to each athlete's total conditioning program, providing elements specific to the exercise regimen and practice for the particular sport.

Descriptions of Exercises

The illustrations in figure 6-1 provide additional pages for the booklet you will give each athlete. They explain each exercise, emphasizing proper form and safety hints. Each of the exercises mentioned in all four of the programs outlined in section 5 is illustrated and explained. When combined with the warming-up exercises, the manual movements, the weight-training programs, the sport-specific charts, and the other materials in this section, they provide the substance for an excellent booklet to give each of your athletes.

Don't rely, however, on the booklet alone. Be sure to demonstrate each exercise early in the total program, mentioning safety points as you go. By watching you or

Figure 6-1

DESCRIPTIONS OF EXERCISES

Each of the exercises mentioned in the previous four programs is illustrated and explained on the following pages. Study each exercise carefully and pay particular attention to the proper form and the safety points. In addition, the coaches will explain each exercise before you actually start the program.

Exercise 1

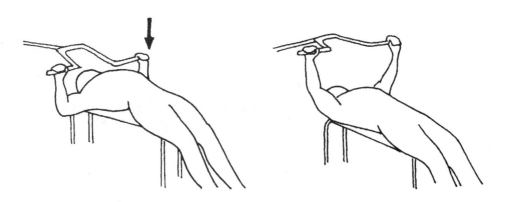

NAME: Bench Press

PROCEDURE: If a Universal machine is available, use it first. The machine makes the spotter's job easier and it provides better balance for the lifter. When you feel you have become sufficiently strong, ask me or another coach to introduce you to the free-weight bench press. The technique is similar to both the machine and the free weights: Lie flat on the bench with your legs hanging off the side of the bench, your feet flat on the floor. Positioning your hands about six inches wider than your shoulder width, your thumbs inside, grab the bar. Lower the bar to your chest, just below your pectorals and push the bar back to arm length.

ADJUSTMENTS: Narrow your grip on the bar (place your hands closer together) to emphasize work on your triceps; place them farther apart to emphasize work on your pectorals. You can also—with the help of a spotter!—lie on the floor, arch your back to do a neck bridge, then do bench presses. This exercise is particularly helpful for wrestlers.

SAFETY HINTS: Do not relax or drop the weight onto your chest; lower it in a controlled fashion. Inhale as you lower the bar to your chest; exhale as you push it back to arm's length. Always keep your head on the bench and do not arch your back too sharply or raise your hips off the bench.

© 1995 by Michael D. Koehler

Exercise 2

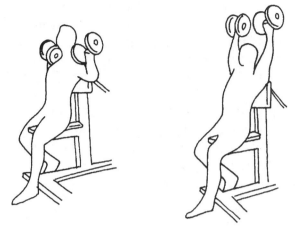

NAME: Seated Back-supported Military Dumbbell Press

PROCEDURE: Raise the barbells to your shoulders and sit on any kind of structure that will give support to your back. Be sure that your elbows are facing out and that the palms of your hands are facing forward. Slowly push the dumbbells upward until your arms are fully extended. Then lower the dumbbells slowly to the original position.

ADJUSTMENTS: You can also use a barbell for this exercise. It may be easier the first time you do it. Once your deltoids become stronger, switch to the dumbbells. They will challenge the entire muscle group.

SAFETY HINTS: As with all exercises, inhale when you lower the weight and exhale forcefully when you raise it. Keep your feet on the floor at all times and your back against the support. Keep your body as straight as possible. This way, you will prevent injury to your back.

Exercise 3

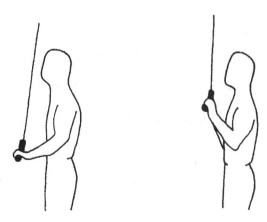

NAME: Standing Triceps Extensions

PROCEDURE: Face the machine bar with your feet approximately shoulder width. Grip the bar with your palms down, your hands at shoulder width. Emphasize a full range of motion by having the bar almost as high as your neck. Slowly lower the bar,

© 1995 by Michael D. Koehler

exhaling forcefully throughout the motion. Inhale as you allow it to raise back to neck height. Remember to lower and raise the bar slowly and deliberately.

ADJUSTMENTS: Use a barbell if the lat machine is unavailable. Raise the barbell over your head, your palms facing the ceiling and your elbows slightly in front of your face. Allow the barbell to *slowly* lower behind your head, making sure your elbows stay slightly in front of your face. Inhale while you lower the bar; exhale forcefully while you raise it.

SAFETY HINTS: Keep your arms tight to your sides throughout the exercise or, if using a barbell, keep your elbows slightly in front of your face, tight to your head. Be sure your hands are approximately shoulder width throughout the exercise, and if you feel any pain during or after the exercise, be sure to see a coach. You may have to use less weight. Always remember: any pain—at any time—*stop the exercise immediately!*

Exercise 4

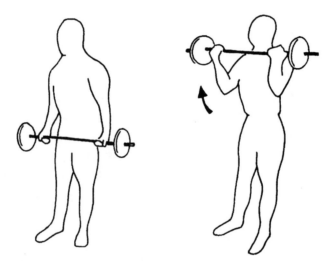

© 1995 by Michael D. Koehler

NAME: Standing Barbell Curl

PROCEDURE: Stand with your back against a wall. Using the appropriate weight for your level of conditioning, grasp the barbell with your palms facing forward—your thumbs facing out. Keeping your back against the wall, slowly raise the barbell, exhaling forcefully throughout the motion. Slowly lower the barbell to its original position at arm's length, inhaling throughout the motion. Remember: both the raising and the lowering should be done slowly and deliberately.

ADJUSTMENTS: You may use dumbbells for this exercise instead of a barbell, and you may alternate the lifts—first one arm, then the other. You can also sit with your back supported, using dumbbells, either simultaneously or alternately.

SAFETY HINTS: Don't allow the weight to fall ballistically after lifting it to the height of your shoulders. You might drop it or pull a muscle. If you find that the weight is too difficult to lift or tires you too quickly so that you are unable to perform the exercise safely, *use less weight*. See a coach first.

Exercise 5

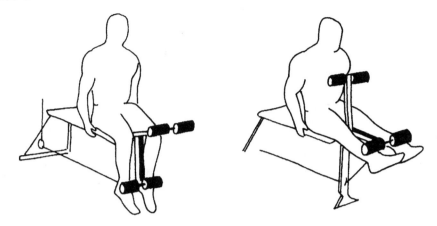

NAME: Leg Extensions

PROCEDURE: Place the top part of your ankles under the pads of a leg extension machine as shown in the illustration. Be sure the front of the seat is tight against the backs of your knees. Grip the seat as illustrated and exhale while raising the weights to the point where your legs are parallel with the floor. Inhale as you lower the weights.

ADJUSTMENTS: If a leg extension machine is unavailable, have a partner provide steady resistance by applying pressure to the fronts of your ankles as you sit on a bench.

SAFETY HINTS: If sitting on a bench, be sure to put a towel on the front part of the bench so that you don't scratch the back of your knees during the exercise. Again, be sure to use an appropriate amount of weight; see a coach if you have any questions.

Exercise 6

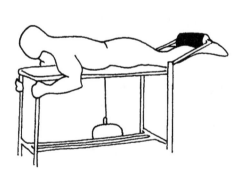

NAME: Thigh Curls

PROCEDURE: Lie face down on the leg extension machine and place your heels under the top pads. Your legs should be parallel to the floor. Slowly bend your legs as you grip the sides of the table for leverage. Exhale as you lift; inhale as you lower your legs to the starting position.

ADJUSTMENTS: If the leg extension machine is unavailable, have a partner apply pressure to the back of your legs as you perform the exercise as described above.

SAFETY HINTS: To avoid injury, be sure the partner applies pressure to your heels, not your Achilles tendons. Also, be sure to place a towel under your legs if using a bench to avoid possible abrasions to your knees and thighs.

© 1995 by Michael D. Koehler

Exercise 7

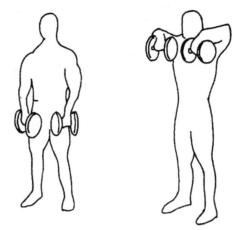

NAME: Standing Upright Rowing with Dumbbells

PROCEDURE: Using a closed grip (your thumbs facing each other), grip two dumbbells, your arms to your sides, the dumbbells resting on the outside of your thighs as in the illustration. Exhale forcefully while lifting the dumbbells straight up as in the illustration. After lifting, your elbows should be as high as your head. Pause for a second at the top of the lift, then slowly lower the dumbbells, inhaling through the motion.

ADJUSTMENTS: The same exercise can be performed with a barbell. Be sure to adjust your grip on the barbell so that your palms are facing your body and your hands are resting on your thighs.

SAFETY HINT: Avoid injury by being sure not to drop the dumbbells ballistically after each lift. They must be lowered slowly to their original position. Use the right amount of weight for your level of conditioning. You're not competing with anyone else to lift the most weight; you're working to improve your own strength levels.

Exercise 8

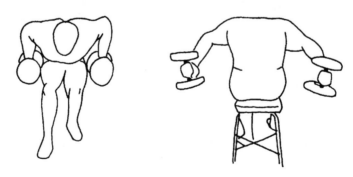

NAME: Triceps Kickbacks

PROCEDURE: Grasp two dumbbells with your palms facing your body. Sit on a bench with your feet solidly on the floor and bend over so that your chest is resting on the tops of your thighs, allowing the dumbbells to hang at your side. Kick the dumbbells back deliberately until the biceps part of your arms and your forearms are parallel

© 1995 by Michael D. Koehler

to the floor. Exhale forcefully as you perform the exercise. Hold the dumbbells in the kicked back position for a second, then slowly return them to the hanging position, inhaling as you do so.

ADJUSTMENTS: This exercise may also be done from a standing position, and the dumbbells may be kicked back alternately. Do it initially from the sitting position, however, because of the support it provides.

SAFETY HINT: If you prefer to do kickbacks from a standing position, find a bench or the arm of a chair to support your head while performing the exercise. It will help provide better leverage.

Exercise 9

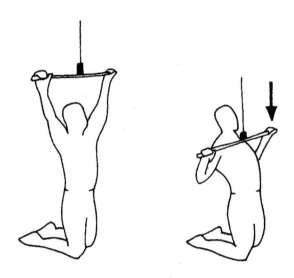

NAME: Lat Pulldowns

PROCEDURE: Kneel underneath the bar of a lat machine and grip the outside ends of the bar so that your thumbs are facing each other. Your arms should be fully extended and your hands about two feet apart. While exhaling forcefully, pull the bar straight down to your chest. Inhale as your return it to its original position. This exercise is designed to work on the upper lats.

ADJUSTMENTS: You can work on your lower lats by closing your grip on the bar so that your hands are only 7 or 8 inches apart. Perform the exercise the same way. Another variation for upper lat work is to grip the bar so that your hands are 2 feet apart and lower the bar behind your head. If the lat machine is unavailable, modified chin-ups can provide many of the same benefits. Refer to that section of your booklet or see your coach.

SAFETY HINTS: Place a folded towel under your knees to avoid soreness. If pulling the bar down behind your head, be sure to execute the exercise carefully and deliberately so that you don't hit your head with the bar. This is a common problem with this particular exercise.

© 1995 by Michael D. Koehler

Exercise 10

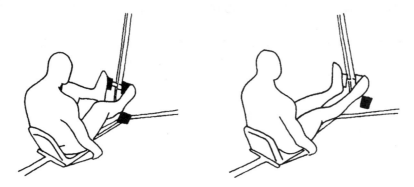

NAME: Leg Press

PROCEDURE: Adjust the seat on the machine so that your thighs are vertical to the floor when your legs are bent. Firmly grasp the handrails under your seat, then press the weight until your knees are in the locked position, exhaling through the motion. Inhale as you slowly lower the weights to their original position.

ADJUSTMENTS: If a leg-press machine is unavailable, see your coach for alternatives or refer to the squat exercises illustrated later in this section.

SAFETY HINTS: Be sure to adjust the seat to maximize the benefits of the exercise and never use more weight than you can lift throughout the number of repetitions in your individual program.

Exercise 11

NAME: Inclined Bench Press with Barbell

PROCEDURE: Lie down on an inclined bench, holding the barbell with as wide a grip as possible. Depending upon the width of the bar, your hands should be approximately 4 to 6 inches inside each weight. The wide grip will enable you to work on your outer and upper pectorals. Push the bar to arm's length, exhaling forcefully through the strain, then slowly lower it to a point just below your neck. Keep your elbows back, in line with your head. Repeat the procedure.

ADJUSTMENTS: If you are doing this exercise at home or if the inclined bench is unavailable, do regular bench presses, using the wide grip as described above.

© 1995 by Michael D. Koehler

SAFETY HINTS: Always use a spotter with this exercise; never do it alone! After raising the bar, lower it slowly. Use an appropriate amount of weight; too much weight increases the chance of injury. Also, keep your head on the bench and do not arch your back. Again, *use a spotter!*

Exercise 12

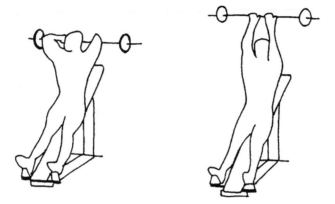

NAME: Seated Closed-grip French Curl

PROCEDURE: Sit on the end of a bench, your back straight and your feet on the floor. Grasp the middle of the bar, your hands in a closed grip (your palms facing you), approximately 5 to 7 inches apart. Hold the bar above your head at arm's length and slowly lower it behind your head, keeping your upper arms as vertical as possible throughout the exercise. Slowly raise the bar to arm's length, exhaling through the effort and keeping your elbows close to the side of your head.

ADJUSTMENTS: You can perform the same exercise while standing. Be sure to keep your legs straight throughout the exercise.

SAFETY HINTS: Again, use a spotter and be sure to use an appropriate amount of weight.

Exercise 13

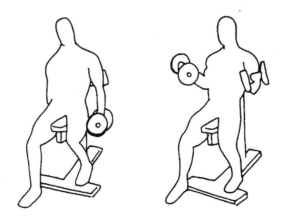

NAME: Seated Dumbbell Curl

PROCEDURE: Sit on a chair with a back support or on the bench with your back against the wall. Keep your back straight and your feet on the floor. Allow the dumb-

© 1995 by Michael D. Koehler

bells to hang at your side, then slowly curl them to shoulder height, exhaling through the strain. Slowly lower them, inhaling through the motion. Keep the dumbbells close to your sides throughout the exercise.

ADJUSTMENTS: Curl the dumbbells alternately, concentrating on your biceps throughout the exercise.

SAFETY HINTS: Be sure you have adequate support from your chair or bench. Set the dumbbells on the floor between each repetition.

Exercise 14

NAME: Wide Stance Squat

PROCEDURE: Place a bench behind you, your heels even with the end. With the barbell on your back, your hands gripping it as wide as possible and your feet a little wider than shoulder width, slowly bend your knees and lower the weight until your buttocks touch the bench. Exhaling, raise yourself to a standing position. Keep your head up and your back straight throughout the exercise, your feet flat to the floor. Do not sit on the bench during the exercise. Simply touch it, keeping tension on your thigh muscles.

ADJUSTMENTS: A wider stance, as in this exercise, enables you to work on your inner thigh muscles. Adjust the exercise by closing your stance to work on the outer thigh muscles. You also can perform the same exercise without a barbell by crossing your arms in front of you and executing the same motions.

SAFETY HINTS: Never bend lower than the height of the bench. Lowering yourself to a point where your thighs are not parallel to the ground places undue stress on the knees. Always use the bench as a reminder. You will also want to be sure you use a belt during this exercise. As we have said repeatedly, however, the use of a belt is wise during *every* exercise in this booklet.

© 1995 by Michael D. Koehler

Exercise 15

NAME: Behind-neck Barbell Press

PROCEDURE: Sit on a bench or a chair that will provide safe support for your back while you perform this exercise. Be sure your back is straight and your feet firmly on the floor. Gripping the barbell as wide as possible, lift it overhead to arm's length and lower it slowly behind your head. Push it back to arm's length, exhaling forcefully through the motion.

ADJUSTMENT: If a bench or chair is unavailable, the exercise can be performed in a standing position. Use an appropriate amount of weight when standing. This is a difficult exercise.

SAFETY HINTS: Use back support whenever possible to provide a solid base while performing this exercise. Also be sure to have a spotter behind you in the event you need help lifting the weight.

Exercise 16

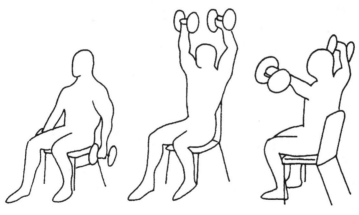

NAME: Dumbbell Raises

PROCEDURE: Sit on a bench or chair that provides support for your back. With your feet flat to the floor, allow a dumbbell in each hand to hang at your sides. Keeping your arms straight, raise the dumbbells in front of you until they are directly overhead. Exhale forcefully through this motion. Inhale while lowering them to your sides, then raise them laterally—straight out to each side—until the dumbbells are approximately shoulder high. Exhale through this motion, then inhale while lowering them again. Continue with the forward motion and the lateral motion as you complete your repetitions.

© 1995 by Michael D. Koehler

ADJUSTMENTS: The exercise can be performed while standing or sitting without back support. It is best, however, to support your back while performing this exercise.

SAFETY HINTS: If in doubt, use less weight while performing this exercise. The number of repetitions you do will provide enough benefit, even if the weight is less than you are accustomed to.

Exercise 17

NAME: Front Lunge

PROCEDURE: Rest a barbell on your shoulders as if you were going to do some squats. With your feet approximately shoulder width, step forward first with your right leg, keeping your left foot planted firmly on the floor. You should step forward far enough so that your right thigh is almost parallel with the floor. Next, step back to your starting position and repeat the motion with your left leg. Continue through the appropriate number of repetitions.

ADJUSTMENTS: This exercise can be performed without a barbell. If you decide to do it without a barbell, place your hands on your hips and execute the exercise as described above.

SAFETY HINTS: Do not use too much weight and be sure to have a spotter with you when you perform this exercise.

Exercise 18

NAME: Barbell Rowing

PROCEDURE: Grasp a barbell on the floor in front of you, your hands just less than shoulder width (close grip) and your thumbs facing each other. With your legs bent and

© 1995 by Michael D. Koehler

your back approximately parallel to the floor, exhale while you lift the barbell straight up until it touches your lower chest. Inhale as you lower the bar almost to the floor. Do not allow it to touch the floor. Continue as described throughout the proper number of repetitions.

ADJUSTMENTS: Perform the same exercise as described above with the following adjustments:

1. Place your hands approximately two feet apart on the bar (medium grip).
2. Place your hands as wide as possible on the bar (open grip).
3. Perform the same exercise with the same variety of grips while lying face down on a bench, the bar lying on the floor underneath you. Lift it until it touches the underneath part of the bench.
4. Perform the same exercise with the same variety of grips with your back bent, your forehead resting on a bench in front of you.

SAFETY HINTS: When supporting your forehead, be sure to use a bench with a soft seat or place a towel under your forehead to avoid abrasions. Also be sure to keep your knees bent and your back straight.

Exercise 19

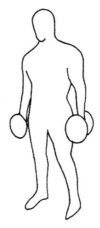

NAME: Dumbbell Dead Lift

PROCEDURE: With your feet 8 to 10 inches apart and holding dumbbells at your sides, bend at the waist until the dumbbells almost reach the floor. Keep your head up and your legs straight throughout the exercise. Inhale while lowering yourself and exhale while returning to the standing position. This is an excellent exercise for the lower back and thighs.

ADJUSTMENT: Grasp the dumbbells at your sides and do a dead lift (bend at the knees) instead of bending at the waist straight-legged. Both exercises—the dead lift and the stiff-legged dead lift—can also be performed with a barbell.

SAFETY HINTS: Be sure to stretch your hamstrings sufficiently before doing the stiff-legged dead lift. You want to stretch before doing *any* exercise, but it is especially important with this exercise.

© 1995 by Michael D. Koehler

Exercise 20

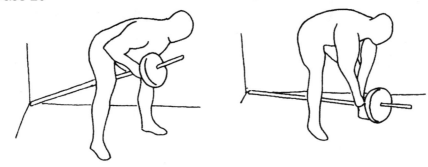

NAME: T-Bar Rowing

PROCEDURE: Place one end of an empty barbell in a corner of a room or somewhere that will stabilize it. Place the desired amount of weight on the other end. Straddle the bar and bend until your back is parallel to the floor, your head directly over the weighted end of the bar. Grasp the bar just inside the weights and lift it until the plates touch your chest, exhaling through the effort. Inhale as you lower it. Don't let the weighted end touch the floor once you begin the exercise.

ADJUSTMENTS: Using the appropriate amount of weight, perform the same exercise using only one arm at a time.

SAFETY HINTS: Keep a slight bend in your legs throughout the exercise to keep some of the pressure off your back and hamstrings. Use the proper technique, stretch yourself, and warm up first.

Exercise 21

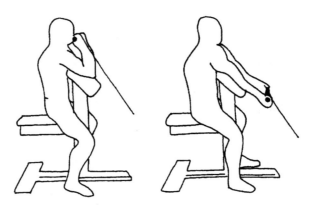

NAME: Preacher Curls

PROCEDURE: Sit behind the Scott Bench or an improvised inclined board holding a dumbbell in each hand as illustrated. Extend your arms completely with your palms up. Slowly raise the dumbbells until they are almost touching your chin. Exhale forcefully through the motion and inhale as you lower them to their original position. Concentrate on each motion, trying to isolate the effort in the biceps.

ADJUSTMENTS: The same exercise can be performed with a pulley or a barbell. If you use either, have your spotter help you get set up before the exercise.

SAFETY HINTS: No matter what piece of equipment you use, be sure you work with a spotter. This exercise is designed to exhaust the biceps. You may need the spotter to take the weight at the end of a set.

© 1995 by Michael D. Koehler

Exercise 22

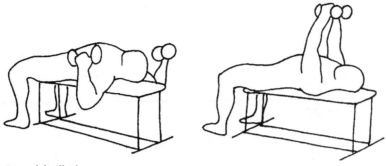

NAME: Dumbbell Fly

PROCEDURE: Lie on your back on the floor or on a bench. Hold two dumbbells at arm's length directly above you, your palms facing inward. Keep the dumbbells almost directly in front of your shoulders. Use the appropriate amount of weight so that you can keep your arms as straight as possible as you lower the dumbbells so that they are in line with the side of your head. Raise the dumbbells on the same path, exhaling forcefully through the motion. Inhale as you lower them.

ADJUSTMENTS: This exercise can be performed as well on an inclined bench.

SAFETY HINTS: Work with a spotter and use only as much weight as you can lift with the proper technique.

Exercise 23

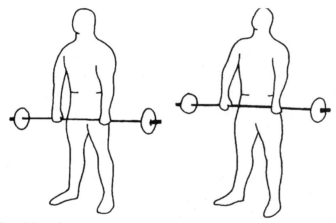

NAME: Shoulder Shrug

PROCEDURE: Hold two dumbbells, thumbs inward, alongside your thighs. Keep your arms relaxed and slowly shrug your shoulders, raising them forward, then rolling them backward as you lower the weights. When you have completed each shrug, you should be standing "at attention," your shoulders back, prepared for the next repetition.

ADJUSTMENT: You can use a barbell instead of two dumbbells. If using a barbell, grasp the bar so that your thumbs are facing each other, your hands a little wider than shoulder width.

SAFETY HINTS: Be deliberate with the motion. Raise and lower the bar slowly; do not drop it back to its original position. Because this exercise allows the use of a considerable amount of weight, be sure to bend your knees when you return the weight to the floor.

© 1995 by Michael D. Koehler

© 1995 by Michael D. Koehler

NAME: Heel Raises

PROCEDURE: Resting a barbell behind your head on your shoulders as in the illustration, slowly raise your heels off the floor so that you are on your tiptoes, then slowly lower your heels back to the floor. Continue with the proper number of repetitions.

ADJUSTMENT: To maximize the benefits of the exercise, place the ball of each foot on a two-by-four and slowly raise and lower yourself as explained above.

SAFETY HINTS: Don't place the balls of your feet on anything higher than 2 inches. The inch and a half side of a two-by-four is generally about the right height. You want to exercise the muscle, not strain it. Also, have a spotter stand behind you to provide support by simply placing his or her hands on your back as you perform the exercise. That will help you maintain balance. The spotter can also help you put the weight on and off your shoulders.

NAME: Cleans

PROCEDURE: Place a barbell on the floor in front of you. With your feet approximately shoulder width and your shins almost touching the bar, grasp the bar—palms down. Your hands should also be shoulder width and your legs bent so that your thighs are almost parallel to the floor. Keep your head up and your arms straight, then inhale forcefully as you pull the bar straight up until you stand in an erect position. As illustrated, after you have flipped the bar so that your hands are under the bar, your palms are facing up, the bar should be shoulder height and resting on your chest when the movement is completed. Exhale as you return the bar to the floor.

SAFETY HINTS: Be sure to use an appropriate amount of weight. If you try to lift too much, you can damage your back. As always, make sure you have a spotter with this exercise and that you use a belt.

**NEVER—WITH ANY OF THESE EXERCISES—
NEVER FORGET OUR *SAFETY FIRST* PRINCIPLE.
YOU ARE PERFORMING THESE EXERCISES TO IMPROVE YOUR HEALTH
AND FITNESS, NOT TO INJURE YOURSELF!**

© 1995 by Michael D. Koehler

someone else who can model proper form, your young athlete will *see* what you mean about elements of safety, and you will be providing further emphasis on the improved performance and the safety of your players. There are some very practical and *legal* considerations in this advice. Most important, however, the expressed concern for the safety of your athletes reflects the reasons for your working with them in the first place.

Finally, be sure to encourage each athlete to work on the entire program—*all* the exercises in that program. They are designed to provide total fitness and strength conditioning. Some young athletes are inclined to work only on those muscles that have immediate aesthetic value. A prominent dancer once told us that the calf muscle is extremely important to dancers because of its importance in jumping. It is *at least* as important to athletes, if less inspiring on the beach. So are the other muscles, so push your athletes to develop all of them.

The Downside of Body Mass

One of history's great college football coaches, Lynn "Pappy" Waldorf, once commented that he didn't necessarily want big football players; he wanted *good* ones. We've all seen football teams with enormous offensive and defensive lines get manhandled by smaller, quicker, and stronger opponents—sometimes by lopsided scores! Size may be desirable in some football players, but it invariably takes a back seat to strength, speed, and intelligence.

While the leaner, stronger player is entering the fourth quarter almost as fresh as at the beginning of the game, the bigger player, if not properly conditioned, is gasping for air and probably getting pushed all over the field. With an insufficient supply of oxygen getting to a player's muscles, strength is sapped, and size is useless.

Many athletes, especially young ones, believe that body mass will give them more strength. In a sense, they're right; Olympic powerlifters and other competitive weightmen require body mass to promote power. Their focus, however, is on five or six lifts to win a gold medal. They don't have to sustain their focus through an entire soccer game and have enough left during the last five minutes to make a maximum effort.

Body mass, therefore, is to be discouraged in young athletes. Strength training should be promoted by coaches as a complement to the other elements in a conditioning program.

Can Athletes Overtrain?

The quick answer to this question is YES. Of course an athlete can overtrain. Too much of anything, no matter how healthful, can have unhealthy results. Athletes can have some involuntary reactions to too much training. They shut down psychologically as well as physically. Muscles *and* motivation weaken, and the strength training regimen suddenly takes a back seat to something else.

There are a good many personal trainers and coaches who keep a close watch on the intensity, duration, and frequency of the workouts they expect of their clients. The old "no pain, no gain" exhortation has fallen by the wayside as players and coaches have traveled down the road to improved physical conditioning for themselves and their players. In fact, many of them have identified symptoms of overtraining that warrant watching.

Elevated blood pressure and an increased morning pulse rate are sure signs of overtraining. Irritability, mood swings, and periodic depression in teenagers are also indications of overtraining, so watch for them. So are fatigue and the increased incidence of colds and flu. Finally, watch for decreased motivation, loss of appetite—even insomnia—as signs of overtraining.

Much like our safety principle, IF IT HURTS, STOP, the general rule of thumb for overtraining is IF YOU JUST CAN'T DO IT, DON'T! Sometimes kids are just exhausted from homework, studying, working, involvement in other activities, or a combination of all four. They may be stressed out, caved in, banged up, or knocked down. At these times, they should not work out.

This is not to say that we don't push young people beyond their sometimes natural inclination to sit back and think about their workouts, but we use common sense when we do it. We also assure that they are alternating hard and easy days and that the athletes are using the proper equipment correctly. We also watch their diets, the subject of section 7.

The Computer Is Your Friend

To prevent overtraining and to provide a specific program that reflects the short and long-term goals of athletes, coaches are encouraged to develop or purchase computer programs that move athletes gradually and reasonably toward the realization of their goals. Many programs are available commercially, or coaches can request assistance from the athletic departments in one or more of their local universities. College coaches, especially if they expect to recruit a school, are always willing to share anything that will keep a foot in the door.

Each of the programs should be designed to provide a progression of exercises that increase gradually in intensity and lead to one or more target maximums. They should be similar in appearance to the programs provided in figure 5-8. The computer provides the important advantage of gradually increasing the intensity of each exercise on a weekly basis.

Sport-Specific Charts

The specific exercises you develop with your players will be determined by their long- and short-range goals and their strength needs to play certain positions on your team. Refer to the chart(s) in figure 6-2 to find the specific exercises that are appropriate for individual athletes. Use these to supplement the total fitness programs outlined in levels A, B, C, and D in section 5. Athletes should be encouraged to follow the programs outlined on the charts just before the start of the season and at selected times during the season.

Figure 6-2 Sport-Specific Exercises

FOOTBALL EXERCISES
LINEMEN

To the Athlete: About a month before the start of the season, perform each of the following exercises at 70% of your maximum strength. Gradually increase the intensity each week. By the start of the season, you should be lifting at 80% to 85% of your maximum strength, concluding each exercise with one or more 100% efforts. Be sure to see me for periodic strength testing to determine maximums and to guarantee safety.

During the season you should follow the same regimen, but at 50% of your maximum strength, doubling the number of repetitions, if you can do so with the proper form. Remember, these exercises are limited. They are specific to your playing position and are not substitutes for your total conditioning program.

Exercises	Muscle(s)	Purpose(s) & Qualifications
Two abdominals	abs	Maximum mobility
Bench press	pectorals and deltoids	Blocking strength particularly pass blocking Emphasize wide-grip to maximize benefits
Upright row	deltoids	Hand shiver during pass blocking
Military press	deltoids	Pass and run blocking
Shoulder shrug	upper trapezius	Forearm shiver and protection for shoulders
Dead lifts	all back muscles	Blocking efficiency Perform this exercise only after you have mastered the Level D program
Behind-neck press	trapezius	Protection for neck
Triceps extension	triceps	Pass and seal blocking
Squats	quadriceps	Lateral mobility and upward thrust
Leg press	quadriceps and gastrocnemius	Leg drive during blocking
Heel raises	gastrocnemius	Driving power during run blocking

More as prescribed by coach. . . .

ALWAYS USE BELTS AND PROPER FORM

© 1995 by Michael D. Koehler

Figure 6-2 (cont.), Ex.2

FOOTBALL EXERCISES
RUNNING BACKS

To the Athlete: About a month before the start of the season, perform each of the following exercises at 70% of your maximum strength. Gradually increase the intensity each week. By the start of the season, you should be lifting at 80% to 85% of your maximum strength, concluding each exercise with one or more 100% efforts. Be sure to see me for periodic strength testing to determine maximums and to guarantee safety.

During the season you should follow the same regimen, but at 50% of your maximum strength, doubling the number of repetitions, if you can do so with the proper form. Remember, these exercises are limited. They are specific to your playing position and are not substitutes for your total conditioning program.

Exercises	Muscle(s)	Purpose(s) & Qualifications
Three abdominals	abs	Improved mobility
Dumbbell curls	biceps	Reduction of fumbles
Preacher curls	biceps	Reduction of fumbles
Push-ups and triceps flybacks	triceps	Forearm strength while running and blocking
Palms-up wrist curls	forearm flexors	Hand strength for holding ball
Neck flexion and neck extension	neck muscles and upper trapezius	Blocking strength and neck protection while running ball
Bent-over rowing	latissimus dorsi, teres major, and biceps	Upper-body strength for warding off tacklers
Military press	deltoids and triceps	Upper-body strength to ward off tacklers and improve speed
Squats	quadriceps, gluteus, and leg abductors	Explosion from start and high-knee drive
Heel raises	gastrocnemius	Leg drive while blocking and running

More as prescribed by coach. . . .

ALWAYS USE PROPER FORM

© 1995 by Michael D. Koehler

Figure 6-2 (cont.), Ex. 3

WRESTLING EXERCISES

To the Athlete: About a month before the start of the season, perform each of the following exercises at 70% of your maximum strength. Gradually increase the intensity each week. By the start of the season, you should be lifting at 80% to 85% of your maximum strength, concluding each exercise with one or more 100% efforts. Be sure to see me for periodic strength testing to determine maximums and to guarantee safety.

During the season you should follow the same regimen, but at 50% of your maximum strength, doubling the number of repetitions, if you can do so with the proper form. Remember, these exercises are limited. They are specific to your sport and are not substitutes for your total conditioning program.

Exercises	Muscle(s)	Purpose(s) and Qualifications
Three abdominals	abs	Improved general mobility
Squats and leg presses	quadriceps, gluteus, and leg abductors	Improve power from bottom position and for driving through opponent
Heel raises	gastrocnemius	Driving through opponent
Bench press	pectorals, deltoids, and triceps	Take-downs and pushing opponent away
Triceps extensions	triceps	Keeping opponent at arm's length
Dead lift	entire back, legs, and biceps	Improved pulling power
Upright and bent-over rowing	latissimus and biceps	Improved strength to control opponent
Palms-up and palms-down wrist curls	hands and forearm muscles	Gripping strength
Shrugs	trapezius	Neck strength for bridging
Bridge bench press	neck muscles	More bridge strength

More as prescribed by coach. . . .

AWAYS USE PROPER FORM

© 1995 by Michael D. Koehler

Figure 6-2 (cont.), Ex. 4

BASKETBALL EXERCISES

To the Athlete: About a month before the start of the season, perform each of the following exercises at 70% of your maximum strength. Gradually increase the intensity each week. By the start of the season, you should be lifting at 80% to 85% of your maximum strength, concluding each exercise with one or more 100% efforts. Be sure to see me for periodic strength testing to determine maximums and to guarantee safety.

During the season you should follow the same regimen, but at 50% of your maximum strength, doubling the number of repetitions, if you can do so with the proper form. Remember, these exercises are limited. They are specific to your sport and are not substitutes for your total conditioning program.

Exercises	Muscle(s)	Purpose(s) and Qualifications
Three abdominals	abs	Improved general mobility
Heel raises	gastrocnemius (calves)	Quick jumping ability
Squats	quadriceps	Improved vertical jumping ability
Lunges	quads and gluteals	Jumping
Military press	deltoids and triceps	Increased ability to hold arms over head for quick rebounding
Behind-the-neck press	trapezius and deltoids	Arm strength for rebounding
Dumbbell raises	deltoids	Arm strength for rebounding and shooting
Front chin-ups and reverse-grip chin-ups	biceps, forearm, and hands	Improved hand strength for rebounding and shooting
Leg extensions	quadriceps	General leg strength for defensive movements
Leg curls	hamstrings	General leg strength
Upright rowing	latissimus dorsi, rhomboids, and biceps	Upper-body strength for rebounding and defensive maneuvering

More as prescribed by coach. . . .

ALWAYS USE PROPER FORM

© 1995 by Michael D. Koehler

Figure 6-2 (cont.), Ex. 5

BASEBALL/SOFTBALL EXERCISES

To the Athlete: About a month before the start of the season, perform each of the following exercises at 70% of your maximum strength. Gradually increase the intensity each week. By the start of the season, you should be lifting at 80% to 85% of your maximum strength, concluding each exercise with one or more 100% efforts. Be sure to see me for periodic strength testing to determine maximums and to guarantee safety.

During the season you should follow the same regimen, but at 50% of your maximum strength, doubling the number of repetitions, if you can do so with the proper form. Remember, these exercises are limited. They are specific to your sport and are not substitutes for your total conditioning program.

Exercises	*Muscle(s)*	*Purpose(s) and Qualifications*
Three abdominals	abs	Improved general mobility
Front chin-ups and reverse-grip chin-ups	biceps, forearms, and hands	Arm strength for bat speed
Modified preacher curls	forearms and hands	Position your arms on the board as if doing regular curls. Instead, lift the weight by bending your arms only at the wrists, putting all the strain on the forearms. This exercise will improve your hand and forearm strength for better bat speed
Leg extensions	quadriceps	Leg strength for improved throwing
Squats	quadriceps	Leg strength for throwing and running
Heel raises	calves	Improved base running
Dumbbell dead lift	quadriceps, gluteals, and erectors (back)	Improved stance for defensive positioning, especially for catchers
Inclined bench press	pectorals, deltoids, and triceps	Upper-body strength for initial speed
Lat pulldowns	latissimus dorsi and biceps	Upper-body strength for quickness
T-Bar rowing	rhomboids, deltoids, lats	Upper-body strength for batting power

More as prescribed by coach. . . .

ALWAYS USE PROPER FORM

© 1995 by Michael D. Koehler

Figure 6-2 (cont.), Ex. 6

GYMNASTICS EXERCISES

To the Athlete: About a month before the start of the season, perform each of the following exercises at 70% of your maximum strength. Gradually increase the intensity each week. By the start of the season, you should be lifting at 80% to 85% of your maximum strength, concluding each exercise with one or more 100% efforts. Be sure to see me for periodic strength testing to determine maximums and to guarantee safety.

During the season you should follow the same regimen, but at 50% of your maximum strength, doubling the number of repetitions, if you can do so with the proper form. Remember, these exercises are limited. They are specific to your sport and are not substitutes for your total conditioning program. Because of gymnastics' unique demands, you may need to supplement this workout with exercises specific to your event(s). See me to discuss these additional exercises. You will also need to work intensively on your flexibility. Refer to that section of your booklet.

Exercises	Muscle(s)	Purpose(s) and Qualifications
Three abdominals and more as needed	abs	General mobility; exceptionally important for gymnasts
Dips	deltoids, pectorals, and triceps	Arm strength for horizontal and parallel bars
Push-ups	deltoids, pectorals, and triceps	Upper-body strength for floor exercise
Military press	deltoids and triceps	Upper body strength for floor ex and other events
Chin-ups	hands, forearms, biceps, and lats	Pulling strength for all bars
Squats	quadriceps	Leg strength for floor ex
Heel raises	gastrocnemius (calves)	Improved jumping ability
Dumbbell fly	pectorals, triceps, deltoids	Upper-body strength for rings, pommel horse, and others
Lat pulldowns	latissimus dorsi and biceps	Upper-body strength for bars and rings
Preacher curls	hands, forearms, and biceps	Grip and arm strength for bars and rings
Triceps extensions	triceps	Pushing strength for bars and floor exercise
Behind-neck-press	trapezius, deltoids, and triceps	Upper-body strength for bars, rings, and floor exercise

More as prescribed by coach. . . .

ALWAYS USE PROPER FORM

© 1995 by Michael D. Koehler

Figure 6-2 (cont.), Ex. 7

VOLLEYBALL EXERCISES

To the Athlete: About a month before the start of the season, perform each of the following exercises at 70% of your maximum strength. Gradually increase the intensity each week. By the start of the season, you should be lifting at 80% to 85% of your maximum strength, concluding each exercise with one or more 100% efforts. Be sure to see me for periodic strength testing to determine maximums and to guarantee safety.

During the season you should follow the same regimen, but at 50% of your maximum strength, doubling the number of repetitions, if you can do so with the proper form. Remember, these exercises are limited. They are specific to your sport and are not substitutes for your total conditioning program.

Exercises	Muscle(s)	Purpose(s) and Qualifications
Three abdominals	abs	Improved general mobility
Leg extensions	quadriceps	Leg strength for jumping
Squats	quadriceps	Leg strength for jumping
Heel raises	gastrocnemius (calves)	Lower leg strength for jumping
Front lunge	quadriceps and gluteals	Improved quickness
Upright rowing	lats, rhomboids, deltoids, and biceps	Arm strength for hitting ball
Military press	deltoids and triceps	Arm strength for killing ball
Barbell rowing	lats, deltoids	Upper-body strength for jumping and blocking shots
Dumbbell dead lift	quadriceps, gluteals, and erectors	Jumping ability and quickness
Cleans	deltoids and rhomboids	Upper body strength for jumping

Others as prescribed by your coach. . . .

ALWAYS USE PROPER FORM

© 1995 by Michael D. Koehler

Figure 6-2 (cont.), Ex. 8

GOLF/FIELD HOCKEY EXERCISES

To the Athlete: About a month before the start of the season, perform each of the following exercises at 70% of your maximum strength. Gradually increase the intensity each week. By the start of the season, you should be lifting at 80% to 85% of your maximum strength, concluding each exercise with one or more 100% efforts. Be sure to see me for periodic strength testing to determine maximums and to guarantee safety.

During the season you should follow the same regimen, but at 50% of your maximum strength, doubling the number of repetitions, if you can do so with the proper form. Remember, these exercises are limited. They are specific to your sport and are not substitutes for your total conditioning program.

Exercises	*Muscle(s)*	*Purpose(s) and Qualifications*
Three abdominals	abs	Improved general mobility
Modified preacher curl	hands and forearms	Hold a barbell on board as if to do preacher curls. Instead, lift the weight by bending the hands at the wrists, concentrating on the muscles in the forearms. This will improve grip strength and ability to control the stick/club
Dead lift	quadriceps, gluteals, and erectors (back)	Improved back strength to control ball while running downfield and to increase power of stroke
Bench press	pectorals, triceps, and deltoids	Upper-body strength for improved stroke
Military press	deltoids and triceps	Same as above
Squats	quadriceps	Upper-leg strength for improved speed
Heel raises	gastrocnemius (calves)	Lower-leg strength for quickness
Front lunge	quadriceps and gluteals	Total leg strength for quickness
Thigh curls	hamstrings	Improved quickness
Dumbbell fly	pectorals and deltoids	Upper arm strength for stronger stroke

Others as prescribed by coach. . . .

ALWAYS USE PROPER FORM

© 1995 by Michael D. Koehler

Figure 6-2 (cont.), Ex. 9

SWIMMING EXERCISES

To the Athlete: About a month before the start of the season, perform each of the following exercises at 70% of your maximum strength. Gradually increase the intensity each week. By the start of the season, you should be lifting at 80% to 85% of your maximum strength, concluding each exercise with one or more 100% efforts. Be sure to see me for periodic strength testing to determine maximums and to guarantee safety.

During the season you should follow the same regimen, but at 50% of your maximum strength, doubling the number of repetitions, if you can do so with the proper form. Remember, these exercises are limited. They are specific to your sport and are not substitutes for your total conditioning program. In addition, be sure to do flexibility exercises at least 20 minutes *before* and *after* doing these exercises. For a swimmer, flexibility is as important as strength.

Exercises	*Muscle(s)*	*Purpose(s) and Qualifications*
Three abdominals	abs	Improved general mobility
Leg extensions	quadriceps	Leg strength for improved kick
Leg curls	hamstrings	Leg strength for improved kick
Lat pulldowns	latissimus dorsi and biceps	Upper-body strength for stroke
Shoulder shrug	upper trapezius	Same as above
T-bar rowing	latissimus dorsi, deltoids, and rhomboids	Back strength for stroke
Dumbbell fly	pectorals and deltoids	Shoulder strength for stroke
Upright rowing	latissimus dorsi, rhomboids, and biceps	Same as above
Triceps kickbacks	triceps	Pulling strength for stroke
Dumbbell raises	deltoids	Shoulder strength for stroke
Dips	deltoids and triceps	Shoulder strength for stroke

Others as prescribed by coach. . . .

ALWAYS USE PROPER FORM

© 1995 by Michael D. Koehler

Figure 6-2, Ex. 10

TENNIS EXERCISES

To the Athlete: About a month before the start of the season, perform each of the following exercises at 70% of your maximum strength. Gradually increase the intensity each week. By the start of the season, you should be lifting at 80% to 85% of your maximum strength, concluding each exercise with one or more 100% efforts. Be sure to see me for periodic strength testing to determine maximums and to guarantee safety.

During the season you should follow the same regimen, but at 50% of your maximum strength, doubling the number of repetitions, if you can do so with the proper form. Remember, these exercises are limited. They are specific to your sport and are not substitutes for your total conditioning program.

Exercises	Muscle(s)	Purpose(s) and Qualifications
Three abdominals	abs	Improved general mobility
Dead lift	quadriceps, gluteals, and erectors (back)	Improved ability to stay in crouch
Leg extensions	quadriceps	Improved upper-leg strength
Squat	quadriceps	Improved upper-leg strength
Leg curls	hamstrings	Improved quickness
Heel raises	gastrocnemius (calves)	Improved foot speed
Dumbbell raises	deltoids	Upper-arm strength for improved stroke
Dumbbell fly	pectorals and biceps	Total arm strength. This exercise simulates stroke motion and helps prevent tennis elbow
Lat pulldown	latissimus dorsi and biceps	Improved upper-back strength for stroke
Front lunge	quadriceps and gluteals	Leg strength for stretching for shots
French curls	triceps	Improved strength for serve

Others as prescribed by coach. . . .

ALWAYS USE PROPER FORM

© 1995 by Michael D. Koehler

Figure 6-2 (cont.), Ex. 11

TRACK EXERCISES
SPRINTERS AND RUNNERS

To the Athlete: About a month before the start of the season, perform each of the following exercises at 70% of your maximum strength. Gradually increase the intensity each week. By the start of the season, you should be lifting at 80% to 85% of your maximum strength, concluding each exercise with one or more 100% efforts. Be sure to see me for periodic strength testing to determine maximums and to guarantee safety.

During the season you should follow the same regimen, but at 50% of your maximum strength, doubling the number of repetitions, if you can do so with the proper form. Remember, these exercises are limited. They are specific to your sport and are not substitutes for your total conditioning program.

Exercises	*Muscle(s)*	*Purpose(s) and Qualifications*
Three abdominals	abs	Improved general mobility
Leg extensions	quadriceps	Upper-leg strength
Thigh curls	hamstrings	Pulling strength in legs
Squat	quadriceps	Power out of the blocks
Heel raises	gastrocnemius (calves)	Pushing power during running motion
Lunge	quadriceps and gluteals	Power for improved stride
Military press	deltoids and triceps	Upper-body strength for power out of the blocks
Upright rowing	latissimus dorsi, rhomboids, and biceps	Upper-body strength for power during running motion
Dumbbell raises	deltoids	Upper-body strength for running motion
Triceps kickbacks	triceps	Increased power for running motion
Cleans	deltoids and rhomboids	More upper-body strength

More as prescribed by coach. . . .

ALWAYS USE PROPER FORM

© 1995 by Michael D. Koehler

Figure 6-2 (cont.), Ex. 12

TRACK EXERCISES
FIELD EVENTS

To the Athlete: About a month before the start of the season, perform each of the following exercises at 70% of your maximum strength. Gradually increase the intensity each week. By the start of the season, you should be lifting at 80% to 85% of your maximum strength, ending each exercise with one or more 100% efforts. Be sure to see me for periodic strength testing to determine maximums and to guarantee safety.

During the season you should follow the same regimen, but at 50% of your maximum strength, doubling the number of repetitions, if you can do so with the proper form. Remember, these exercises are limited. They are specific to your sport and are not substitutes for your total conditioning program. Because of the variety of field events, be sure to see your coach for additional exercises that are specific to your event.

Exercises	Muscle(s)	Purpose(s) and Qualifications
Three abdominals	abs	Improved general mobility
Bench press	pectorals, triceps, and deltoids	Improved push for shot and other throwing events
Upright rowing	latissimus dorsi, rhomboids, and biceps	Good for throwing events and arm lift for jumping events
Dumbbell raises	deltoids	Also good for throwing events and for arm lift for jumping events
French curl and triceps kickback	triceps	Both good for running motion and all throwing events
Military press and behind-the-neck military press	deltoids, trapezius, and triceps	Excellent for throwing events and for arm lift for jumping events
Squat	quadriceps	Leg power for throwing and jumping
Heel raises	gastrocnemius (calves)	Lower-leg power for both throwing and jumping events
Lunge	quadriceps and gluteals	Excellent for jumping events; also good for throwing events
Dumbbell fly	pectorals and biceps	Good for throwing events
Cleans	deltoids and rhomboids	Upper-body strength for all events

More as prescribed by coach. . . .

ALWAYS USE PROPER FORM

© 1995 by Michael D. Koehler

The preseason work should gradually increase in intensity. During the three weeks prior to the first day of the season, athletes should be working up to their maximum weights, completing each exercise with a maximum lift. In essence, this is their peak time, the time in their weightlifting regimen when they are at their strongest and when they are making maximum efforts to improve their strength.

Once the season starts, the athletes should continue working on the exercises in the charts, but they should decrease the amount of weight and increase the number of repetitions. The increase in repetitions will provide *aerobic* muscle conditioning, which is designed to prevent injury and maintain strength. Remember that strength increases are not the primary focus of in-season weightlifting. Although some increases are possible, the main purpose of weightlifting in-season is to supplement performance and prevent injury.

Your preliminary input and encouragement throughout all the programs are very important. Refer to figure 5-7 for a way to develop such goals. Also acknowledge that athletes may surpass computer programs by continuing to develop their own maximum strength testing. It's wise for you to supervise such early strength testing to assure safety. In addition, when youngsters do deviate from predesigned programs, make certain that their exercises remain sport specific. The charts will help them maintain this focus.

Finally, notice that each chart specifies a workout regimen for individual positions on the team. Because the athletes playing these positions have different strength levels, it will be appropriate for the coach to individualize the workout further by indicating the degree of intensity for each player. The strongest player at that position, for example, will perform the exercises at 80 percent of maximum with a 25-second rest period between sets, the weakest at 50 to 60 percent of maximum with a 45-second rest period.

A Word About Myths

Like the rest of the sports world, strength training involves almost as much fantasy as fact. Young athletes, for example, shouldn't have to worry about becoming muscle-bound if they work to increase both strength and flexibility. World class gymnasts are among the sports world's strongest athletes; their flexibility is one of their most obvious assets.

Your athletes don't have to worry about developing big muscles. The right weightlifting regimen will increase strength without exaggerating size.

The relative and absolute strength of men and women may favor the men, but the muscular endurance of both may be about the same. It's a matter of record that many women perform better than many men in activities requiring muscular endurance, such as marathon running and long-distance swimming.

Coaches will be heartened to know that they can exercise alongside their players during weightlifting sessions. Decreases in muscular fitness are more the result of lifestyle than of any movement of the clock or calendar. Our habits can age us a whole lot faster than Father Time. In fact, by age 65 the average person has lost only 15 percent of his or her strength potential.

How about the idea that athletes are born, not made? Not true. If it were true, why would we be working so hard to improve our performance? Some of us are more gifted than others, but we've all seen athletes with lesser gifts outplay their more talented counterparts because they're in better condition. On the flipside, what about the idea that the more you train, the better your fitness levels? To the contrary, excessive training can break down muscle development and even cause illness.

Another misconception is the idea that once fit, always fit. This myth is, perhaps, one of the biggest reasons why many of us rationalize away good fitness habits. Consider the once great running back in the NFL who couldn't finish the half mile run in a recent Superstars competition. Physical talent wasn't his problem; the banquet circuit was.

Does muscle turn to fat when you stop working out? No. Fat doesn't turn to muscle when you exercise vigorously, and muscle doesn't turn to fat when you stop. Fat and muscle cells are not interchangeable. A related myth is the belief that muscle development requires more protein. Certainly it requires some protein but not in excess of Recommended Daily Allowances. Too much protein is stored in the body as fat.

Finally, what about the notion that rigorous exercise can be harmful because it enlarges the heart? Well, exercise certainly makes it stronger, but actual harm to the heart comes from attacks that result in an inadequate supply of blood to the brain and other parts of the body. A well-exercised heart forces more blood into the system and causes the arteries to become larger, lessening the chance of blockage and heart failure.

Most coaches are familiar with these misconceptions. Many players, maybe most, are not. It's a good idea, therefore, for coaches to dispel such ideas by explaining them away and by exhibiting their own personal conditioning habits. A part of the coach's role, therefore, is to model as well as direct the training activities of his or her players.

What Are the Other Elements of the Coach's Role?

It's probably not too surprising that Joe Paterno said it best. He told one of his Nittany Lion teams one year that his job was to push his players as hard as he could. He didn't want them coming back to him at some time in the future saying that they could have won a national championship if only he had pushed them harder. A high school girls basketball coach recently shared Paterno's sentiments when she told us that she wanted her girls' to look back on their playing careers with no regrets, that only a maximum effort would satisfy their acceptance of what they had accomplished.

Both coaches are equally aware, however, that the "hard pushes" and the "no regrets" apply to the classroom as well as the field, court, and weight room. Just as athletes require a commitment to a total conditioning program, they must make a similar commitment to their academic development. The information shared in figure 6-3 may help them develop the right perspective.

Figure 6-3

SOMETHING TO THINK ABOUT

The world is full of statistics. Some are helpful; some are not. *These are very helpful!!* Read them carefully; take them home to share with your parents; talk them over with me or the other coaches. They will definitely influence your class work and your involvement in sports. They involve the likelihood of your ever playing a sport in college or the pros. Regarding college:

Did You Know?

1. A major university may mail as many as 5,000 to 8,000 questionnaires each year to prospective athletes in football. And they give only 20 scholarships. They may mail an equally high number in basketball, but they give only 2 or 3 scholarships each year. Other sports give fewer scholarships.
2. A high school football player who receives a questionnaire may still have odds as high as 320-1 against his receiving a scholarship. It's tougher in other sports, particularly for girls. Their sports are often underfunded.
3. Of the approximately 265,000 high school seniors who play football each year, only 1% will receive a scholarship to play for a major university.
4. Only 1.5 % of the nation's high school basketball players will receive a scholarship; most of those will be partial scholarships.
5. The budgets of the other college sports programs are smaller than budgets for these major sports. They have less opportunity to recruit and fewer scholarships to offer.
6. Only .07% of athletes earning All-Conference honors receive scholarships.

What About the Pros?

1. Only 7/1,000 of 1 percent of today's high school football players will play in the pros.
2. That number is only 4/1,000 of 1 percent of basketball players.
3. The average pro career is only three years.

HIT THE BOOKS!!

YOUR FUTURE IS IN ACADEMICS!!

© 1995 by Michael D. Koehler

Let's Wrap It Up

A few important points warrant additional mention. The principle, IF IT HURTS, STOP, cannot be overemphasized. Jimy Taylor, as tough as he was at Green Bay, was not the only athlete with a high tolerance for pain. We learned a long time ago that you don't have to *look* tough to *be* tough. You can find ballerinas who tolerate more pain than middle linebackers. You and I must be especially alert, therefore, to any signs of pain in our students during exercise. If the grimace lasts beyond the exertion, the athlete is in pain. That's the time to stop him or her, find out what's wrong, and take whatever corrective action is necessary.

Safety first must prevail at all times. Acknowledging pain is one thing; preventing it is another. Be sure that each athlete is following the proper procedures during any exercise, especially if it involves weights. One careless moment can result in a lifetime of disability and pain. Those of you who have forced your body beyond its limitations in the name of athletic competition also realize that the pain resulting from a careless moment may not become obvious until middle age. Protect your athletes from such possibilities in the weight room. Get their attention by paraphrasing a popular saying: "Pay me now—or later in life."

That's why we have included in the passouts the proper adjustments and the important safety tips for each exercise. If you decide to make a booklet of the warming-up exercises, the manual exercises, the weightlifting program, and the sport-specific chart(s) that highlight special exercises, it will contain everything the students need to tailor the program to their needs. By assisting them with the development of the program and watching them during their workouts, you will help them realize their goals.

These goals are very important because, as illustrated in figure 5-7, they emphasize the relationship between the exercise program and the student's enhanced appearance or improved athletic performance. As important, when athletes establish their own goals, they commit to them more readily. It's a whole lot easier for coaches to remind kids of their goals than to coerce them into strenuous activities that they neither want nor understand.

Above all, coaches and athletes must *have fun.* Part of the enjoyment comes from the athletes' recognition that they are strengthening their bodies. For coaches and parents, the enjoyment is multifold. They recognize that their kids are improving neuromuscular connection and skeletal structure; fighting off genetic predispositions; improving discipline, confidence, and self-esteem; and fighting off many ailments that accompany an unhealthy lifestyle.

Finally, figure 6-4 provides a poster that we use to remind our athletes of what it takes to realize physical fitness. Post it prominently; it works. And remind your athletes that the philosophy that inheres in the words DO IT extends into every aspect of their lives. Self-discipline and a considerate but healthy aggressiveness accomplish more than talent. You have the opportunity to teach them a very important lesson in life. Good luck.

Figure 6-4

**IF YOU WANT TOTAL CONDITIONING,
YOU NEED**

Dedication from parents, coach, teacher, and **YOU**.

Organization to guarantee continued improvement.

Intensity to guarantee improved strength, and

Technique to guarantee safety and good form.

DO IT

© 1995 by Michael D. Koehler

EATING YOUR WAY

TO SUPERIOR PERFORMANCE

First, a quick story. It must seem like only yesterday that most of you middle-agers were eating a lean piece of beef, dry toast, tea, and honey for your pregame meal. We all must have shared a similar experience. At an early-morning meeting, our coach, usually red-eyed and breathless, would growl something like: "The beef'll get the taste of blood in your mouth!" We would obediently snarl in agreement, then gather in packs to attack the training table and its unsuspecting steaks.

Little did any of us realize that each morsel of undigested meat would later wreak its revenge. While we were warming up for the game, trying desperately to increase the flow of oxygen and energy to our muscles, much of the blood in our bodies was racing to our stomachs to digest our pregame meal. Our coach had unsuspectingly weakened us by substituting his "taste of blood" for actual blood in our muscles.

What's worse, some of today's coaches, sustained by the memory of their old coaches and unable to break the vice grip of tradition, maintain the same practice. Others, however, are recognizing the importance of nutrition in athletic performance and are providing easily digested, carbohydrate-rich diets before games and throughout much of the week to guarantee appropriate energy levels for their players.

Such is the focus of this section.

How Does Nutrition Fit into the Big Picture?

Nutrition is to an athlete's body what fuel is to a high-performance engine. Neither will win anything without the right supply of energy. In fact, such an analogy may be the best way to think of nutrition and performance. Muscles are the body's engine;

155

they operate at peak performance with the right fuel mix and "run out of gas" when the supply is inadequate. No matter how powerful the engine, its proper performance requires the right fuel.

The job of the coach is to encourage young athletes to give their engines the right fuel. Coaches are unconcerned that fat is a series of carbon molecules with hydrogen and oxygen molecules attached along the chain. Some of them *are* concerned that fats are either saturated or unsaturated, and most are concerned that fat provides energy to the body in combination with sugars that release it.

This latter fact is one of the keys to athletic performance. Coaches realize, therefore, that diet is an important element whenever we build the total athlete. That athletes realize it is even more important. Their knowledge of the importance of a proper diet will not only improve their total performance but have value for them for the rest of their lives.

Rethinking the Importance of Nutrition

Nutrition is an aid not only to performance but to the *opportunity* to perform. Consider the athlete who needs to drop three or four pounds to make weight in wrestling, or the one who wants to add a few pounds to improve her ability to box out under the boards. Each of these examples—and there are a whole lot more—suggests that nutrition as an element of physical conditioning extends well beyond performance.

At this point, the relationship of nutrition to athletics suggests opportunities for young athletes to respect or to abuse their bodies, a reality that warrants the constant vigilance of all coaches. As indicated in section 6, the desire to lose weight quickly often results in the loss of water and lean muscle tissue rather than fat. Conversely, the desire to add weight quickly can tempt youngsters to use steroids or, at the least, provoke immoderate eating habits.

The coach's job is to guard against both possibilities by assuring appropriate levels of involvement for each player. This is, of course, easier said than done. Youngsters have their dreams. The 175-pound wrestler believes that if he wrestled at 145, he would become an All-Stater. The 5'9" forward is convinced that if she grows 5 inches and plays center, she will improve her chances to be recruited by her state university.

To make our jobs more difficult, we learned a long time ago that we are not in the business of destroying dreams. Without visions of crowd-pleasing and self-satisfying performances, kids have little more than hard work to expect from sports. We know that it involves a whole lot more than that, but it also involves the physical well-being of our athletes. Significant weight changes, therefore, are to be avoided by young athletes—certainly discouraged by coaches.

The Chemistry of Eating and Exercising

More must be said about proteins and carbohydrates relative to fitness and performance, but let's avoid the esoteric terminology that obscures our understanding of effective nutrition. Our purpose is to keep it plain and simple, to outline the right kind of diet for young athletes who want to enhance their appearance and performance and who need to maintain proper nutrition for the inevitable growth they will experience during junior and senior high school.

Consider this observation:

> The harder you work an engine, the more fuel it requires. . . .When a man is trying to build himself up by means of exercise, he simply has to take enough food to repair the tissue which is broken down while exercising. . . . Most of the men who are noted for their strength eat three meals a day, and their diet is a mixed one. . . .I believe that a mixed diet is the best one for an athlete.

These suggestions were offered in an article entitled, "Body-Building and Muscle-Developing Exercises," published by the Milo Bar-Bell Company in 1915. Not much has changed in eight decades. The advice regarding the actual weightlifting exercises is also similar to much of what we suggested in section 6.

The graduate student in a nutrition class may require a sophisticated knowledge of chemistry, but *our* understanding of good eating involves little more than common sense. If muscles are the engines that enable our execution of physically demanding athletic skills, they require the kind of fuel that promotes peak performance. This section outlines ways for young athletes to get that fuel.

Using Common Sense with Nutrition

When people start exercising regularly, their appetites increase. When young athletes burn fuel during practice or competition, they want to replenish it as soon as possible, often with junk food on the way home. Coaches, therefore, are well advised to encourage their athletes to fill up on the right foods at the end of the day. Some coaches, for example, provide boxes of bananas for the players after contests. The kids can eat one in the locker room after a shower and take another for the trip home.

Having the right food on hand is ideal but often impractical. The best bet for coaches, therefore, is simply to tell their athletes to load up on water and hurry home to refuel their engines with the foods mentioned in figure 7-1. Include this information in the packet you provide every player early in the season. It lists the foods and explains the reasons for eating them.

Notice that it also mentions the role of proper nutrition for the growth that occurs during adolescence. Most young athletes are concerned about their size. Their eyes are not only bigger than their stomachs; their dreams are bigger than their bodies. They are well motivated to do much of what is necessary to "grow into" their dreams.

Most teenagers can work up an appetite just by opening the refrigerator door. Their bodies demand food. The coach's job is to assure that they are eating the *right* food. That the athletes understand the nuances of nutrition is unimportant. They require only brief explanations so that the foods mentioned in figure 7-1 make sense to them. Coaches, however, must know more in order to answer the inevitable questions from so many inquiring young minds.

Figure 7-1

EATING YOUR WAY TO IMPROVED PERFORMANCE

THE BODY'S NUTRIENTS

The basic nutrients of the body are proteins, carbohydrates, fats, vitamins, and minerals. Look at the following chart to understand how they work:

NUTRIENT	NEEDED FOR	CAN BE FOUND IN
Fat	Continuing energy	Meat and dairy products
Carbohydrates	Energy, especially quick energy. Also help to burn fat	Preworkout: Apples, ice cream, raw carrots. Postworkout: Bananas, honey, raisins, bread. Most fruits, vegetables, and grains
Proteins	Muscle growth and repair	Meat, (including fish and poultry), eggs, and most beans
Minerals and vitamins	The body's metabolism	A well-balanced diet

All athletes who eat well-balanced diets, including appropriate servings from the bread, vegetable, fruit, milk, and meat groups, will take in all the vitamins and minerals they need to sustain their growth and promote their athletic performance. They also will consume the carbohydrates and the proteins they need for practice and competition. Athletes or their parents who have specific questions are encouraged to see the family doctor.

© 1995 by Michael D. Koehler

What Coaches Must Know

First of all, let's recognize that the Recommended Daily Allowances (RDA) offered by the Food and Nutrition Board of the National Research Council represent a starting point for any considerations of proper nutrition. We may have to adjust this standard somewhat in order to satisfy the nutritional needs of young athletes, but RDAs generally provide sufficient amounts of nutrients to meet the needs of healthy people.

Such a standard is especially important, given the wide range of dietary fads that can be found on the market. Like the "miracle elixirs" and snake oils that nineteenth century hucksters foisted on the gullible, today's "guaranteed" diets provide more bluff than benefit. To combat such advertising claims, coaches must know about the basic building blocks of nutrition. Fortunately, they are uncomplicated.

Understanding Nutrients

Nutrients are obtained from food and are necessary for the growth, repair, and maintenance of the body. The five basic nutrients are proteins, carbohydrates, fats, vitamins, and minerals. Let's add water as another essential, particularly as it carries other essential elements to parts of the body. Proteins, fats, and carbohydrates are the nutrients that provide energy for all of us. They are the focus for growing, active adolescents.

Metabolism is the process of converting food—proteins, fats, and carbohydrates—into energy. These three nutrients are the primary elements in the maintenance and repair of the body. The harder youngsters work during practice or competition, the greater their metabolism and the more nutrients they require not only to repair tissue and to replenish energy supplies but to promote normal growth.

Vitamins, minerals, and water assist in the metabolic process by transporting food substances to tissues and carrying waste products from them. Each is important for other reasons as well. Our focus, however, is energy, so this section considers the essential elements of nutrition from that perspective. In a well-balanced diet, carbohydrates provide about 50 percent of our energy supplies; let's look at them first.

Carbohydrates are found in food starches and sugars. Potatoes are rich in starch; sucrose (table sugar) and lactose (found in milk) are rich in sugars. Because they provide an immediate energy source, they are especially important before and after practice and competition. Some nutritionists and exercise physiologists encourage well-conditioned athletes to eat a candy bar and drink a lot of water immediately after vigorous exercise in order to replenish the energy that is so important to the heart and other muscles.

Interestingly, the sugars found in candy find their way to the muscles of well-conditioned athletes and to the hips and stomachs of nonathletes! In fact, after vigorous exercise, the heart absorbs such energy sources before any other muscle in the body. It receives top priority from Mother Nature in the event strenuous exertion is necessary again. Once the heart replenishes its energy stores, it lets all the other muscles have their share.

For those of us who don't exercise regularly, candy bars are stored in the body as fat. Because basal metabolism—the minimum amount of energy required to maintain life—doesn't do much to burn off bon bons and chocolate doughnuts, such sugars remain potential energy by sitting in fat cells—waiting for the body to "get moving." Because young athletes move vigorously, they become the envy of sedentary parents and other adults; they can empty the refrigerator almost daily but stay slim.

Young athletes do, however, require a balanced diet to provide appropriate nutrients, to satisfy their performance and developmental needs. It's one thing to acknowledge that young athletes use body fat more efficiently than many of the rest of us; it's another to assure that they receive the nutrients required to sustain those levels of efficiency.

Fats and carbohydrates satisfy the vast majority of our energy needs and, as such, are critical to young athletes. To a lesser extent, proteins also provide energy, but their primary importance is found elsewhere. They are important to the growth and repair of muscle tissue.

Proteins Help Balance the Diet

Just what are proteins? Specifically, they are organic structures like carbohydrates and fats, having the same molecular building blocks. Whereas carbohydrates consist of a carbon backbone with oxygen and hydrogen attachments, proteins have an additional nitrogen attachment. It is this attachment that is so important to the growth and repair of body tissue.

Our job as coaches is to charge our athletes with the responsibility of maintaining a diet that satisfies the energy as well as the growth and maintenance needs of their bodies. Figure 7-2 explains the importance of proteins and amino acids and complements the information provided in figure 7-1. Notice the reference to protein as an energy source. Without an adequate supply of carbohydrates and fats, the body burns protein as an energy source. At this point its most important contribution to the body is wasted.

It is critical for the growth and repair of human tissue. Every time a young athlete lifts weights or runs vigorously, he or she tears down muscle tissue. Protein is needed to repair that tissue and to build it up as a result of the exercise. Interestingly, the repair and growth of muscle tissue requires energy; athletes, therefore, burn calories while resting after strenuous exercise. Their bodies are repairing the small muscle tears that result inevitably from strain.

That's another reason why exercise is so important for all of us and why protein is so essential in our diets. Protein also transports nutrients into cells and in and out of the blood. Because antibodies are made of protein, it is also a major part of our immune systems. Coaches, therefore, want to make sure that athletes get a sufficient supply not just to build and repair their bodies but to avoid unnecessary illness.

A Word About Amino Acids

Proteins are formed by chains of amino acids, which are released to assist with the growth and repair of body tissue when food protein is digested. Because amino

Figure 7-2

PROTEINS AND PROTEIN SUPPLEMENTS

WHAT ARE THEY?

Proteins are critical for the growth and repair of muscles. Whenever we exercise vigorously, we tear down muscle tissue. Protein is needed to repair it and build it up as a result of the exercise. Antibodies, those agents in our bodies that fight infection, are made of protein. It is especially important to us, then, to help build us up and to prevent illness from breaking us down!

HOW DO THEY WORK?

Proteins are composed of amino acids, which are classified as essential and nonessential. The foods that contain large quantities of both essential and nonessential amino acids are called *complete* proteins. Complete proteins are found in dairy products and meats (including fish and poultry). *Incomplete* proteins, those that don't provide all the essential and nonessential amino acids, are found in most fruits and grains.

WHAT DOES ALL THIS MEAN TO ME?

You need enough protein to repair your muscles after vigorous exercise and to help promote their growth. You also need carbohydrates to meet your energy needs, hence your need for a *balanced* diet, one that provides enough protein for the development and repair of muscles and enough carbohydrates for energy.

CAN I CHEAT BY TAKING AMINO ACID SUPPLEMENTS?

NO! A balanced diet will meet all your needs, unless you have a condition requiring such supplements, in which case you have already received a doctor's prescription. Just to prove the point, consider this fact: some athletes spend money on two amino acids that help promote the development of muscles, lysine and arginine. Most don't realize that just a 3-ounce portion of lean beef contains about 1,700 mg of arginine and 2,200 mg of lysine. These athletes would have to take about 18 capsules of these amino acid supplements to get the same amounts!

STICK TO A BALANCED DIET!

© 1995 by Michael D. Koehler

acids play a vital part in the development and repair of muscles, coaches must have a basic understanding of their function. Fortunately, coaches need not define the roles of methionine and glutamine; they need only understand that these kinds of amino acids constitute protein and are essential for young athletes.

The athletes themselves need to understand only that protein is an essential part of a balanced diet. Coaches might want to enhance that knowledge by providing information like that in figure 7-2. Some amino acids, for example, are classified as nonessential because the body can produce them independently of food intake. The essential amino acids are provided only by food intake.

The quality of food intake is a factor as well. *Protein quality* is a term that refers to the ratio of essential amino acids to nonessential amino acids. If a food, for example, provides a significant amount of the 9 essential amino acids and the 11 nonessential amino acids, it is termed a complete protein. Incomplete proteins are found in foods with lower protein quality—those that provide a lower ratio of essential to nonessential amino acids.

Examples of foods containing complete proteins are milk, meats, fish, and poultry. We will refer to them as animal protein. Incomplete proteins are found in such foods as corn, wheat, rice, barley, and oats. These are classified as vegetable protein. Generally, fruits, grains, and vegetables are incomplete proteins. They meet the carbohydrate needs of athletes but they satisfy their protein needs only in combination with other kinds of vegetables in the diet.

For example, a vegetarian diet can meet protein needs if rice is eaten with beans or if the following combinations are eaten: split peas and rice, chick peas and bulgur wheat, black-eyed peas and rice, baked beans and corn bread, and peanut butter and bread. Most youngsters, however, will maintain a diet that includes varying portions of animal protein, such as milk and cereal, vegetables with lean beef, nonmeat lasagna with cheese topping, or poultry or fish and vegetables.

Such combinations of food meet most of the needs of young athletes involved in vigorous exercise. An emphasis only on carbohydrates in the diet fails to meet the development and repair needs of muscle tissue. An emphasis only on a protein diet fails to meet the energy needs of active youngsters. In the case of sedentary youngsters, it's interesting to observe that excess protein turns to fat. Exercise, therefore, is the complement that lets food work its miracles for all of us.

What About Amino Acid Supplements?

Body-building magazines are replete with advertisements peddling amino acid supplements that promise weight gain, weight loss, or improved sleep. Such claims are potentially very dangerous for young athletes, many of whom are so preoccupied with physical appearance and performance that they will eat or drink anything that promotes their idealized self-images.

Some people have disorders that may be responsive to amino acid treatments, but teenagers who take immoderate doses of amino acids to promote muscle growth may be risking serious side effects. Consider the relatively recent manufacture and sale of an amino acid that was said to induce sleep. Ultimately, the Federal Drug

Administration (FDA) banned its non-prescription sale after 20 people died of a serious muscle disorder allegedly resulting from its use.

One of the largest vitamin manufacturers in the United States recently was fined $40 million for claiming that some of its products burned fat, that others added weight quickly. Its products could be proven to do neither. People continue to buy them, however, undoubtedly in an attempt to get fit faster and more easily. Josh Billings was right when he said, "The best way to convince a fool that he is wrong is to let him have his own way."

We as coaches, however, can't do that with our kids. Fortunately, our jobs are made easier by one simple truth. A well-balanced diet provides all the vitamins and minerals and amino acids that any active youngster needs to improve his or her appearance and athletic performance. An average diet provides all the animal protein a young athlete requires to develop and repair muscle tissue.

How Much Protein Is Enough?

Nutritionists have developed a variety of complicated ways to rate the quality of proteins: biological value, protein efficiency ratio, or net protein utilization. Coaches require no such measurements to be of help to their athletes. All we need to know is that all of us need about 10 to 12 percent protein in our daily caloric intake. An RDA chart can provide helpful information in this regard.

Many body builders take in more protein than they require for muscle development. Young athletes must be warned about the possible side effects of too much protein. Excessive doses of protein can cause damage to the liver and kidneys. They can result in calcium loss and increased cholesterol due to the fact that complete proteins come from animal sources. Excess protein also is stored in the body as fat, a factor that compromises the young athlete's attempts to improve his or her appearance.

Encourage your youngsters to trust RDA charts; even show them how to calculate an appropriate daily intake of protein. Most of them won't want to make daily calculations, so work with them to develop a general diet that will satisfy both their carbohydrate and their protein requirements in order to satisfy the needs of their bodies during and after vigorous exercise. The athletes who get into serious body building probably will want to calculate their protein intake periodically.

Bulking Up the Right Way

Several considerations apply.
   • Young athletes who want to increase their body mass must first determine if, in fact, the demands of their sport require it.

This sounds like an obvious first step only because it is. Many young athletes, especially boys, want to be bigger. They equate size with performance and assume "the bigger, the better." As indicated elsewhere in this book, smaller, better-conditioned athletes often push their larger counterparts all over the court or field. The first thing coaches must do, therefore, is discuss with each young athlete the "why" of bulking up. If more bulk does promise to improve performance, they must consider the next important question.

• How much bulk is the right amount?

This question can be answered only after first assessing the athlete's body fat percentage. Refer again to figure 4-2 to make the appropriate determinations, then decide exactly how much weight needs to be gained.

• How will we gain it?

The most obvious answer to this question involves the simple nutritional truism that people who take in more calories than they burn will gain weight. It also relates to the fact that muscle is heavier than fat. Young athletes must understand, therefore, the relationship of exercise to weight gain. Vigorous exercise tears down muscle tissue; protein helps repair it; and the muscle itself, in order to prevent further breakdown, increases in size and strength (hypertrophy). This increased size promotes weight gain.

It follows, then, that vigorous exercise accompanied by a well-balanced diet that provides more calories than those expended in exercise and in normal growth will result in weight gain. The old notion of drinking milk shakes and eating foods high in protein is somewhat valid, particularly as "unused" protein turns to fat, but the best advice for any young athlete who wants to increase bulk is to visit the family doctor to determine the appropriate diet and to receive the periodic supervision required for healthy weight gain.

Most important, always ensure that young athletes make some preliminary assessment of body fat percentages and avoid weight gains if those percentages are too high. Just because a youngster wants to put the shot in track doesn't mean that he or she has the body type to be able to do it successfully. The same is true of the boy who wants to be the starting tackle on the football team or the girl who wants to play power forward.

Our job as coaches is to help kids realize their dreams but always somewhere in the *real world*. With the appropriate weight loss and the right levels of conditioning, the girl may become a perfect point guard and the boy the starting nose guard on defense. We must help them *shape* as much as *realize* their dreams. With younger athletes, oftentimes that job starts by carefully coordinating physical capability with the desire to play. As the child grows, adjustments can be made, always within a realistic assessment of the child's capabilities.

The Flipside: Losing Weight the Right Way

Immoderate weight gains certainly can be harmful to general health, but careless weight loss can be even more serious. Fasting deprives the body of necessary nutrients. The calories we ingest each day are used to fuel the heartbeat, the activity of the lungs and nervous system, and such things as the repair and growth of muscles, hair, and nails. In essence, *basal metabolism* represents the energy the body expends during such activities.

Fasting jeopardizes these activities. To compensate, the body actually begins to feed on itself. In order to satisfy its need for quick energy, the body will break down its own proteins into amino acid components and synthesize them into glucose. What this means to most young athletes is the loss of valuable muscle tissue (protein) for practice and competition. In addition, weight that is lost quickly invariably is gained back just as quickly.

A good principle for young athletes, therefore—especially wrestlers, boxers, and others who are conscious of their weight—is "the more slowly you lose weight, the longer it stays off." A loss of one to two pounds a week is usually a good rule of thumb, unless, of course, the youngster already is at or below an ideal weight for his or her body fat percentage. In such cases, when weight loss is inadvisable, coaches and others must step in to promote a reevaluation of the reasons for such weight loss.

The Reality of Eating Disorders

This brings up a related point. Adolescents are often preoccupied with their body images—at times, extremely critical of their appearance. Boys tend to think of themselves as too small or too light; girls tend to think of themselves as too tall or too heavy. Some surveys indicate, for example, that as many as 20 percent of all college women may have an eating disorder. The two most common are anorexia nervosa and bulimia—the former an unwillingness to eat at all, the latter a desire to overeat, then purge oneself of the food.

Both are dangerous and potentially fatal and normally begin during adolescence. Coaches, therefore, must be alert to signs of eating disorders in their athletes, particularly in sports like wrestling and gymnastics. Many girls who compete in gymnastics also engage in dance activities, both of which emphasized weight loss and muscle tone. This is not to say that gymnasts are anorexics. As with wrestlers, however, the need to avoid weight gain can play into their preoccupation with body image and result in an eating disorder.

Coaches who suspect youngsters of an eating disorder are encouraged to contact counseling personnel or other qualified persons to diagnose the existence and the extent of the problem. The sooner a potential or an actual eating disorder is discovered, the easier it is to resolve. Coaches are encouraged to work with others in the school, therefore, when these and other kinds of emotional interferences are suspected.

The Diet During Strenuous Exercise

Most sports in junior and senior high school involve two to three weeks of preseason workouts designed to condition and instruct athletes. Each session purposely pushes athletes to the edge of exhaustion to improve their levels of conditioning and to encourage the self-discipline that is so important for young athletes. In order to perform up to expectation and to maximize the learning that takes place during each session, athletes must replenish energy supplies between and during practice.

Even when many of them run their way through the off-season, the combination of anxiety and maximal effort can sap even the strongest and best-conditioned kid on the team. When machines run at 75 percent to 100 percent of maximum output, even the most efficient require high-performance fuels. Carbohydrates to replenish energy and proteins to repair and develop muscles are two musts in every diet.

Most important, young athletes require water to increase the number of energy-carrying cells in the blood and to promote urination, which eliminates toxic substances from the body. Water also increases the volume of the blood and promotes perspiration, which acts as the body's cooling mechanism. It's also important to note that just a 10 percent loss of the body's water can lead to heatstroke; a 5 percent loss can lead to heat exhaustion and a significant loss of mental capacity. Few of us, coaches included, can afford such a loss!

So keep water on hand at all times during practice and competition. Be sure athletes have an adequate supply of water to replace what they lose during vigorous exercise. The reproducible in figure 7-3, "Practice and the Diet," should be distributed to each of your players before the first practice, especially if you plan to work them hard during the preseason.

The Pregame Meal

The pregame meal involves another important nutritional consideration for young athletes. Figure 7-4 provides important information for the young athlete who may be tempted to eat too much before a contest. The reproducible in figure 7-4 should be distributed to players the night before the first contest to impress upon them the importance of eating light on the day of a contest.

It emphasizes as well that the most important pregame meal is the one eaten the night before the contest. It is the one that provides most of the energy that will be needed during competition. The meal eaten on the day of competition will provide some energy if it is easily digested, but its most important characteristic is that it is light; then the blood in the body is not digesting the meal but is available to the muscles to provide energy.

The reproducible also emphasizes the need for water during competition. It serves as an excellent reminder for young athletes. The best reminder, however, is the water that is placed prominently somewhere on the sidelines or near the athletes. Managers, if available to you, should also be encouraged to provide water to players when they exit the field or court.

Coaches are also well advised to have young players visit the family doctor to secure the permission they need to engage in the kind of activity that characterizes competitive sport. The information available in this section, therefore, involves general considerations that apply to most young athletes. Any with special needs should receive the input they require from the family doctor.

A Few Myths About Nutrition

Given the nation's preoccupation with dieting, we might expect a myth or two about nutrition and the body. Here are a few that coaches should keep in mind—for themselves as well as their athletes.

Figure 7-3

PRACTICE AND DIET

There's nothing strange about being tired during two-a-days. If you're not tired, you're not working hard enough! But you can help yourself with the proper diet. Recognize that you draw on energy stored in your muscles as carbohydrates. During one day of double sessions, you can use up all your carbohydrates. If you don't replace them at night, you won't have any for the next day's practices. So read the following information and use it during double sessions as well as when the season gets underway. We will be providing similar information later regarding your pregame meal.

Foods High in Carbohydrates

Be sure to eat a lot of cereals, breads, pasta, muffins, pancakes, rolls, and other grain products. Fruits and vegetables are also high in carbohydrates. Yogurt, milkshakes, milk, cocoa, and ice cream also have lots of carbohydrates. Cakes, pies, cookies, soft drinks, and other sugary foods are high in carbohydrates but low in most other nutrients. Be sure, therefore, to use these only as supplements to your diet.

Other Foods

Recognize that foods from the Meat Group are relatively low in carbohydrates, but they are important in your overall diet. So eat a variety of foods from each of the four food groups (Milk, Meat, Fruit/Vegetable, and Grain) in order to provide all the nutrients your body requires.

Water

Drink a lot of water! It will prevent cramping and will maintain the flow of oxygen to your brain and muscles. Research indicates that the loss of even 5 percent of your body fluids can result in a significant loss of your mental capacity. Some of us can't afford that! So drink a lot of water. We'll take care of your water needs on the field; you take care of them at home.

A Reminder

Be sure to see your family doctor regarding your unique nutritional needs or to identify the best possible diet for you while you are participating in this sport. This handout is designed to provide general information to get you started.

© 1995 by Michael D. Koehler

Figure 7-4

PREGAME MEAL

Points to Keep in Mind

The pregame meal that is most important to you is the one you have the night before the game. Because of the energy you will require the next day, it's always a good idea to eat a meal high in carbohydrates: milk, yogurt, navy beans, pinto beans, bananas, carrots, grapes, corn, raisins, pasta, whole wheat breads, crackers, bagels, and so forth. These will provide the energy you need to perform to the best of your ability on the following day. The actual pregame meal really won't provide that much energy, considering the amount of time it takes to get into your system, so eat a light meal designed to make you comfortable during the game. Carbohydrates are again a good idea because they are easily digested. A good breakfast of orange juice, corn flakes with sliced bananas, whole wheat toast with jelly, and skim milk will provide everything you need to play a good game. Pancakes are also a good source of carbohydrates.

Remember

1. Eat your pregame meal three to four hours before the game. Eat nothing up to one hour before the game. A full stomach during the game brings blood to your stomach to help digest food and away from your muscles—where you most need it.
2. Don't eat candy bars for quick energy just before the game. They may produce low blood sugar, which may leave you tired and weak.
3. Water is always available on the field and sidelines. Drink as much of it as you can—in moderation. Be sure to replace the moisture you lose through perspiration. Don't bloat yourself, but also be sure to drink a healthy supply of water before the game.

Also

Any athlete with a physical condition requiring medical attention may require a modified diet for training and competition. In such instances, we encourage you to meet with your family doctor to secure his or her input regarding your nutritional needs.

© 1995 by Michael D. Koehler

- *Our stomachs shrink.* Many adults and young people believe that fasting shrinks our stomachs. Normal stomachs will not shrink with less food. Your appetite may decrease, but your stomach will remain approximately the same size.

- *Pasta provides healthful carbohydrates.* This is more a mistake than a myth. Pasta is an excellent source of carbohydrates, but most of us tend to be overgenerous with sauces. Like other pastas, fettucini is an excellent source of energy and is low in fat, but with Alfredo sauce, it has as much saturated fat as three pints of the richest ice cream you can find in the local deli. So tell your kids to eat pasta but to avoid Alfredo and other cream sauces.

- *Fasting promotes permanent weight loss.* It's no secret that fasting does result in weight loss, but most of the loss is water and muscle tissue. During a fast, the body burns glycogen from the muscles and then actually stores more fat in order to protect itself against future fasts! Exercise and an appropriate diet—the only combination of effective and healthful weight loss!

- *Seafood helps reduce cholesterol in the diet.* Some fish, particularly those with white meat, are low in fat and cholesterol. Others, like salmon, are relatively high. Some few, however, elevate cholesterol to new heights. Consider the fact that if you or any of your athletes order fried calamari for an appetizer in your favorite restaurant, you're likely to consume more cholesterol than you'll find in a four-egg omelet.

- *Cramps are caused by insufficient salt intake.* Not true. During vigorous athletic competition, cramps are caused by inadequate water. The athlete who takes salt tablets during competition and then drinks water will have all the water find its way to the salt tablets, not to his or her muscles where it is needed.

- *Only vigorous exercise burns calories.* To the contrary—any increase in activity burns calories. Many of us may suspect that running burns a lot of calories; it does, up to 700 an hour. But it's also encouraging to realize that two hours of golf can burn up to 600 calories. Even if you sit behind the typewriter or keyboard for four hours, you'll burn 100 calories. And all those housecleaners out there can smile with the knowledge that an hour of vacuuming burns 150 calories. They'd smile a whole lot more if they could get someone else to do all that vacuuming!

The point is, many of the above problems result from an ignorance of nutritional facts. And sometimes that ignorance is compounded by a willingness to rationalize away some very obvious realities. We've done it ourselves. Pasta is an excellent food source, but not with Alfredo sauce. A lean piece of beef is rich in protein, but it can become potentially harmful when it's bathed in Bearnaise sauce.

There's an old saying: Fish must swim three times to taste good. They must swim first in water, then in butter, then in wine. Well, that may be true for those of us who love French cuisine, but if healthful nutrition is the goal, we'll buy fish with white meat and bake it or grill it using any one of a wide variety of tasty and healthful recipes. We'll do the same with fowl and pasta and the other foods listed in this section.

Suddenly, we're reminded of the humorist who indicated that if we eat healthy foods and exercise regularly, we'll all live to be a hundred—we'll just *wish* that we were dead! Laughter is good for us, too, but being funny doesn't make poor nutrition acceptable. Encourage your young athletes—and their parents—to take the time to find that rich array of tasty and healthful foods and to maintain a humane exercise regimen. You'll be helping your program and doing a lot to promote lifelong health for entire families in your community.

Let's Wrap It Up

All of us tend to hear about nutrition in bits and pieces. Sometimes we hear that a carbohydrate diet is low in fat and provides sufficient energy to meet the needs of even the most active youngster. Then we hear that diets high in fiber are important because of their positive effects on our bodies. Then we hear that diets high in proteins help repair and develop muscle tissue, even that diets high in amino acids prevent things like canker sores!

Well, it just may be that all these claims are true, which suggests the need for all of us to maintain a balanced diet, one low in sugar and fat, high in fiber, and with sufficient carbohydrate and protein mixes to satisfy the energy and growth needs of our bodies. Such a diet also obviates the need for vitamin and mineral supplements and gives young athletes everything they need to promote their growth and athletic performance.

We as coaches influence young lives in profound ways. We do so by modeling the values that are important to us, one of which is the maintenance of a healthy lifestyle. We also instruct and sometimes demand that youngsters do what is in their own best interests as well as the best interests of the team. When such demands involve healthful nutrition, we do a whole lot more than help them become good athletes. We promote habits that will benefit them for their entire lives.

Section Eight

DRUGS:

KEEP SAYING NO

First, a quick story: A good friend who coached high school football for more than 30 years tells the story of a team that ran into a big problem during his second year as a head coach. Word came to him that midway through the season several of his players had gotten drunk at a local party. He confronted the entire team at the beginning of their next practice, explaining that the accusations seemed to be well founded and that he planned to do something about them.

He told the team that he would have to suspend each guilty player for two games, unless some of them had earlier violations, in which case those players would be dropped from the team. He then proceeded to move from player to player, asking each "if the shoe fit." Those who said yes were instructed to leave the field immediately, turn in their gear, and not return for two weeks. Two boys were dropped from the team completely.

The team never rebounded from the disruption of having so many kids miss practice. They had won their first four games of the season but lost four of the next five because of missing players and a subsequent loss of team unity. Expecting in the preseason to win the conference championship and to enter playoff competition, they ended the season 5 and 4 and, to this day, talk bitterly of the party that destroyed their dreams for a championship season.

At the time, the coach shared their disappointment. His strength of character, however, carried him through the next 28 years of his career and resulted in a win-loss record of 234-64, 15 conference championships, 3 runners-up to the state champs, and one state championship. Even those few community members who, at the time, criticized his decision realize today that the message he sent to future teams helped develop what became one of the finest programs in the state.

Still coaching, he is as adamant today as he was then: "Drugs kill! There is absolutely nothing good about the kinds of recreational or illegal drugs that kids think will make them feel better or enhance their performance! I will not allow the drugs or the kids who use them to be even remotely associated with our program!" His is a stand that all coaches must take, if the messages we send to kids are to be clear and strong enough to influence their life choices.

What Is a Drug?

One of the first things we must do about drug use is educate youngsters. The best place to start is with a definition. The word *drug* is a generic term that refers to any substance used in medicine to cure, alleviate, or prevent disease or deficiency by enhancing, lessening, or stopping the normal functioning of components of the body. Most generally, it is any chemical agent that affects the body. Such a definition accommodates steroids and narcotics—both of which are recurring concerns of coaches.

Narcotics are a concern because of their pronounced effects on the nervous system—altered states of perception, addiction, and even death. Over the last several years, steroids have become a concern because of their potentially harmful effects on the body, which can include altered psychological states ("roid rages") and damage to the reproductive organs, the liver, and the heart.

Coaches must know a great deal about drugs and their effects on the body if they are to influence the behaviors of young athletes. Certainly, a part of that influence is to get kids to know more about drugs in order to combat the misguided but very convincing "street" lore that pushes them in the direction of anything that relieves pressure or enhances their performance. We must also reflect in *our* behaviors a position that doesn't provoke unnecessary pressure in kids and their perceived need to enhance performance.

This is the starting point for coaches. Each of us must do some serious soul searching because drug abuse, although a problem in itself, probably is more symptomatic of a larger problem. In an idealized world, where the joy of participating is still more important than winning and where all of us, even in a losing cause, gain a profound sense of personal satisfaction from a maximum effort, drugs are unnecessary. Happy people don't want their senses dulled, and youngsters who are satisfied with a maximal effort don't need to enhance performance.

Don't Be the Victim of Someone Else's Needs

O.K., back to the real world. Even the most dedicated coach will never be able to guarantee happiness and personal satisfaction for all his or her young athletes. Too many factors beyond our control influence their development. We can, however, make a dent in a very big problem. It is within the power of each of us to ameliorate society's demands to win and to be "the best" at whatever it is we do.

Winning must always take a back seat to the *desire* to win, the willingness to work hard and to commit oneself to a maximal personal and team effort. Young athletes must understand that such efforts are their own reward, regardless of the outcome, and as Vince Lombardi said, they ". . . are more important than the events that occasion them." According to Lombardi, the game is only an opportunity to display the *desire* to win and the hard work that went into its preparation.

Imagine, for example, a society composed of people who have learned the value of hard work and cooperation and who realize their satisfactions in life from trying to be the best they can be, as parents, citizens, husbands and wives, workers. Compare such a society to one that emphasizes winning for its own sake, one that emphasizes competition and mutual antagonism and provokes the need in its citizens to have more money or more status than their friends or neighbors.

Drugs are unnecessary in the former society; they are unavoidable in the latter. The same is true of communities, schools, and athletic teams. Resolution of the drug "problem," therefore, starts with each of us, to the extent that we promote athletic participation for the right reasons. Having looked in the mirror and made whatever changes are necessary in ourselves and our programs, the next step in combating drug abuse in our athletes is to assure their understanding of our philosophies and to encourage the kind of self-esteem that enables them to avoid being the victims of someone else's needs:

Peer Group

Figure 8-1 provides an important perspective for young athletes and, if possible, should be shared with your players early in the school year, certainly during the first meeting of the season. It discusses the kinds of influences that youngsters receive from their peers and the reasons behind some of them, and it reinforces many of their reasons for engaging in competitive sports in the first place.

Those of us dealing with young athletes in their early teens already understand their preoccupation with self. Personal appearance, levels of maturity, and social acceptance are important to them. Such preoccupations, although developmentally normal, suggest that they are more motivated by the social rather than the physical or psychological effects of drugs. Combined with undeveloped social skills and an orientation more to the present than to the future, these characteristics are prime factors in causing young teens to experiment with drugs.

Role models are influential in the lives of students at this time in their lives, and coaches are among the most influential role models in the school. When the school provides information about drugs in science, traffic safety, and health classes, when intervention systems are developed, when coaches and others in the building teach refusal skills, and when sports teams and other extracurricular activities promote leadership activities and self-esteem, young teens are less inclined to experiment with drugs.

The same is true of older teens, generally juniors and seniors in high school. At this stage in their lives, young athletes seek greater independence from adult figures, especially parents. Because they are still oriented to role models, coaches remain among the most influential people in their lives. Older teens tend to be more interested in the psychological than the social effects of drugs, and their positive sense of self is a prime factor in deterring them from drug abuse. Again, athletics and fitness programs provide the ideal setting for the development of not only the physical but the psychological strength to say NO to peer influences.

Figure 8-1

A FEW WORDS ABOUT PEER GROUPS

A QUICK LOOK AT THE OBVIOUS

You're already familiar with the kinds of influences peer groups have on teenagers. You know, for example, that many are positive as well as negative. Unfortunately, many adults tend to think of peer group influences as negative, probably because they often hear about them in relation to drug use. Certainly, peer groups can cause some teens to use drugs or to break the law in other ways. If "everyone" is doing it, it can be very difficult to "say no," even when "saying yes" can be so harmful to us. That's where positive peer group influences come in.

LOOKING AT THE POSITIVE

We all know how important social acceptance is, and anyone who understands teenagers knows that your appearance is very important to you. For that matter, social acceptance and appearance are important to all of us, young or old. It's just that, for most adults, peer group influences aren't as strong as they are for teenagers. All of us must consider our own values, as well as those of family and friends, when deciding to behave in certain ways. The strength of our personalities, for example, is most evident when we go against the expectations of our peer groups if we know they are doing something wrong.

That's what athletics are all about, pride and strength of mind and body. When teams of young adults focus on such pride, they influence each other in positive ways. That's what we want to accomplish this year—individual and team pride. Once we do, we can't do anything but win.

PEER GROUPS AND WINNING

Maybe the greatest coach in the history of professional football, Vince Lombardi, once said, "The will to excel and the will to win, they endure. They are more important than any events that occasion them." Lombardi is reminding us that the game itself is not that important. The will, the desire to excel, to commit to do your best, these are the most important things about athletic competition. And they are the most important things in life, the kinds of things that sometimes make us say no to a peer group that is dragging us down by the things it does.

The peer group that commits to personal excellence, no matter what the event is—a party or a game, invariably wins. As Coach Lombardi indicated, it may not always win the game, but it develops the kind of attitude and personality strength that make all its members stronger.

**USE YOUR PEER GROUP, BUT LET IT BUILD YOU UP;
NEVER ALLOW IT TO TEAR YOU DOWN!**

© 1995 by Michael D. Koehler

Parents

Let's admit it—some parents gain a narcissistic boost from the successes of their children. Some dads, for example, unable to make the first team as teenagers, push a son into football, then can't understand why he doesn't work hard enough to become an All-Stater. Even the encouragement of parents, however—wishing only the best for their children and seeking to develop the right values in them—is often misinterpreted by teenagers as unfair pressure and becomes a problem in the home.

As older teens are taking shaky, if determined, steps away from a real and perceived dependence on their parents, the parents are grateful to the coach, teacher, or counselor who can provide a helping hand and a sense of direction at this stage in their children's lives. This is yet another factor that helps sell the value of athletics to the parent community.

The Community

Booster Clubs and community organizations help athletic programs and other school activities immeasurably. Their moral and financial support are often invaluable. They also can intensify the pressure to win. In that regard, junior and senior high school boosters are potentially as dangerous as college boosters. Perhaps the last real stronghold of amateurism in our society, junior and senior high schools, especially in large metropolitan areas, are often plagued by intrusive adults who find their satisfactions in manipulating youngsters.

They help recruit talented junior high school athletes for certain secondary schools; they provide money under the table; some few even introduce young athletes to steroids and other performance enhancing drugs. Although most boosters are reasonable—guilty only occasionally of an excess of zeal—their enthusiasm for their school's success can result in unnecessary pressure for youngsters. Even though the vast majority would shudder at the thought of encouraging kids to use drugs, the inadvertent pressures many create have a similar effect on kids.

Coaches must be careful, therefore, to do all they can to maintain the proper perspective when accepting favors from boosters. Their involvement in your program, even when well intentioned, can have negative effects. We must also recognize the powerful influence *we* exert on kids, certainly enough to help parents with their jobs and to combat the insidious influences of elements within the peer group.

Tobacco and Alcohol Are Drugs

One of the most insidious influences facing all teenagers is the temptation to drink and smoke. Federal government statistics indicate that approximately 3,000 teenagers have their first cigarette each day. Statistics also indicate that teenagers purchase almost one billion packs of cigarettes annually. Combine those statistics with estimates that the average age for a youngster's first drink is 11 and that more than half of all seventh graders have tried alcohol, and the scope of the problem in this country is obvious.

For the coach working with junior high school athletes, such statistics are particularly startling when one considers a young person's susceptibility to alcoholism. Adults who drink excessively run the risk of becoming alcoholics in from 5 to 15 years. Because their livers are not completely developed, teenagers run the same risk in 6 to 18 months, preadolescents in only 3 months. The coach who works with seventh and eighth graders, therefore, must be especially sensitive to rumors of alcohol abuse among his or her players. It's conceivable that the seventh grader who starts drinking shortly after the first day of school could be an alcoholic before Thanksgiving.

It's especially true if the predisposition exists in his or her family. Studies have shown that certain ethnic groups are more prone than others to alcohol addiction. The problem involves enzymes found in certain ethnic groups, the presence or absence of which influences the effects of alcohol on persons in that group. Preteens with family predispositions, therefore, warrant special attention.

It's especially true if the predisposition exists in his or her family. Studies have shown that certain ethnic groups are more prone than others to alcohol addiction. The problem involves enzymes found in certain ethnic groups, the presence or absence of which influence the effects of alcohol on persons in that group. Pre-teens with family predispositions, therefore, warrant special attention.

Smoking involves similar concerns. Recent studies indicate that cigarettes may be the first substance youngsters use en route to significant alcohol and drug abuse. Be careful not to scoff at such statistics; these are not just scare tactics. A researcher from Indiana University recently claimed that youngsters who smoke a pack or more of cigarettes a day are 45 percent more likely than nonsmokers to use marijuana and 79 times more likely to use cocaine.

Certainly, knowledgeable researchers are not suggesting a causal relationship between cigarettes and cocaine use. To predict future drug abuse of the casual or experimental smoker would be irresponsible, but it makes sense to establish statistical linkages between cocaine users and youngsters who smoke more than a pack a day, particularly as such linkages serve as warning signs to parents, coaches, and other school personnel.

That's why the information in figure 8-2 is so helpful to young people and their parents. Share it with them at a preseason meeting or early in the school year during any of several orientation meetings. The handout is informative and has excellent public relations value for your program and school.

Most important, such information may help change statistics that identify alcohol as the leading cause of death in adolescents. Well over half of the people killed in drunk driving accidents are teenagers, even though they account for only 20 percent of all licensed drivers. In fact, the only age group in this country whose life expectancy is actually *decreasing* is that of teenagers.

Why Are Some Drugs Harmful?

Recent attempts by schools and the media to educate youngsters about the potential dangers of drug use have met with some success. Smoking, for example, seems to be declining among segments of the African-American community. Heroin, LSD, and

© 1995 by Michael D. Koehler

Figure 8-2

ALCOHOL AND TOBACCO:
SOMETHING TO THINK ABOUT

DID YOU KNOW THAT

- Adults who drink excessively can become alcoholics in 5 to 15 years.
- Teenagers who drink excessively can become alcoholics in 6 to 18 *months!*
- Preteenagers who drink excessively can become alcoholics in only *3* months!
- Recent research claims that teenagers who smoke a pack or more of cigarettes a day are 45 percent more likely to use marijuana than nonsmokers.
- Over half the people killed in drunk driving accidents are teenagers, even though they account for only 20 percent of licensed drivers.
- The only age group in this country whose life expectancy is actually *decreasing* is that of teenagers!

Someone once said that alcohol is what put the wreck in recreation. All the statistics out there agree. We know, for example, that the greatest enemy of today's teenagers—is today's teenagers. They are killing each other in gang activity, each other's cars, and at parties when they encourage each other to drink too much. We also know that teenagers are also their own best friends. Friends watch out for each other because they care. Let's find *good* friends, then, the kind that really care about us, and listen to them.

We only magnify our problems when we look at them through the bottom of a glass. We help resolve them when we see them through the eyes of a good friend. Alcohol and tobacco use violate training rules, but that's only one reason not to use them. The best reason is that they just aren't good for you, especially if you hope to develop the lung capacity so important for athletics and lifelong health.

REMEMBER:
ALCOHOL AND TOBACCO ARE POISONS;
TREAT THEM ACCORDINGLY.

crack cocaine are much less appealing to youngsters interested only in experimenting with drugs. Recent studies, however, indicate that we still have a long way to go. A federal government study indicates that only half of the nation's 12- to 17-year-olds see any risk in marijuana use.

Most of them don't realize that the potency and toxicity of today's marijuana is 10 to 20 times stronger than in the '60s and '70s. Some studies have even indicated that one joint damages the lungs as much as 100 cigarettes and that it contains as many as 421 chemicals. When lit, that number jumps to 2,000! If kids do have a growing concern about what they are putting into their bodies, these figures should get their attention. Figure 8-3 provides a wealth of information about the potential dangers of marijuana use.

Coaches can underscore these facts by explaining to young athletes that marijuana is fat soluble, which means that it stays in the body for up to three weeks. This continuing toxicity, combined with its synergistic effects when used in conjunction with other drugs and its potentially significant damage to the respiratory tract, is a very potent argument to avoid it, particularly when a youngster wants to improve athletic performance. Similar arguments apply to other drugs, too.

The Case Against Cocaine

Most obviously, crack cocaine is immediately addictive. Youngsters who use it once suddenly find themselves chained to a habit that can push them out of school and often into crime to support the addiction. Because coke is perceived as the drug of upward mobiles, it has achieved an element of social acceptance that often makes it more attractive to teenagers. It is expensive, however, so isn't common in junior and senior high schools, although its current popularity is alarming. Some estimates indicate that as many as 5,000 people try cocaine for the first time each day.

Crack cocaine is less expensive and every bit as dangerous as "base" cocaine. Its manufacture and distribution have strong ties with gang activities, so youngsters who experiment with it may find themselves not only addicted to the drug but involved in gang activities that often result in imprisonment or death. The reproducible in figure 8-4 provides information on cocaine and most of the other drugs that sometimes tempt youngsters.

Coaches should have a thorough knowledge of the information not only in the reproducible but in the remainder of this section. Many junior and senior high school students may not know the name of the current vice president, but they're familiar with "black beauties" and "dexies." In fact, the scope of their knowledge is often shocking, so thorough that parents and coaches who rely on exaggerated scare tactics fight a losing battle.

Such a reality has special meaning to coaches. If we preach inaccuracies about drug use, our players' subsequent mistrust of everything else we say will spill over into coaching techniques, strategy, and team and personal values. Teens and preteens have a low tolerance for inaccuracies. The facts are scary enough. Let's be sure we use them when discussing drugs with young athletes and others.

Figure 8-3

TAKING A CLOSER LOOK AT
MARIJUANA

Doy You Care About What You Put into Your Body?

If so, think about these facts:

- Compared with 10 to 20 years ago, today's marijuana is 10 to 20 times more poisonous to your system.
- Yet marijuana has become so acceptable to unsuspecting teenagers that a recent government study discovered that only half of the nation's 12- to 17-year-olds see any risk in using it.
- Some recent statistics have indicated that one joint can damage the lungs as much as 100 cigarettes.
- One joint contains as many as 421 different chemicals.
- When lit, that same joint can contain as many as 2,000 chemicals!
- Marijuana is fat soluble, which means that it can stay in your system for anywhere from one to three weeks.
- Such continuing toxicity can cause significant damage to your respiratory system.

Fortunately, growing numbers of people in our society are becoming very careful about what they put into their bodies. Even if you weren't an athlete, you certainly would be concerned about the poisons your body would absorb every time you smoked just one joint. Maybe that's why one study indicates that marijuana use has dropped off 35 percent to 40 percent among some college students.

For athletes, however, marijuana use is especially damaging because of what it does to your lungs. If you are serious about your sport and really do care about your health and fitness levels, you would have to search long and hard and still would be unable to find even one reason to justify smoking even one joint.

THINK ABOUT IT.

© 1995 by Michael D. Koehler

Figure 8-4

THE CASE AGAINST COCAINE AND OTHER DRUGS

THE ARGUMENT AGAINST USING COCAINE IS AS CONVINCING AS ANY ARGUMENT YOU WILL EVER HEAR! THINK ABOUT THIS:

- Crack cocaine can be *immediately* addictive. Think about it—use it once, and you're dependent, subject to the pity and, unfortunately, even the laughter of classmates and acquaintances.
- The manufacture and distribution of cocaine have strong ties with gang activity, which can lead to a whole new set of problems for users.
- Cocaine does promote momentary happiness and increased awareness, but both are followed by depression, which sometimes can require the involvement of psychologists and psychiatrists.
- Cocaine carries the potential for addiction, paranoia, even seizures.
- Cocaine is potentially damaging to the heart and lungs, making it especially harmful to athletes.

OTHER DRUGS

Drug Type	Name of drug	Slang Name	Harmful Effects
Stimulants	Coffee, tea, cola, caffeine, cocaine, amphetamines, nicotine	Coke, speed, uppers, crank, dexies, black beauties	Legal issues, depression, dependency, and lung damage
Depressants	Barbiturates, tranquilizers, sedatives, alcohol, narcotics	Downers, ludes, reds, yellow jackets	Dependency, decreased reflexes, and depression
Hallucinogens	LSD, PCP, peyote, STP, mescaline	Ecstasy, acid	Negative effects on perception, flashbacks, terrifying reactions

© 1995 by Michael D. Koehler

For example, it's fair for us to indicate to players that cocaine may induce a brief euphoria and a heightened sense of awareness, but it is followed inevitably by depression, sometimes psychologically significant, and its potential for addiction, paranoia, and seizures make it especially dangerous. For athletes, as indicated in figure 8-4, cocaine can damage the heart and lungs, which is yet another reason to avoid it.

Other Drugs and Why They Hurt Performance

The same is true of other *stimulants*: amphetamines, smoking or smokeless tobacco, and caffeine in over-the-counter drugs, coffee, tea, and cola. They involve not only legal issues and the usual up/down cycle of euphoria and depression, but they exhaust the body's own energy supplies more quickly due to an increased heart rate, provoking a psychological and physical "crash" that immobilizes youngsters. Such crashing results in the sure signs of drug use, all of which will be described later in this section.

• *Depressants:* As listed in figure 8-4, the sedatives and hypnotics include barbiturates like phenobarbital, nonbarbiturates like Quaalude™, minor tranquilizers like valium, and alcohol. Narcotics are also depressants and include opium and its derivatives morphine, codeine, Demerol™, and heroin.

Depressants reduce sensitivity to stimulation, can induce sleep, and can promote a sense of confidence and relaxation. They, too, however, can result in depression, weight loss, and diminished reflexes and responses. Such physical reactions are damaging enough for young athletes, but narcotics also carry the potential not only for overdose but for hepatitis and AIDS because of the possible use of unsterile needles.

• *Hallucinogens:* Also referred to as psychedelics, such drugs include LSD, certain kinds of mushrooms, DMT, peyote, mescaline, STP, and PCP. They are exceptionally strong stimulants that increase brain activity, which results in euphoria and altered perceptions of reality. Aside from the immediately negative effects on perception and thinking, hallucinogens can also provoke not only flashbacks but unwanted, even terrifying reactions and experiences.

• *Inhalants:* Many common household items carry dangerous potential for chemical abuse. Rubber cement, airplane glue, paint thinner, varnish, lighter fluid, gasoline, hair spray—even typing correction fluid—can induce the dizziness or the "rush" that some youngsters seek. Figure 8-4 does not list the specific items because we sometimes don't want to provide too much information to impressionable youngsters. Coaches and parents must be familiar with them, however, because of their popularity among some teenagers.

Inhalants are especially dangerous because of their potential for sudden death, significant loss of muscle control, suffocation, permanent damage to the central nervous system, and, in cases of long-term use, damage to the liver, kidneys, heart, blood, and bone marrow.

The Case Against Steroids

There are other drugs that harm youngsters, some of them even found in the kitchen (nutmeg is one such spice). Steroids, however, are causing the greatest concern among coaches and much of the athletic world because of their potential for physical and psychological damage. A couple of recent stories illustrate.

A high school football player in Ohio recently died of a heart attack—according to the county coroner, the result of a diseased and enlarged heart. In combination with puncture wounds on the young man's thighs and the atrophying of his testicles, the heart attack caused the coroner to pronounce steroid use as the cause of his death. The young man collapsed during football practice and died shortly afterward in a nearby hospital.

On the college level, a football player from the Southeast Conference recounted his continuing battle against the ravages of anabolic steroids when he admitted to aggressive behavior and considerations of suicide. In the pros, several players, including the late Lyle Alzado, attributed illnesses like cancer and heart enlargement to their abuse of steroids.

More generally, stories of steroid users beating up, even killing, acquaintances and friends are too common to be discounted as media hype. The psychological effects of steroids are as significant as the physical effects. Periods of severe depression follow heavy use of steroids, and psychiatrists across the country have documented some psychotic behavior among steroid users, even auditory hallucinations. Fortunately, when people stop taking the drug, their symptoms usually disappear.

How Widespread Are Steroids?

Estimates indicate that 15 percent to 80 percent of NFL players have used steroids at one time in their careers. The low end of the range generally is reported by the athletes themselves, the upper end by sportswriters and observers of sport in this country. Estimates go as high as 60 to 80 percent of the world's premier track and field athletes. Of particular concern to coaches of young athletes, sports psychologists have indicated that as many as half a million junior and senior high school athletes could be using steroids to enhance their appearance and athletic performance.

A Few Warning Signs

Obviously, some of the drugs discussed in this section are more harmful to youngsters than others. Immediately addicting drugs like crack cocaine are of particular concern to parents, coaches, and other school personnel. Hallucinogens like LSD that carry the potential for flashbacks weeks after their initial use are also of concern to us.

We must be careful, however, to avoid explaining to our young athletes the *relative* harm or potency of different drugs. To indicate that crack cocaine or LSD may be more dangerous than other drugs is to suggest that the others are *less* dangerous.

That's why the information in figure 8-4 explains the danger of each drug and its negative effects on athletic performance without reference to degree of harmfulness.

This brings up another point. Parents, coaches, and any others who work with youngsters are well advised to avoid any reference to the *potency* of drugs. Some reports in the media, for example, indicate that today's marijuana is 10 to 20 times more potent than the marijuana of the 60s and 70s. That it is more *potent* may, in fact, be more an advantage than a disadvantage to some youngsters. When discussing marijuana, therefore, as well as the relative harm and potency of other drugs, it is wise to refer only to their dangers, unwanted side effects, and toxicity. To say, for example, that today's marijuana is 10 to 20 times more *harmful* and *toxic* than the marijuana of the '60s and '70s is potentially more alarming to youngsters than to impress them with statistics about potency.

Share figure 8-5 with your players, probably early in the season or school year, to reemphasize the dangers of drug use, to affirm their sense of concern for each other, and to let them know that *you* know about the warning signs of drug use. The signs of steroid use in boys, for example, are relatively obvious even to the uninitiated. Significant increases in size and muscle mass, puffiness around the eyes, more facial hair, and more acne are generally indications of potential problems.

For females, the symptoms may involve the development of facial hair, deeper voices, and masculine physiques. These signals are not necessarily determinative; some girls are biologically predisposed to the development of muscle mass, while others are not. Title IX has opened the door to young women athletes. Admittedly, it could be opened wider. As good as it has been for young women who want to compete, it has been bad for those who seem willing to alter their bodies in order to compete at artificially high levels. It seems, then, that Title IX was introduced for women but that "chemically-created" men are finding much of the spotlight.

Fortunately, other warning signs are as obvious. School counselors and other support services personnel have known for a long time that class cutting, truancy, and misbehavior in the classroom are sure indications of problems in a youngster's life. Those problems may involve personal issues such as physical or sexual abuse, divorce, or the loss of a family member. They may also suggest conflict with schoolmates, some kind of learning interference, or the use of drugs.

Coaches, therefore, must be as alert to these signals as anyone else in the school, probably more so because of the length and quality of contact with youngsters. Once a problem is suspected, they must make appropriate referrals to others in the school for help with diagnoses. Youngsters have enough trouble struggling through the developmental tangle of adolescence without further obscuring any sense of direction with mind-numbing drugs.

The alteration of personal appearance in both young and old is often a sign of trouble. It is one of the surest signs of depression and, on that basis, can be a signal of drug use in teens. For that matter, all the signs mentioned in figure 8-5 are reliable indicators, particularly as they occur in combinations. Isolated symptoms may or may not signal problems, so coaches must be careful not to generalize symptoms. It's a good idea to mention concerns to support services personnel to elicit their help in determining whether a youngster's behavior is indeed symptomatic.

Figure 8-5

THE WARNING SIGNS OF DRUG USE

INTRODUCTION

Coaches, parents, and students should all be aware of the warning signs of drug use. We must know them in order to recognize symptoms, then to help the drug user in whatever way we can. We all know that drugs, no matter how desirable they may seem to us, have the potential to kill. Parents, coaches, and *real* friends don't want teammates and close friends taking such chances with their lives. A friend who lacks the pride and self-confidence to avoid drugs needs our help. Please read this sheet very carefully so you will be in a better position to provide that help. Your coaches already are familiar with these signs.

NAME OF DRUG	WARNING SIGNS
Alcohol	Slurred speech, unsteady walk, slowed reflexes, relaxed inhibitions, glazed eyes
Cocaine	Restlessness, increased excitement, glass vials, glass pipe, razor blades, syringes, needle marks
Marijuana	Red eyes, dry mouth, excitement, laughter, increased hunger, rolling paper, pipes, odor of burnt hemp rope
Hallucinogens	Focus on detail, anxiety, panic, nausea, capsules, tablets, blotter squares
Inhalants	Nausea, dizziness, headaches, poor coordination, drowsiness, poor muscle control, smell of inhalant on clothing and breath
Narcotics	Nausea, dizziness, drowsiness, inability to feel pain, pinpoint pupils, cold and moist skin, needle marks
Stimulants	Alertness, talkativeness, loss of appetite, weight loss, irritability
Depressants	Drowsiness, lack of coordination, capsules, confusion, slurred speech, needs more sleep
Steroids	Significant weight gain, acne, altered moods, increased anger, puffiness in face, hair loss for men, increased facial hair and deeper voice in women

© 1995 by Michael D. Koehler

In fact, each time you have a concern about a youngster's possible drug involvement, mention it first to a counselor or someone in the support services, even an administrator. If a parent contact is appropriate after meeting with the counselor, be sure to describe the student's behavior anecdotally. For that matter, any written referrals or other forms used by you should contain anecdotal information, not opinion.

Written Referrals

Figure 8-6 provides an example of an appropriately written referral. Because federal law gives parents access to school forms, teachers, coaches, and others who use them must be careful to avoid comments like "Tom was high" or "Jill had to be on drugs. . . ." These kinds of comments are inflammatory and can provoke a world of trouble for the teacher or coach making the referral. It is always best to describe the behavior: "Tom had trouble maintaining his balance" or "Jill's speech was slurred." Leave the rest up to the counselor or the administrator, and any interpretation of your description up to the parent(s).

Where Does the School Stand on Drug Use?

Even marginal or implicit acceptance of drug use in school provokes problems everywhere in the building. Apparent laxity in one area causes youngsters to doubt the resolution of the school in all areas. Once that happens, the school has lost control of the ability to combat a very serious challenge to the health and well-being of its students.

The sheer persistence of drug use within the past several years has granted it a degree of immunity in many schools. Schools and communities have been worn down by an insidious problem that seems to defy resolution—and what becomes commonplace becomes unnoticed. Drug use must never go unnoticed, especially by coaches. Refer to figure 3-2 in section 3 for a reproducible that explains the school's reasons for training rules and then to figure 3-3 for the Athlete's Pledge—his or her commitment to the rules.

To be prepared for possible violation of training rules—and to warn students and their parents—you should:

- Identify all violations, including specific reference to all forms of tobacco, alcohol, marijuana and other illegal drugs and related paraphernalia, even abuse of inhalants and other prescription or nonprescription drugs. The rules might also make reference to "look-alikes," pills and capsules that generally have the same color and appearance as illegal stimulants and depressants.

- Detail the consequences of all violations, including first, second, and third offenses. Some schools may allow three offenses, others only two. Whatever your school chooses to allow, the final offense must result in the most severe consequence, generally the loss of athletic eligibility for one full calendar year.

Figure 8-6

WRITING REFERRALS

"WHY" REFERRALS?

Often, we need the help of other professionals in the school to diagnose and help treat problems we may observe during our associations with young athletes. Drug use is one of the most serious.

"WHEN" REFERRALS?

We should write referrals whenever we become concerned about the behavior of a young athlete or other student and feel we need another perspective from a qualified official. The closer we work with other school personnel, the more we will be able to help youngsters who may need extensive professional help.

"HOW" REFERRALS?

Over the years, parents have been given increased access to their children's school files. Referrals to other school personnel, therefore, must be written very carefully. Always write them objectively and anecdotally, if possible. When possible, take students immediately to school authorities, and study the following examples:

How NOT to Write a Referral

Rarely give your opinion or interpret the symptoms you are reporting. Leave that up to the professionals. For example:

- Don't say: "Tom was drunk in class today."
- Don't write: "Bill was high today during practice. He must have been on something."
- Don't recommend a future specific course of action: "Sue needs to be drug tested."

How to Write a Referral

Be as descriptive and as anecdotal as possible. For example:

- Write: "Tom was disoriented in class today, stumbling over desks and laughing uncontrollably."
- Indicate: "Bill had no coordination in practice today. His speech was slurred and his pupils were pinpoints."
- Recommend: "Please talk to Sue as soon as possible. I have observed drowsiness, red eyes, and drug paraphernalia in her possession."

© 1995 by Michael D. Koehler

- Include reference to a student's voluntary admission of an infraction. Sometimes parents and students feel that the school should overlook an infraction if the student admits to it before school personnel become aware of it. Schools are well advised to acknowledge voluntary admissions but to affirm the intraction. Then, as needed, they can lessen the consequences for the violations.

- Make reference to mandatory conferences with counselors, social workers, or substance abuse specialists. Such a requirement affirms the school's desire not only to administer appropriate consequences but to solve the student's problem. Some evidence of student involvement in such a conference should be required before the student is reinstated to athletic competition.

- Require that students *and* parents sign the document. This can be done at any of several orientation meetings held at the beginning of the school year, or it can be mailed to the home of each student who has expressed interest in participation in interscholastic athletics. The form should include spaces for the student's full name, year of graduation, dates of signing, and student and parent signatures.

Experts on gang activity advise that communities have zero tolerance of any gang involvement in their schools; they want the problem eliminated through immediate expulsion or suspension of those actively involved, followed by expulsion of students who have documented gang affiliation. Once gangs infiltrate schools, they are virtually impossible to eliminate, so schools must be careful not to let such problems get started.

Much the same is true of drug abuse. Aside from the fact that the sale and use of drugs is closely associated with gang activity, drug use itself is a relentless disease that eats away at the energy and vitality of students and schools. Athletic programs are particularly vulnerable to the destructive force of drugs. Like the coach in the story at the beginning of this section, therefore, coaches are encouraged to be intolerant of drugs or the players who use them.

Good Communication Is a Must

Use every opportunity to remind students and their parents of training rules. If opportunities don't exist, create them.

- *School orientation meetings:* Every fall, most schools provide orientation meetings for freshmen and transfer students and their parents. The Athletic Code is an important element in any school's culture because it discusses topics like those in figure 3-3 and outlines the specifics of the training rules. Such meetings are a good time to introduce such materials to all students new to the school.

- *PTO, PTA, and Booster Club meetings:* These kinds of meetings provide the opportunity to introduce and explain the Athletic Code and training rules to the parents of upperclass students and to others who are interested in student activities.

- *Preseason team meetings with athletes and their parents:* Just before the start of the season, most coaches meet with players and their parents to provide information about the program, including equipment, rules regarding travel, absence, tardiness, team discipline, and the specifics of the training rules. Such meetings are not only informative but helpful in meeting the legal requirements of substantive and procedural due process, both of which involve the clear communication of rules leading to possible adverse action.

• S*peeches at junior high schools:* High school coaches are always welcome speakers at meetings involving junior high school students and their parents. Such speeches can be motivational regarding such things as drugs or study habits, or they can be informational regarding team procedures and training rules. Coaches who provide such a service to junior highs perform a service to the community and a valuable public relations activity for their programs.

• *Speeches at local fraternal, business, or community organizations:* Groups like Kiwanis, Rotary, Lions, Optimists, and the League of Women Voters often seek speakers for luncheon meetings. Local sports programs are always of interest to such groups. Well-prepared speeches relating the nation's concern with drug abuse to the self-discipline resulting from athletic participation, and specifics like the training rules not only entertain but inform important members of the community and elicit their financial and moral support.

• *Comments during practice or after a contest:* These are among the best times to remind athletes of the importance of training rules and the inevitability of consequences. Win or lose, youngsters can find reasons to break training rules after a tough contest, especially if it's during the weekend. That's why it's always a good idea to remind them not to let one irresponsible moment jeopardize everything the team has worked so hard for since the beginning of the season.

Common sense dictates that frequent reference to training rules enhances their importance. Coaches must take advantage of every opportunity to remind young athletes and parents of their importance. More will be said of these opportunities and their public relations value in section 10.

Where Do the Athletes Stand?

Like the rest of us, young athletes are more invested in decisions when they have some input into them. Even when schools have developed a solid set of training rules and have grown comfortable with them, therefore, it's a good idea to convene a committee of athletes, coaches, parents, and other school personnel to review the rules periodically and to make necessary changes. When the committee concludes its efforts, the changes, if any, may be insignificant, but the ownership felt by athletes and parents will revitalize the rules.

Athletes also gain ownership of the training rules when they share opportunities with coaches to speak about drugs and alcohol to community organizations and junior high school and elementary students. No one is more effective than the local high school hero telling younger students about the dangers of drug abuse, and no one is more positively affected by the experience than the local high school hero.

Remember, however, that she may stand an impressive 6 feet and score an equally impressive 25 points a game, but she may need a little practice time before the big day, to deliver the speech as well as she does points under the basket. And the younger students will listen to her. She'll do wonders destroying drug abuse and building up your program. When well-respected youngsters speak out against drugs and for the values learned in athletic competition, everybody wins.

Self-Worth as a Deterrent to Self-Indulgence

Self-indulgence is to the soul what gluttony is to the waistline. What feels good at the moment eventually weighs us down. Self-worth involves restraint, self-discipline teaches it, and coaches teach self-discipline. We live, therefore, in the best of all possible educational worlds. Most of our young athletes come to us expecting hard work and discipline. All we have to do is deliver, in a way that promotes self-fulfillment and self-worth.

It's not an easy task, but when done well, it makes kids feel good about themselves. When they feel good about themselves they find it much easier to say no to drugs. We're reminded of an earlier comment: the harder a youngster works, the more impossible it is for him or her to be a failure. We might add that hard work also makes drugs unlikely. If we agree that society's drug problem is symptomatic of a loss of love and self-worth in many of our youngsters, then coaches are encouraged to remember Coach Kelly's advice to let the kids know you care while you promote their hard work.

Let's Wrap It Up

Unfortunately, some coaches are more a part of the drug problem than its solution. These coaches don't deserve all the blame, but they are key elements in a problem that looks at young athletes only as depersonalized elements in a game plan that promises recognition and a bigger piece of the financial pie for the school—and possible but improbable shots at million-dollar contracts for the athletes. Such coaches, usually unintentionally, promote the use of steroids to enhance performance and other drugs to relieve stress.

Consider just one of the recent results found in the University of Pittsburgh's Epidemiology of Sports Injury Study. The researchers looked at 12- to 16-year-olds in a Pittsburgh-area community who indicated that they did not drink. One year later, whereas only 7 percent of the boys who did not play a team sport said they were now drinking, 17 percent who played one or two sports and 23 percent who played three sports said they were now drinking.

The researchers were quick to deny any generalizability of their results, but they did indicate that high levels of physical activity did not protect students against the development of unhealthy behaviors. Perhaps that's why the NCAA has implemented year-round, random drug testing procedures for some of its sports, most notably football and track and field. Athletes found positive will be ineligible for one year and must continue to test negative throughout the year to assure restoration of eligibility.

Such random drug testing seems to be working. Recently, Joe Browne, the NFL's vice-president of communications, was quoted in the *Boston Globe* as saying: "There is a large body of evidence that clearly indicates that steroid use in the NFL has dramatically decreased in recent years due to our year-round random testing program." Fortunately, the same seems to be true of intercollegiate athletics.

A recent study at a major Midwest university indicates that steroid use among college athletes has dropped off about 50 percent in the last four years. On the negative side, alcohol use is still high, somewhere around 88 percent. The use of all forms of cocaine has declined considerably, from 17 percent eight years ago to 1.1 percent most recently. The use of marijuana also declined by some 35 to 40 percent.

As usual, therefore, the good news outweighs the bad news. Just as most coaches play by the rules and care genuinely about the well-being of their athletes, most athletes recognize the dangers of drug use and seek athletic participation for the pleasures it provides. Those of us who work with junior and senior high school athletes, however, do not enjoy the assistance of random drug testing procedures from national regulatory organizations.

We must do all we can, therefore, to familiarize ourselves with the signs of drug abuse and work closely with other school and community personnel to provide diagnostic help and intervention when needed. As important, we must use fitness activities to communicate the dangers of drug use and, through our associations with young athletes, provide the enjoyment and promote the self-worth that preclude their need for drugs.

Section Nine

BEYOND ATHLETICS

First, a couple of stories: The first involves a high school football player who, during the summer preceding his senior year, was helping his father operate some heavy equipment and was told to siphon some gas from one truck to another. He found a nearby tube, inserted one end in the gas tank and put the other end into his mouth to start the gas flow.

The gas shot through the tube into the young man's mouth and lungs, and he went into shock almost immediately. Fortunately, one of the workmen saw what happened, picked him up, and took him immediately to an emergency room, where they pumped his stomach and put him on oxygen. He was a mighty sick young man, particularly when the family doctor told him that his lungs were so damaged that he might not be able to play football during his final year of high school.

The second story involves an acquaintance, now a middle-aged coach for a local high school. She was an outstanding athlete in college, a starter for her basketball team as a freshman, an eventual all-conference selection, then a coach for one of the top girls' basketball programs in the state. Driving home one night after a game, she was struck by a drunk driver, and was taken by police to a nearby hospital with a cerebral hemorrhage, where she remained in a coma for 33 days. When she regained consciousness, she had to learn to walk and talk again, a process that involved months of therapy.

Like the young man in the first story, she eventually was told by her family doctor that she probably would have to give up coaching because the regimen would be too much for her, and she would be unable to demonstrate fundamentals to her players. She, too, was devastated, but she began an exercise program to regain as much of her former conditioning as possible.

Both these young people were among the most courageous we have ever met. Faced with the prospect of lifelong debility and the loss of a self-defining activity, each began a workout program that promised nothing but hard work and a great deal more pain than they had ever experienced before. Both committed themselves to their programs, working daily to regain a dream that seemed at times impossible to them.

Ultimately, the young football player became the starting fullback for his team, and the coach went on to become coach of the year in her state. In each instance, their doctors informed them that their recoveries were made possible by their levels of physical conditioning before their accidents and by their dedication to conditioning programs afterward. In essence, their bodies were strong enough, first of all to enable them to survive their accidents, then not only to resume their former activities but to realize a great deal of success with them.

Total Conditioning as a Way of Life

We don't want to encourage youngsters to commit themselves to total conditioning in anticipation of such potential tragedies, but we do want them to understand that a commitment to lifelong conditioning has a full range of expected and unexpected benefits. Figure 9-1 lists many of these benefits; it is an excellent reproducible to distribute to every student in your school, not just the athletes. You might give it to teachers, too. This handout represents an excellent way to sell your program.

Following is a more detailed explanation of each of the specifics on the handout:

• *Maintain or achieve healthy blood pressure levels.* Doctors have been praising exercise for years as a significant way to lower blood pressure. Young athletes can avoid high blood pressure and adults can improve it by engaging in a regular program of aerobic activity. This may not be a salient selling point to youngsters, but it will be to their parents, some of whom will use it to push their children into your program.

• *Strengthen the heart and lungs.* A related benefit involves a general strengthening of the heart and lungs, which results in improved blood flow and the transportation of oxygen throughout the body. More oxygen results in more energy, improved muscle strength, and increased endurance for athletic as well as other kinds of activities, including schoolwork and community involvement.

• *Improve relationship between "good" and "bad" cholesterol.* The body's HDL ("good cholesterol") fights LDL ("bad cholesterol"). A regular exercise program increases the size and strength of the HDL "army" and actually lowers LDL counts.

• *Tone muscles and strengthen bones.* Exercise that includes strength training not only tones muscles but strengthens bones, a factor that is critical in the reduction of injury during practice and competition.

• *Achieve or maintain a desirable weight.* Exercise and proper diet are the two most important factors in losing weight. Because excess weight is a proven cause of major diseases, exercise and proper nutrition are essential for a healthy life style and for the prevention of such problems as coronary heart disease and adult-onset diabetes. The youngster who establishes proper exercise habits now will be likely to avoid serious health problems later in life.

• *Improve or maintain energy levels and productivity.* Well-conditioned people are not only more active than their sedentary friends but have energy to engage in

© 1995 by Michael D. Koehler

Figure 9-1

INTERESTED IN TOTAL FITNESS?

DID YOU KNOW THAT TOTAL FITNESS:

- Maintains or achieves healthy blood pressure levels?
- Strengthens the heart and lungs?
- Improves the relationship between "good" and "bad" cholesterol?
- Tones muscles and strengthens bones?
- Achieves or maintains a desirable weight?
- Improves or maintains energy levels and productivity?
- Improves sleep habits?
- Improves self-confidence as reflected in posture and appearance?
- Improves self-discipline?
- Reduces depression and promotes a sense of well-being?
- Improves athletic performance and reduces injury?

If you didn't realize these benefits of improved fitness and want to cash in on them, join the fitness program now. Once you do, you're going to feel a whole lot better about yourself and discover a pool of untapped energy you didn't realize you had.

You'll also meet some great people, so join us now. If you're interested, contact me at:

more activities. The well-conditioned young athlete can perform well in school, after school during practice, and at home after supper to complete homework assignments or to study for tests. Energy is like friendship; the more we give, the more we get. This is not to say that young athletes don't need rest. Sleep is very important to them; we'll discuss its importance later in this section.

  • *Improve sleep habits.* Interestingly, the harder we exercise, the better we sleep. We may not sleep longer, but we'll sleep better. Again, this will be discussed at more length later in this section.

  • *Improve self-confidence as reflected in posture and appearance.* Young people who look good and feel good about themselves are generally more poised than their schoolmates. Their commitment to a demanding exercise regimen results not only in improved appearance and performance but in the self-confidence that accompanies new-found competence.

  • *Improve self-discipline.* None of us will ever reach our full potential without discipline, especially self-discipline. It provides the boundaries and the sense of direction that make accomplishment possible. Coaches have no guarantees that regular exercise and sports will promote the self-discipline that influences the lives of young people not only on the court or field but in the classroom and at home. Many of us have learned, however, that if accompanied by the right values, self-discipline acquired through sports will spill over into all areas of a young person's life.

  • *Reduce depression and promote a sense of well-being.* Aside from the positive psychological effects of improved appearance and self-esteem, vigorous exercise releases nature's tranquilizers—endorphins—into the bloodstream. The relaxation and sense of well-being they promote are an added benefit of vigorous exercise.

  • *Improve athletic performance and reduce injury.* These have been discussed elsewhere in this book.

Taking a Careful Look at Stress

The harmful effects of stress are well documented in medical literature. So are the positive effects of exercise in reducing stress. Smart coaches realize that their programs do both: reduce stress through exercise and create it through competition. The psychological and biochemical advantages of stress-reducing exercises are obvious selling points for your fitness and sports programs. Capitalize on them whenever possible.

  Because stress, however, is also a byproduct of competition—maybe an inevitable consequence—coaches must help their young athletes deal with it. In fact, discovering the self-control that results from dealing with stress is another major advantage of athletic participation. Fortunately, the process is relatively simple.

  A good friend once told us: "You know, worry really works! Every time I worry about something, it never happens!" His comment made a lot of sense. What each of us thinks is critically important to what we are and do. Those among us who accomplish the most are those who think and believe they will be successful. Some people call it a positive mental attitude; others call it positive thinking. Some sports psychologists call it *self-talk*.

Self-Talk

Self-talk is what happens in our heads each time we consciously think about something. Being aware of this internal dialogue is important for all of us but especially for young athletes, many of whom worry about their appearance or their likelihood of failure. Stress results from such worry. Exercise can help eliminate much of the stress if the activity results in improved appearance or successful performance.

Even more important, however, athletic activity can teach young athletes to engage in positive self-talk in order to eliminate thoughts of poor appearance or failure. Such negative thoughts generally result from a preoccupation with the past or the future: "I wish I had exercised all summer so I would be in better shape now" or "If I make 30 points tonight, I'll be leading the conference in scoring." Such thoughts are self-defeating. They disregard the moment, that slice of time when performance occurs, when action affects outcome.

The thought that occurs prior to that action is all important. It might relate to the actual performance of a skill: "Remember to follow through on your free throws." Or it might involve the sense of confidence youngsters need to sustain the right attitude: "I always come through under pressure" or "No one on their team is going to be able to tackle me today."

Whatever the self-talk involves, it must be positive. Folks laughed at Muhammed Ali when he said, "I'm the greatest!" But boxing fans appreciated watching him pummel opponents in the ring. Muhammed Ali's self-talk led to success. So does "Remember to follow through on your free throws." The athlete who tells himself or herself to avoid "pulling the string" on free throws invariably pulls the string when it's time to sink the big one. He or she has been conditioned by the kind of self-talk that involves negative images.

Youngsters must associate daily with positive images. Coaches who compliment and support their young players do much to counteract the negative impressions they sometimes receive from peers, parents, or teachers. Adolescents and preadolescents also create idealized images for themselves—and often fall short of them. Ours is a world of diverse and sometimes contradictory expectations; it is also a society of broad and highly visible accomplishment.

Both can combine to push and pull youngsters in a number of different directions, many of which are often beyond their control. All this means stress. Regular exercise and knowledgeable, sensitive coaches can help kids combat it. The reduction of stress through regular exercise and positive self-talk can become a lifelong habit that protects youngsters and adults from the sometimes serious mischief of one of our society's biggest pests.

Looking at Exercise and Sleep

A related issue involves the need for sleep. We've already indicated that exercise can promote a sleep that is physically and psychologically renewing. In fact, according to some behavioral psychologists, sleep is the body's primary restorative activity. It is a behavioral adaptation to the environment, an opportunity for diminished responsibility and renewed strength. It is, therefore, essential that teenagers—especially those involved in competitive sports programs—get the proper amount of sleep each night.

To most teenagers, sleep is a whole lot more important in the morning than at night. Reluctant to go to bed when they should, they're next to impossible to get out of bed when they must. At these moments, the importance of sleep is most evident. In fact, researchers across the country have determined that sleep disorders may affect 13 percent of the adolescent population, causing underachievement in significant numbers of them.

The daytime side effects of inadequate sleep can impair intellectual functioning, promote mood swings, and increase the potential for negative self-imaging, even delinquent behavior. Building the total athlete, therefore, involves regular exercise, proper nutrition, and the restorative benefits of sleep. Share the reproducible in figure 9-2 with your athletes; they will benefit from it both on and off the field or court.

The Downside of Suntanning

Young athletes need to be reminded that well-trained bodies include good heads, the kind that understand that the 20-million-degree thermonuclear furnace we call the sun accounts for 90 percent of the skin cancers in this country (see figure 9-3).

If they're well informed, they also realize that overexposure to the sun can damage the skin without a sunburn, that the harm isn't evident for 20 to 30 years, and that the damage is irreversible. Skin can become dry, leathery, wrinkled, and discolored. The cancers that are provoked by such overexposure range from basal cell carcinoma to malignant melanoma and can result in disfiguration and death.

Fortunately, the sun's most dangerous rays are absorbed by the atmosphere, but the ultraviolet B (UVB) and ultraviolet A (UVA) rays do penetrate the environment and can cause sunburn and cancer, even cataracts. The added bad news for athletes is that, during periods of overexposure, exercise should be avoided because it can increase the potential for overheating.

The "healthy look" that we receive from overexposure to the sun's rays, therefore, can be very misleading. Consider our friends "down under," who enjoy one of the world's driest and most beautiful climates. Each year, Australians experience approximately 140,000 new cases of skin cancer. In a population of just over 18 million, one thousand people die annually from overexposure to the sun.

In the United States the National Cancer Institute has announced a 50-percent increase in skin cancers within the past 10 to 15 years, most of the increase affecting younger Americans. They have indicated that one in three people living in Sunbelt states can expect to contract some kind of skin cancer. They also indicate that the primary solution to the problem is education. Young Americans must be aware of the problem and must not only change their habits regarding intentional exposure to the sun's rays but take proper precautions during times of unintentional exposure, during outdoor practice or competition.

As important, they must recognize that indoor tanning is much more dangerous than outdoor tanning. Because ultraviolet rays can be 4 to 10 times stronger in tanning beds than under the sun, the risk of skin cancer is greater. In addition, the possibility

© 1995 by Michael D. Koehler

Figure 9-2

GETTING ENOUGH SLEEP?

DID YOU REALIZE THAT

- Sleep is the body's primary activity for renewing strength?
- Sleep disorders affect 13 percent of the U.S. teenage population?
- Inadequate sleep impairs your ability to think properly?
- Inadequate sleep can cause negative mood swings?
- Inadequate sleep can hurt athletic performance?
- Inadequate sleep can harm classwork and interfere with relationships at home?

All of us don't require the same amount of sleep, but we all need to meet the demands of our bodies. If you feel overly tired in the morning and drag your way through your first few classes, you may not be getting enough sleep at night. Without enough sleep, you risk some of the above behaviors, and *they're not worth it!*

If you're finding yourself staying up late at night to complete your homework assignments or study, you *could* be wasting time during the day. If this is a possibility, see me and/or your counselor to find ways to organize your time better. Remember, enough sleep is critical if you want to be at your best in school and during practice and games!

Figure 9-3

THINK TWICE ABOUT THAT SUNTAN!

THINK ABOUT THESE FACTS:

- The sun is a 20-million-degree thermonuclear furnace that accounts for 90 percent of the skin cancers in this country.
- The harm a suntan does to your skin today won't be really evident for another 20 or 30 years.
- The National Cancer Institute has announced a 50-percent increase in skin cancers in this country within the past 10 to 15 years.
- Excessive sun can cause the skin to become prematurely dry, leathery, wrinkled, and discolored.
- Skin cancer can result in disfigurement and death.
- Indoor tanning is more dangerous than outdoor tanning. Tanning beds can produce ultraviolet rays that are 4 to 10 times stronger than the sun.

Be sure, therefore, to use a sunscreen during outdoor practice and especially during the summer months when you are exercising to stay in shape. Avoid overexposure to the sun during vacations and on weekends. We already have indicated the long-range effects of suntanning. The short-range effects can cause lots of pain during practice or games when your uniform is rubbing against a sunburn!

Be smart and don't invite trouble just to get a tan.

IT REALLY ISN'T WORTH IT.

© 1995 by Michael D. Koehler

for damage to the immune system and the increased potential for cataracts make indoor tanning even a greater risk. Admittedly, the facts are not all in regarding such potential problems, but such potential hazards are not worth the momentary enjoyment of a tan.

Solar radiation may be a benefit to mankind in the form of warmth and energy, photosynthesis, vision, and Vitamin D, but its potential for damage to our bodies is a significant factor that must be shared with youngsters. Use the reproducible in figure 9-3 to encourage your young athletes to avoid extended exposure to the sun's rays and to use sunscreens during periods of extended exposure outside. This is yet another valuable lesson they will carry away from their experiences with you.

A Word About Visualization

Visualization can have lifelong benefits for young athletes. Art Costa, a renowned educator at the University of California in Sacramento, has indicated that visualization provides a mental activity that can be the equivalent of actual practice. That's right; along with a range of sports psychologists, he claims that "thinking about" a physical activity can produce benefits similar to its actual performance.

How Thinking Improves Performance

The concept is not to be confused with a Vince Lombardi pep talk or the various "head games" players use to get themselves "fired up." The concept of visualization focuses less on "firing up" athletes then on "sharpening up" their skills. In essence, thinking about athletic performance actually improves that performance, not just because the player tries harder, but because he or she actually gets better.

Costa cites a university study to make his point. Three separate groups of participants were selected. All were equal in ability and skills. They all were coached on how to improve their free-throw shooting. The first group was instructed to actually practice free throws. They were given basketballs and were supervised in a gym. The second group was told to visualize the act of shooting free throws—to mentally rehearse the skill as explained earlier to them. The third group was told to do anything but shoot free throws—or think about shooting them.

It's no shock that the third group didn't improve at all. What is interesting is that the first two groups improved almost at the same rate. The shooters improved most, but the "thinkers" were not far behind. Imagine—the brain sends the same conditioning impulses to our nerves and muscles when we *think* about shooting free throws as when we actually shoot them. It doesn't know whether we're standing at the free-throw line with a ball in our hands or not.

And it won't know if young athletes are throwing softballs, batting, swinging golf clubs, handling field hockey sticks, high jumping, performing swan dives, or punting a football. Youngsters can find practice time in the locker room before a game or at home as they nod off to sleep. The concept of visualization holds great potential for athletes of all ages. Use the reproducible in figure 9-4 to pique the interest of your players, even to share with their parents. Parents may be open to suggestions for improving their golf games.

Figure 9-4

**NEED PRACTICE TIME?
VISUALIZE IT!**

WHAT IS VISUALIZATION?

Visualization is the process of mentally rehearsing an athletic activity or skill. It can be the equivalent of actual practice! People who engage in visualization "watch themselves" perform an athletic activity over and over again. High jumpers, prior to an actual jump, may "watch themselves" approach the bar and successfully execute the jump. Basketball players may stand on the free-throw line and "watch themselves" execute a fundamentally sound free throw. Olympic bobsledders viualize each of their runs just before they actually perform them. Your mom or dad can actually sit at home and visualize a golf swing before heading for his or her favorite course.

HOW DOES VISUALIZATION WORK?

Visualization causes the brain to send the same conditioning impulses to our nerves and muscles as when we actually perform an athletic skill. The nerves actually practice the skill. In effect, our brains don't know if we're actually shooting a basketball, throwing a football, or swinging a golf club. So take advantage of visualization techniques before practice or competition; your brain has a practice field all its own!

SHARE THIS WITH YOUR PARENTS, TOO

How would you like to sit in your easy chair and practice your golf swing? Like athletes in many sports, you can think your way to improved performance. Sports psychologists have learned that thinking about athletic performance actually improves it, not just because the player tries harder but because he or she actually gets better. So find practice time during a short work break. Before you take to the links with your favorite foursome, find a comfortable spot in the living room, mentally rehearse the correct way to swing a golf club—and let your brain "do the driving for you!"

**IF YOU CAN'T ACTUALLY DO IT,
VISUALIZE IT!**

© 1995 by Michael D. Koehler

Lifelong Fitness for Endurance

Habits are generally too weak to be felt until they're too strong to be broken. Fortunately, this is as true for good habits as bad ones. Unfortunately, a sizable number of Americans are unable to maintain fitness habits long enough to benefit from them. Recent studies indicate that Americans are exhibiting less and less interest in fitness training since the trend crested in the 1980s. Specifically, studies indicate that 60 to 70 percent of American adults discontinue fitness programs within one month of starting them.

A recent Harris poll, for example, identified a four-point decline in the percentage of Americans who exercise vigorously and a six-point drop in the percentage of persons who stay away from cholesterol and fatty foods. Another study by the Centers for Disease Control showed a leveling off of the numbers of Americans who smoke. This particular report ended a 26-year decline of smokers in this country.

Many of these people indicate that fitness training involves too much time and effort. Apparently, they have yet to discover that fitness involves only 15 to 20 minutes of mildly vigorous activity three times a week. It seems that the "no-pain-no-gain" principle still prevails among many who do and do not exercise. Unfortunately, for those who exercise, it compromises their aerobic fitness; and for those who don't exercise, it remains an obstacle to lifelong health.

We have the opportunity to teach youngsters that aerobic fitness doesn't require exhaustion, that lifelong fitness is more a routine than a regimen, more exhilarating than exhausting. Certainly, the conditioning programs we impose on them for competitive sports go well beyond "mildly vigorous activity," but the athletes' knowledge of proper aerobic fitness and their commitment to healthful living should help establish the kinds of fitness habits that will sustain their fitness levels well into adulthood.

According to another Harris poll, many Americans also fail to realize that 66 percent of people in this country were overweight last year, compared with only 61 percent the previous year. One of the reasons must involve the fact that only 66 percent of the 10- to 17-year-olds exercise regularly and, more tragically, that only 10 to 20 percent of 18- to 64-year-olds have developed appropriate aerobic exercise habits.

They also fail to realize that just a half hour of moderate activity—raking, walking briskly, even gardening—will improve their fitness levels and actually delay the aging process. Research indicates consistently that most people reach their biological prime at approximately age 30 but that the prime can be extended to age 60 through regular exercise. This is an extremely important point, one that should be shared with students and parents alike.

Sedentary people tire and weaken faster than their active friends. Many of them begin to assume that feeling 20 years older than they really are is a consequence of living in today's society. To some extent, they are right. The American lifestyle has transformed some of our jumping beans into couch potatoes and has failed to teach them that people need lose only 5 percent of their endurance with each decade of age.

Just think, the 60-year-old grandparents out there can be only 25 percent less active than their 10-year-old grandchildren. With moderate and continuing exercise, they need not worry about feeling exhausted whenever the little ones finally go home with Mom and Dad. Interestingly, what this means is that people in our society who appear unnaturally youthful are, in fact, the normal ones. Our bodies are intended for activity and have been conditioned by centuries of survival to expect it. When they remain active, they maintain themselves.

The longer we remain active, therefore, the better we feel—and *appear*—whenever we bump into friends and acquaintances, or the bathroom mirror! Use the reproducible in figure 9-5 to make this point. Share it with parents, teachers, administrators, and nonathletes in your school. It will help them, and it will do wonders for your program.

Beyond Athletics Toward Self-Discipline

Ben Franklin once said, "At 20 years of age the will reigns; at 30 the wit; at 40 the judgment." The challenge for us is to help youngsters make the transition from 20 to 40! Most of us who have been in the business more than a couple of years realize that is no easy task, especially in this society, given the self-indulgence and retarded social development that seem so evident all around us. Whenever he musters up the courage to look down on us, Franklin must be surprised at a society that can claim so many advances, yet backslides in so many different ways. Advances don't guarantee progress. It's a lesson that eludes many of us.

Fortunately, it's a lesson that many coaches try almost daily to teach. Every time we persuade a young athlete to push herself for another half mile around the track or dig deep into his energy reserves for one more goal-line stand, we teach self-discipline. With enough such lessons, punishment in schools and in society becomes less necessary.

Perhaps that's one reason why coaches enjoy visits from former players. They discover, invariably, that many of them have carried the self-discipline learned in sports into their personal and vocational lives and have used it to achieve not only professional success but personal happiness. Young athletes learn that self-discipline, not self-indulgence, makes them feel good about themselves.

Your fitness and sports programs, therefore, involve consequences that reach well beyond the field or court—yet another selling point for the school and community.

Let's Wrap It Up

The human body is capable of remarkable adaptation—to environmental conditions, viral threat, and strenuous physical demands. In fact, our history on this planet is a continuing story of such adaptation. As the saying goes: "What doesn't kill us makes us stronger," and it's safe to say that human beings are stronger today than ever before in our past.

We find ourselves threatened, however, by our own increasing levels of inactivity. The "creature comforts" we create improve our lives but impair our vitality. Some sports psychologists would say that we are less able to really enjoy the improved quality of life we have created for ourselves. Physical activity is now less necessary for

Figure 9-5

FITNESS: EXHILARATION,
NOT EXHAUSTION

SOMETHING TO THINK ABOUT

- Almost 70 percent of adult Americans discontinue fitness programs within one month of starting them.
- Recently, there was a 6 percent drop in the percentage of Americans who stay away from cholesterol and fatty foods.
- The numbers of people who smoke in this country has leveled off in recent years. This leveling off has concluded a 26-year decline in the number of smokers in America.
- Sixty-six percent of the people in this country were overweight last year.
- Only 10 to 20 percent of 18- to 64-year-olds in this country have developed appropriate aerobic exercise habits.
- Most people reach their biological prime at age 30, but that prime can be extended to age 60 with regular exercise.
- People need lose only 5 percent of their endurance with each decade of age.
- Raking, walking briskly, even gardening can provide aerobic exercise—and actually delay the aging process.
- Sedentary people tire and weaken faster than their active friends.

Get in on the action! Develop a regular exercise program for yourself. Better yet, join our fitness program. You'll be doing yourself a big favor!

© 1995 by Michael D. Koehler

food, but it is perhaps every bit as important for survival. It helps treat or control coronary heart disease, overweight, hypertension, respiratory disease, musculoskeletal disorders, even depression.

Yet the message seems lost on many of us—maybe most of us. We find a variety of reasons to avoid physical activity, some of which—fortunately—are funny. Consider these excuses used by patients at the Orthopedic Center of the Rockies to miss their physical therapy appointments (found in the January '93 edition of *The Physician and Sports Medicine*).

- "I have only so many heartbeats left, and I don't want to waste them on exercise."
- "I can't. I have a hyena."
- "I don't want to give my mother the satisfaction of saying I'm taking care of myself."
- And, finally, from an obviously impressionable, if benighted, young woman: "My mother told me not to jog because my uterus would fall out."

It seems we need to sell our programs for a variety of reasons. The next section will help.

Section Ten

SELLING THE PROGRAM

Introduction

    Salespersons are intermediaries. Ask anyone who makes a living peddling products or services. Ultimately, the product does the selling. Good products attract consumers, pay wages, and establish successful enterprises. This is not to say that selling is unimportant; it is vital, as we shall see in this section. The better the product, however, the easier it is to sell. Our purpose in this section, therefore, is to emphasize the quality of the product and then provide some insights into effective ways to sell it.

First Things First: Selling the Program to Students

Presentation is half the selling job. Create a worthwhile product, then present it well, and people are likely to be interested in buying it. We want people to buy our fitness programs. We want the kids to get involved, and we want significant others to provide the support needed to offer the best product available. First, what do we do to encourage the involvement of young athletes?

Making Fitness Necessary and Fun

    The obvious answer for coaches is to tell youngsters they have to be involved if they want to be on your team. Certainly, this tactic works, especially in schools with successful and popular programs that attract large numbers of young athletes. Studies are indicating, however, that numbers of young athletes are falling off in many schools. Many coaches find themselves "beating the bushes" to find players and, when they do, often making compromises in their coaching behaviors in order to keep them.

Common sense dictates, therefore, that we mandate involvement in our fitness programs whenever possible but make them appealing all the time. Following are some suggestions:

• *Audio equipment*. Have tape and/or CD players available in the weight and workout rooms with a variety of tapes selected *by the players*. If you're anything like us, you'll find yourself at times gritting your teeth or leaving the room to escape the racket. Many contemporary tapes are to music what World War II was to peace. But they like it, and it will do much to keep them plugged into your program.

You might also provide tapes that explain high school and NCAA eligibility, appropriate nutrition, even some that contain explanations of offensive and defensive strategies, perhaps your signals or play-calling system or explanations of fundamentals. Such explanations are often invaluable for practicing visualization techniques while young athletes ride the stationary bike or use the treadmill.

• *Video equipment*. Many publishers have a range of commercially available video-tapes that make the time go faster while exercising. Students might enjoy "riding or run-ning through" Hawaii or Yellowstone National Park, or they might enjoy watching one of several qualified nutritionists discuss connections between certain foods and athletic fitness. You might also provide a library of your game tapes or instructional tapes from college coaches. Publishers offer a range of tapes explaining fundamental skills in a variety of sports. They can be very appropriate for the young athlete who seeks a diver-sion while "chained" to the bike or treadmill for half an hour or forty-five minutes.

Many young athletes enjoy aerobic tapes and often learn after one workout the challenges they pose. We've seen programs where boys and girls have engaged in aer-obic exercises together. The boys invariably walk away from the experience with a great deal of respect for the cardiovascular endurance of girls, and both improve their fitness levels while having fun.

• *Mirrors*. Every coach knows that immediate reinforcement provides the best motivation. Nothing in the weight room reinforces more immediately than a mirror. "Looking good" has different meanings for boys and girls. Whatever it means, they both enjoy seeing it when they exercise. The walls in the exercise room don't have to be completely mirrored, but mirrors should be located at strategic spots to give kids a good look at the progress they are making each day.

• *Arrangement of room*. Stationary bikes and treadmills should be located in front of televison sets or windows. Weight machines should be stationed so that athletes can complete a circuit (work muscles progressively) without moving back and forth across the room. Free weights should be located in an area of the room that permits freedom of movement. Towels and water should be located in an accessible area of the room. Movement throughout the room should be unrestricted to minimize interference with exercisers and the potential dangers such interference might involve.

• *Competitions and activities*. Finally, be sure to provide a range of programs that promote competition among athletes and give them opportunities to socialize. Competitions rewarding most weight lifted or most miles run capitalize on the moti-vations of kids. When promoting such activities, however, be sure to establish base-line data for each athlete, so all are comparing their own individual progress. The youngster who progresses the most should be the winner, not necessarily the one who lifted the most or ran the farthest.

Social events like bowling tournaments, handball competitions, picnics with soft-ball games and other physical activities, and bike outings provide exercise and help develop the togetherness that all teams require to be successful. Such activities require a little more planning and perhaps a lot more of your time, but they reveal you in a whole new light and give you opportunities to establish close relationships with your players. They also bring the kids closer together and help promote the family concept that is so critical to any team's success.

These, then, are some ideas for selling the fitness program to your young athletes. Interestingly, they also help sell the need for such a program to administrators, teachers, and parents. When you provide wholesome and healthful activities for youngsters during the school year and throughout the summer months, school personnel and parents welcome your ideas. Adults can be sold on your program for other reasons as well. We will discuss them later in this section. For now, let's continue to look at ways to sell the program to your athletes.

Taking Responsibility for Your Own Life

Teens and preteens, almost by definition, battle the dependency they feel at home—at least we hope they do. The youngster who rarely questions or defies parental or other authority is either enjoying an idyllic relationship with the world or developing a dependency that will interfere with his or her autonomy later on. Most psychologists agree that teenagers need to *counter-depend,* that is, fight the dependency they experience at home or in school.

Fortunately for them and regrettably for many of us, most of them wage this battle with almost supernatural efficiency. They are particulary successful in circumstances where they seem most powerless. Dominating and controlling parents soon learn that they may win an occasional battle, but the counter-depending teen invariably wins the war. Parents and coaches, therefore, are well advised to provide reasonable consequences for the inappropriate behavior of teenagers and to promote opportunities for them to take responsibility for their own lives.

A fitness program is one of the most visible of these opportunities. Some parents can claim credit for much of what their kids do, but even the most narcissistic are hard pressed to take the bows for a youngster's level of physical conditioning. Whenever you promote your fitness program, therefore, as a responsibility as well as an opportunity, you plug into the psychological needs of youngsters to take control of their lives. Figure 10-1 provides an excellent reproducible to distribute throughout the school.

Making the Right Kinds of Friends

The reproducible also promotes the fitness program as a way to make friends in the school. This is an obvious advantage to students as well as their parents. Although parents have no guarantees that athletes are the most decent and trouble-free kids in the school, they can feel confident, by and large, that such kids are hard working and committed to something beyond their own self-indulgence. The dedicated athlete who works hard after school on the court or field and who also gets good grades is doing *something* right and is generally respected by adults as well as other students.

Figure 10-1

TAKE CONTROL OF YOUR LIFE

WHAT OUR FITNESS PROGRAM OFFERS YOU!

If you're involved in sports, our fitness program will get you into the kind of physical condition you require for competitive athletics. All levels of competition, from junior high school to the pros, are getting tougher every year. Athletes are bigger and more talented. To compete with them and to keep yourself injury free, you need to maintain a high level of physical fitness. Our program will help you do just that.

If sports don't interest you, then do it for yourself.

WHY IS IT SO IMPORTANT?

You don't want to be injured or perform at less than your best when you go out for your favorite sport. If you like sports, then your level of physical fitness is important to you. Even if you're not interested in competitive sports, good fitness will help you look good, feel good, and do a good job in the classroom because you'll have more energy and feel better about yourself.

WHAT DO YOU HAVE TO DO?

Take control of your life. You alone are responsible for the level of physical fitness you achieve. When you were a child, Mom and Dad told you what to do—and to some extent they probably still do! Our fitness program, however, expects you to take control because only *you* can make the commitment to do the hard work that will result in your improved appearance and performance—not just on the court or field but in the classroom and community.

Our fitness program wants young adults; it wants *you*. Join now and let's work together to help you realize your goals.

© 1995 by Michael D. Koehler

When athletic and fitness programs are populated by such youngsters, parents seek them out for their own children. At that point, you have the best of all worlds. Your program is sought out by conscientious parents, and it tends to attract the kinds of youngsters you need to develop a winning program. Much of this may sound too good to be true, but those of us who have been in the business for a few years realize that it can happen. And when it does, everybody wins.

Some of the biggest winners are youngsters who may be new to the school. Any experienced teacher realizes that, unless the school has some kind of "peer helper" program, the underachievers and troublemakers in the school tend to be the first ones to reach out to transfer students. Often, even the best youngster finds himself or herself during the first few weeks in a new school being courted by one or more of the "lesser lights." This is a fact of life. Your fitness program can change all that.

Use the reproducible in figure 10-2, then, to give to transfer students at the beginning of the school year. You might leave copies with your school's registrar or the head of the guidance department to give to the student and his or her parents during early discussions about registration and orientation to the school. Notice that the invitation doesn't mention a specific sport, just the value of the fitness program as a preparation for athletics and an opportunity to meet students with similar interests.

Such a form makes several important statements. Explicitly, it emphasizes the fact that young athletes benefit from total conditioning. It suggests the additional advantage for transfer students of making new friends. Implicitly, it identifies you as a proactive member of the staff, someone who reaches out to students to meet all their developmental needs.

As such, the form not only generates interest in your athletic and fitness programs but provides valuable public relations within the school and community. The students will benefit from it, and the parents and administration will appreciate your investment in the kids. Both will be more likely to reach out when the program needs help. Anything that has easily publicized value for the school is desirable to most administrators, and, once publicized, it has immediate value for parents.

These Statistics Don't Lie

Adults will be even more inclined to reach out after you share some relevant statistics with your athletes. Doctors and sport physiologists have identified several primary causes of sports injuries: poor flexibility, muscle imbalance, congenital problems, inadequate training, and poor equipment. Such causes account for most of the nearly 2 million injuries that affect young athletes each year. Fortunately, we can do something about them, even the congenital abnormalities.

As discussed in section 5, any program of total conditioning must emphasize flexibility and the strengthening of every part of the body—all the skeletal muscles and the cardiovascular system. When programs fail in this regard or when student athletes are denied such programs, injuries result. We were approached one year by a local high school coach who had just experienced the fourth separated shoulder on his football team.

Because it was midseason, we couldn't do much but advise him to back off certain contact drills in practice and start his players on a weightlifting and flexibility reg-

Figure 10-2

NEW KID ON THE BLOCK?

FIRST OF ALL—WELCOME!!

Welcome to (Name of school)! You're going to love it here. You might be a little homesick for the first couple of weeks, but you'll soon discover, like everyone else around here, that this is a nice place to be. We all get along very well, and we're all proud of our school. We'd like to get to know you a little better.

HOW CAN WE GET TO KNOW YOU?

Well, the first thing you can do if you enjoy exercise is join our fitness program. You may be interested in a particular sport. We can introduce you to the coaches, and we can provide the kind of exercise program you need to avoid injuries and perform at your absolute best! And if you're not interested in sports, you may still want to look good and feel good about yourself. Our fitness program can help you with that, too.

WHAT ELSE CAN IT PROVIDE?

We're proud to say that some of the best students in this school (also some of the nicest kids) are involved regularly in the program. Some are preparing for athletic competition; others are trying to shed a few pounds; all are improving their appearance and finding more energy to do homework and help around the house and in the community. Join up and meet everyone! You'll find yourself involved in a program that will improve your fitness and introduce you to some of the greatest students in the school.

HOW DO I JOIN?

Stop by my office and let's talk. I have some forms for you to complete, and I'll want to show you around, maybe introduce you to a few more people. Following is the information you need to see me:

My name is (Your name), and you
can find me in (Room Number), or
you can call (Phone Number).

**STOP BY. IT WILL TAKE ONLY A COUPLE OF MINUTES,
AND I'D REALLY LIKE TO MEET YOU.**

© 1995 by Michael D. Koehler

imen before selected practices. We stopped by periodically to talk to his players and help them with the exercises and told them to plan on a total fitness program as soon as the season ended. Most of them worked for the remainder of the school year and into the summer before their next season.

During the next seven consecutive seasons, his players have not suffered one separated or dislocated shoulder. The weightlifting improved the trapezius and deltoid strength of every player and eliminated a problem that plagued his program and that promised years of recurring pain for several of his players. Because the weightlifting program emphasized total body strength as well, he also noticed a sharp decline in the number of twisted ankles and knees.

In fact, the reduction of total injuries during the past seven years of his program has been startling, given recent statistics indicating that high school football players face a greater risk of injury than all other student athletes. Of the almost million and a half athletic injuries faced by high school students, the majority occur in football, basketball, tennis, soccer, and track and field, this latter sport experiencing some of the most damaging injuries.

Track and field, like dance and most running activities, place considerable strain on muscles and joints. Success in such activities is dependent on cardiovascular as well as skeletal strength, so most athletes and dancers push themselves for extended periods of time to achieve the levels of endurance so necessary to their activities.

Research has indicated that overuse is the cause of more than two-thirds of all sports injuries, hence the problems with running and aerobic dance, even tennis. Interestingly, in a study of 10,000 injuries at the Center for Sports Medicine at San Francisco's St. Francis Memorial Hospital, researchers discovered that more fractures were caused by aerobic dance than any other activity. The prevention of injury in today's society, therefore, is dependent on the education of recreational as well as interscholastic and intercollegiate athletes.

Coaches, particularly those who provide total fitness programs, can do much to help in that regard. Every time we remind a young athlete to stretch well prior to vigorous exercise, we help establish the kinds of habits that carry over into adulthood. Even nonathletes involved in fitness programs benefit from reproducibles like those in section 2, especially figure 2-1. The reproducible in figure 10-3 provides related information.

All athletes are well advised to walk away from exercise as from the dinner table—neither too full nor too hungry. Too much exercise can be as damaging as too little. Anyone who exceeds humane expectations of his or her body during exercise runs the risk of injury, sometimes debilitating injury. It's not surprising, then, that aerobic dance, while important for aerobic fitness, can cause stress fractures that are damaging to total health.

Teenagers Are Especially Susceptible

Anyone who works with teens and preteens knows only too well that moderation is not one of their strong suits. In fact, they tend to be *excessive* in either their pursuit or neglect of it! Consider, for example, their tendency to exercise, even overexercise

Figure 10-3

EVERYTHING IN MODERATION!!

WHAT IS MODERATION?

Moderation is a personal quality that enables you and me to avoid extremes. You already know, for example, that eating too much can be unhealthy, so we all try to eat *moderate* amounts of food. We also try—at parents' request—to spend a moderate amount of time on the phone! We moderate the amount of time we spend with our friends on weekends, so we can find a moderate amount of time to do our homework!

WHAT ABOUT EXERCISE?

Moderate exercise is important, too. We're not saying to back off so that you don't get enough exercise; physical fitness still involves a lot of hard work. We *are* saying, however, that too much exercise, like too much of anything, can be harmful.

HOW ABOUT SOME SPECIFICS?

Recent research is telling us that "overuse" is causing more injuries in sports than anything else. We overuse our shoulder muscles and the shoulder joint itself by throwing a baseball or a football too much. We overuse our elbows by hitting too many tennis balls for too long a time. And we overuse our legs by running, jogging, or aerobic dancing too long and too vigorously.

More and more women, for example, are experiencing stress fractures in their legs because of *im*moderate aerobic dancing.

WHAT CAN YOU DO?

Let's talk. We've indicated all along that *safety first* is one of our guiding principles. Immoderate exercise violates that principle. It's important, therefore, that you and I discuss the workout program that's just right for you, particularly if you exercise at home as well as in the fitness room. See me. Stop in with your parents. I'd like to meet them.

© 1995 by Michael D. Koehler

one muscle group over others. The pectorals and the arms tend to be the focus for boys, the hips and thighs for girls. Certainly, this isn't true of all kids, but it's true of enough of them to cause coaches some concern. This kind of excess can be a real problem for young athletes.

Consider just the knee joint. It probably is the most vulnerable area of the body, especially for athletes. Gayle Sayers, Bobby Orr, and Mickey Mantle represent three different sports, and all are as famous for their knee injuries as their remarkable accomplishments in sports. They discovered, as have so many other talented athletes, that a knee injury can immobilize even the most gifted athlete.

The knee is composed of four ligaments, the anterior and posterior cruciates and the medial and lateral collaterals, which act as rubber bands joining the body's two largest bones, the femur and the tibia. In addition, two pieces of cartilage absorb shock and two muscles, the hamstring and the quadriceps, hold the joint together. Like any system, then, the knee is dependent upon the efficient interaction of all its parts. When one of them breaks down, the system fails.

It makes sense, then, for all serious athletes, particularly the younger ones, to strengthen every part of their bodies, especially those parts that are most susceptible to injury. Consider a recent study of injuries related to volleyball. Predictably, ninety per cent of them were located in the legs, 23 percent in the ankles and 59 percent in the knees. The fitness program that shares such statistics with young athletes, their parents, and school authorities does much to sell itself to kids and find adult support.

Advertising Prevention and Treatment of Injuries

Injury prevention is as important to athletes as performance enhancement. Some orthopedic surgeons, for example, have gone so far as to indicate that loose-jointed youngsters should avoid contact sports like football, soccer, and field hockey—and that tight-jointed athletes should avoid running and swimming activities. Experienced coaches certainly must agree with them—and all of us must make sure that information on this important aspect of injury prevention is disseminated to athletes and their parents as well.

All of us have seen young athletes who seem predisposed to ankle, elbow, or knee sprains and pulled or torn muscles and tendons. They seem to injure easily and require more than the usual amount of time in the training room to use the whirlpool or get their ankles wrapped. Such young athletes require comprehensive fitness programs to avoid such injuries, alert coaches who are sensitive to their physical predispositions, and treatment programs that help resolve problems.

Selling Total Fitness

The advantages to a young athlete of total fitness offer a big selling point for your program. Potential for injury is reduced by providing *general* strength-building activities as well as *specific* exercises that respond to the unique needs of certain athletes. According to a physical anthropologist as the University of Texas, young athletes who engage in extensive workouts do not harm their overall physical development. If the workouts become immoderate, however, the potential for damage to muscles and joints is there. Moderation and safety remain key factors in every workout program—and in the publicity you create.

Programs for female athletes require some special consideration. One researcher at the University of Washington and another at Children's Hospital in Boston—among scores of others—have found that teenage athletes run into two primary problems. One involves damage to bones, muscles, and joints in both sexes. The second, however, involves the loss of menstruation in women who exercise extensively, perhaps immoderately. They suffer from brittle bones, which leads to the high incidence of stress fractures in many aerobic dance activities.

A Word About Treatment

Parents, particularly, will want to know that you are keeping abreast of updated treatment techniques, and that you are able to respond quickly and appropriately to injuries in your athletes. In the absence of an athletic trainer, coaches are often the first line of treatment for injured players. They must be familiar, therefore, with programs like RICE (*R*est-*I*ce-*C*ompression-*E*levation) that respond quickly to injury and promote the healing process.

Ice has been important in the immediate treatment of injury for a long time, but only relatively recently has compression been identified as equally important. Studies in England discovered that applying cold or pressure independently of each other had relatively little effect on swelling. Cold *and* pressure, however, reduced swelling by as much as 80%. Similar studies at Penn State University found that using ice under a wrapping reduced swelling by only 33% but that ice on top of compression wrapping decreased blood flow by 75%, thereby reducing swelling.

Such techniques, if applied immediately after injury, can do much to minimize the effects of injury and promote quicker healing of damaged joints or muscles. You'll help your athletes as well as your program; the youngsters will suffer less and return sooner to competitive activity, and the parents and community will be favorably impressed with your sensible—and sensitive—approach to building the total athlete.

Be sure to talk to your team doctor for additional information about RICE and to secure her or his help in circumstances where athletes may have joint trauma, persistent pain, infection, or other symptoms. Also, whenever it is indicated, refer students and their parents to the family doctor for complete diagnosis and treatment.

Promoting Maintenance of Fitness

Another point to keep in mind when selling your program is its ability to sustain the general fitness levels of young athletes who are sidelined because of injury. A dislocated thumb or a mild shoulder separation may prevent athletic competition, but it doesn't have to interfere with aerobic activity on the stationary bike. No coach wants to push a young athlete into any activity that can cause or exacerbate injury; neither, however, do we want to allow injury to nullify the positive effects of months of exercise to achieve high levels of cardiovascular fitness.

To emphasize this point to those concerned, coaches are wise to have parents and athletes ask the family doctor to indicate the kinds of fitness exercises players can perform while recuperationg from injury. Be sure they understand that your fitness program is the perfect place for young athletes, regardless of sport, to maintain their fitness levels while allowing injuries to heal.

Talking About Playing Through Pain

The past 25 years of competitive athletics in this country have witnessed a dramatic increase in the number of potentially debilitating injuries to young athletes. Specifically, youngsters are now being diagnosed with stress fractures, tendonitis, and bursitis, maladies formerly restricted to professional athletes. The reasons are primarily twofold.

1. Organized sports have caused "overuse" injuries, the results of hitting too many tennis balls, throwing too many baseballs and footballs, and running for long distances on unforgiving surfaces, such as streets and sidewalks.

2. Once injured, youngsters choose to play through the pain in order to avoid appearing weak to coaches or teammates.

The combination of these two factors results in the kinds of unreported injuries that can be permanent. You can stress in your program your desire to steer young athletes away from this kind of dangerous behavior.

It is especially important to do so at this level, because the significant influence of college and professional sports has complicated the problem. One of the most enduring traditions of intercollegiate athletics, cherished by young and old alike in the memory of George Gipp, involves sacrificing mind and body in order to win the big game. Coaches have perpetuated the tradition by expecting athletes to play hurt, and professional athletes have reinforced it by sacrificing their youth and—in many instances, their health—to winning the game.

During the 1980s, for example, statistics indicate that 72 percent of the players in the National Football League (NFL) suffered injuries that kept them sidelined for up to 8 weeks. More pointedly, the number of players who ended their careers because of injury has doubled since the 1950s. Many of these players saved enough money to sustain themselves when their careers ended; others did not.

Unfortunately, the legacy they have left today's young athlete endures in misguided notions of playing hurt and emphasizing winning over everything else in their lives. In a recent article by Mark Anderson, a sports medicine specialist at the University of Oklahoma Health Sciences Center, coaches and parents are warned that youngsters can face a lifetime of physical and psychological pain when they suffer a sports injury or fail to meet performance expectations that are imposed on them.

Coaches and parents must be sensitive to such subtle influences. The pressures we consciously or inadvertently impose on youngsters can have far-reaching consequences. Anderson and others remind us that teens and preteens in our society experience enough pressure already. In sports, the one area originally designed to release pressure, they are experiencing some of their greatest stresses.

Figure 10-4, therefore, provides an important message for young athletes. It should be posted prominently in the fitness room and mentioned periodically after practice and contests. Certainly, one of the ways coaches can put athletics in the proper perspective is to encourage players to acknowledge pain and to report it to assure proper treatment. A relatively short period of rehabilitation is preferable to missing the entire season, ending a career, or suffering permanent damage.

When Athletes Imagine or Fabricate Pain

As you promote the emphasis in your program on dealing with pain appropriately while working with teenage athletes, you must also be aware of the flipside— *not* playing *without* pain. Some youngsters fabricate injury to protect themselves from fear or unrealistic expectations, not only in sports but also in the home or the classroom. Excessive fear and relentless expectations can immobilize youngsters, and each young athlete has a different threshold for both. Coaches must be sensitive to such signs and should alert parents to their concerns.

The signs of such behavior involve injuries without physical symptoms, constant complaints, reluctance to perform, excessive and often unexcused absences, and unwillingness or inability to associate with coaches and teammates. Often, the coach's best early response to such behavior is to tell the young athlete and his or her parents to see the family doctor for a complete diagnosis—and hope that the doctor doesn't play into the youngster's imagined illness. To avoid such a possibility, it is wise to get permission from the parents to call the doctor yourself or to have the team trainer call to explain the school's perspective.

Maintaining an Objective Approach

Be careful not to criticize or berate the youngster but to explain objectively and anecdotally your experiences with him or her. Indicate that you or the team trainer or doctor checked the child and are unable to find serious injury. Request the doctor's help to make a diagnosis and either treat the injury or help the child work through whatever fears he or she may be experiencing.

If the young athlete is not injured, when he or she returns to practice, indicate that you have spoken to the doctor and are looking forward to his or her continuing in practice and competition. Then wait. Humoring or criticizing such children often gets them the attention they seek and is counterproductive to getting them back on the team. Back off, remembering that perceived expectations or fear was the probable cause of the problem in the first place.

Allow some peer pressure and the child's interest in the activity to motivate his or her return. If, after several days, this strategy doesn't seem to be working, then meet with the child to force the issue, focusing on the fun the team is having and how much

Figure 10-4

DON'T PLAY WITH PAIN!

LISTEN TO YOUR BODY

Pain is your body's way of getting your attention! Don't ignore it. With the proper treatment and rest, even the most painful injuries heal. Without such attention, they only get worse and could bother you for the rest of your life. When you experience pain, therefore, the kind of pain that limits movement, see your coach immediately. We're not talking about an occasional bruise; those kinds of injuries occur often in sports. We are talking about a pain that is persistent and limits movement in any way. If you are concerned about a pain, so am I. See me right away.

DON'T BE A HERO

Stories of college and professional athletes who "play hurt" would have us believe that they're tougher than everyone else. Well, they may be pretty tough, but so are the athletes who commit themselves to a sport and treat their injuries so they can play at their best and maximize their contributions to their teams. "Playing hurt" just isn't smart. Professional athletes may do it because some of them don't see any alternative. To keep earning big salaries, many of them sacrifice their health, sometimes for the rest of their lives. Even then, they risk their futures and usually don't play at their best.

YOU BE SMART!

We want you to play at your best and to realize the lifelong rewards that accompany good health and fitness. Don't be a baby about an occasional bruise, but always be a responsible young adult when it comes to athletic injury. Don't become the victim of a belief that only tough athletes play with pain. Frankly, it's silly. Again, if you have any questions, see me.

PAIN IS A MESSAGE FROM YOUR BODY.
PAY ATTENTION TO IT.

© 1995 by Michael D. Koehler

they miss him or her during practice or contests. Avoid mention of the child's probable success in the sport; again, this may have been the initial cause of the child's fears and could delay his or her return to the team for several days, maybe forever. With a little "benevolent disregard," imagined injuries tend to heal faster.

Avoiding One-Sport Athletes

Playing one sport in junior and senior high school is the social equivalent of going steady with one person for six or seven years. Both can inhibit social and psychological development, promote unrealistic expectations of the nature of the relationship, and restrict the child's scope of experiences. Young athletes tend to focus on one sport for a couple of reasons. One is that responsibilities at home or in the community permit only one sport.

An extreme example of responsibilities at home is that of a couple of boys on one team in Wisconsin; they were allowed by their parents to come to practice only after school but not to play in the Friday night games! They lived on farms and had chores from 5:00 in the afternoon until dinner time. In spite of the peculiarity of the situation, however, it was a joy working with them. They came to practice each day for one reason—the love of athletics. We sorely missed them on Friday nights, but we will remember them always for their complete love of the game.

Obviously, these kinds of student athletes are rare. There may be other kinds of responsibilities that restrict an athlete's total involvement in a school's athletic program; a big reason, however, involves his or her perception that other sports will increase the probability of injury or interfere with individual progress. Often, coaches or parents contribute to the situation by creating in young athletes the kind of stress that allows only enough psychic energy for one sport.

At other times, coaches may restrict their players to only one sport to prevent injury, to promote team goals, to buy time during the off-season to refine the athlete's specialized skills, to increase opportunities for tournament play, or to improve the athlete's chances for a scholarship. In combination, these reasons tend to create friction among coaches, restrict the athlete's experiences with other coaches and players, result in increased stress on the athlete, and promote unrealistic expectations of the future.

Even when expectations are realistic, this kind of specialization often results in an overemphasis on the value of athletics over academics, inhibiting personal and educational growth. Whether an athlete is performing an athletic skill, lifting a weight, or establishing personal values, *balance* is important. Once the athlete, his or her parents, or a coach creates an imbalance, injury becomes probable. The injury may be physical or psychological; it can be nonetheless debilitating.

Our job as coaches is to encourage our young athletes to develop a range of diverse skills in order to expand upon their options as they approach adulthood. These skills are both athletic and academic. When athletic, they should reflect, whenever possible, broad involvement in the extracurricular opportunities provided by most schools. Such an attitude sells the importance of your fitness program. It promotes development of the total athlete and the total person.

Selling the Program to Adults

Much of what we have discussed in the previous sections will sell the program to adults as well as to young athletes. Once parents and school administrators understand your focus and realize the nature of your involvement with youngsters, they will support your program. Good fitness and athletic programs meet the developmental needs of students, satisfy the expectations of parents, and provide the kind of public relations value that administrators seek in school programs. They tend to provide very sensible advantages for students.

Reduction of Injuries

One of the most obvious advantages is the reduction of injuries for young athletes. Injury prevention is critically important and warrants the attention of young people and adults. Studies conducted by the National Athletic Trainers' Association (NATA) reveal that approximately 1.3 million high school students incur sports injuries each year. An additional several hundred thousand get hurt in junior high schools.

In addition, according to U.S. News and World Report, an estimated one-third of all sports injuries occur in children from 5 to 14 years of age. Injury sidelined more than a third of all high school football players and almost a quarter of girls high school basketball players. This rapid rise of athletic injury is directly attributable to an increased national emphasis on sports competition and, interestingly, the relatively poor physical condition of today's young athletes.

Fortunately, statistics also indicate that approximately 70 to 75 percent of all these injuries are relatively minor and interfere with participation for no more than a week. Of special interest to parents and coaches, however, is the assertion from sports physiologists that many of these injuries result from overuse of particular muscles in the body. Constantly repeated motions damage joints, tendons, ligaments, and muscles. Researchers indicate that, most often, such overuse results from overtraining and concentration on one sport.

Others result from careless training techniques or poor fundamental skills. An obvious selling point for your fitness program is the fact that these same researchers are calling for improved training not only to enhance performance but to cut down on the sharply increasing incidence of injury to young athletes. Use the reproducible in figure 10-5 to share such information with administrators and parents. You might even share it with the local newspapers to garner community support for your program.

A related point involves the improved likelihood of your school's finding appropriate insurance for athletes with the guarantee that they are receiving important fitness care. The NATA has gone on record often, encouraging parents and school officials to provide appropriate health care for student athletes. A comprehensive fitness program may be "just what the doctor ordered."

Figure 10-5

THE ATHLETE'S NEED FOR TOTAL FITNESS

INTRODUCTION

Recent statistics indicate that approximately one and a half million young athletes incur sports injuries each year. In fact, an estimated one-third of all our nation's sports injuries in any given year occur in children from ages 5 to 14. Injury routinely sidelines about a third of all interscholastic football players and almost a quarter of girls' interscholastic basketball players. Fortunately, most of these injuries are minor, keeping young athletes sidelined for only a week. Unfortunately, many of them are severe, resulting in lost participation, curtailed sports activity, and permanent damage.

A COUPLE OF CAUSES

Perhaps the most obvious cause of such injury is the nation's increased emphasis on sports. More and more young adults are competing in athletics every year. Many of them are unprepared for the demands such sports place on their bodies. A related cause involves the levels of fitness young athletes achieve before entering competition. Many do not have access to the kinds of facilities that promote high levels of fitness. The result is increased injury and mediocre levels of performance.

RECOMMENDATION

Our school should (implement a/constantly improve our) fitness program to improve the performance levels of our young athletes and prevent their unnecessary injury. A wide variety of stories and statistics constantly remind us that weightlifting and cardiovascular fitness programs dramatically eliminate the incidence of injury in schools. Our students deserve such protection. Information regarding cost and logistics is available. I would be pleased to discuss each of these issues at a time that is convenient for everyone.

© 1995 by Michael D. Koehler

Needs of Female Athletes

Several researchers recently have discovered that injuries for women tend to be sport-specific as opposed to gender-specific. This is an important finding, given early and dwindling opinion that girls and women are too fragile to engage in competitive sports. Consider, for example, this quote from a sportswriter in the *New York Times* in 1953: "There's nothing feminine or enchanting about a girl with beads of perspiration on her alabaster brow....any self-respecting schoolboy can achieve superior performances to any woman champion."

At the time of this article, Avery Brundage, the president of the International Olympic Committee, was recommending that women be barred from Olympic competition. What Brundage and the *Times* sportswriter didn't realize at the time was that a female Olympic sprinter (Florence Joyner Griffith), several years hence, would have beaten Bobby Morrow, the gold medalist in the 1956 Olympics in Melbourne, only three years after Brundage and his friend were recommending the exclusion of women.

That girls and women have proven their courage and significant skill goes without saying. Many of the finest athletes in the world are women, and the future promises much more of the same, particularly if women's programs can maintain and even improve upon the support they receive currently. Certainly, more needs to be done for them, but the hard-earned opportunities have featured amazing talent and have provided role models for boys as well as girls.

Research, however, makes a couple of additional points. Already mentioned in this section, the loss of the menstrual cycle can cause women's bones to become brittle, resulting in an increase of stress fractures. Overtraining, therefore, must be closely monitored, especially for girls. In addition, doctors at Good Samaritan Hospital in New York indicate that, although women may not suffer significantly different injuries from those suffered by men, they do suffer some at increased rates.

Musculoskeletal disorders may be more prevalent in women than in men. Knee pain resulting from running and cycling may be especially pronounced. Doctors indicate that abdominal injuries may also be more prevalent. Coaches are advised, therefore, to recognize such potential problems and to promote for female athletes the kinds of training activities that remedy and avoid these injuries. Your fitness program addresses these results—offering yet another selling point for total fitness.

Getting into the Community

Finally, the coach who garners community support goes a long way toward securing administrative support for his or her program. Many schools, especially those that enjoy good relationships with parents and businesses, tend to be very responsive to the needs and expectations of the community. They learn early that the community is "the source from which all good things flow," and they do whatever is necessary, within reason, to satisfy parents, particularly influential members of the community.

Keep the following organizations and activities in mind, then, when seeking community support for your fitness program. Many of them can donate needed funds or equipment to start, maintain, or improve the program, and others can encourage or even pressure your school's administration to provide the support you need.

• *Organizations of retired teachers.* Upon retiring, most teachers join local or state organizations for the social, political, and recreational services and programs they provide. Many of these organizations provide periodic luncheons to update members on state or federal legislation that affects them, to discuss relevant issues in education, or to listen to speakers who can share statistics and information about total fitness for young and old. Such groups will benefit from your message and may contain individuals who can use their influence with the board of education or administration to help you.

• *Fraternal and service groups.* Organizations like Kiwanis, Rotary, the Optimists, Knights of Columbus, Lions, and the Jaycees are always seeking speakers for luncheon and other occasions. They particularly enjoy listening to presentations about local athletic programs and discussing issues with coaches. At such times, coaches can share statistics about the nature of injuries in interscholastic athletics—and about the value of total fitness as a way to prevent them. These organizations consist of very influential community members who can be powerful allies as you promote the need for your program.

•*Advisory Councils, PTAs, and Parent and Booster Clubs.* School-parent organizations constantly seek only the best for their young people and are often disposed to finance or supplement the school's efforts to finance projects such as fitness programs. Many members of these groups and the parents of athletes are quick to organize fundraisers within the community to upgrade athletic facilities and programs, particularly once they have been convinced of their need to prevent injury.

• *Women's Clubs, Daughters of the American Revolution, and the League of Women Voters.* Often, the most active and influential people in the community are women. Women's organizations are energetic and generally very receptive to educational needs, especially when such needs are well documented by statistics. Use the reproducible in figure 10-6 to make preliminary contact with them as well as with other groups already discussed in this section. With slight changes, it can be used as well with the community's feeder schools.

• *Elementary schools and junior highs.* Evening meetings with elementary and junior high school students and their parents are effective ways to promote academics, discuss high school orientation, highlight high school athletics, and combat drug abuse. Such meetings provide needy information to families in the community and garner support from a variety of parents, many of whom otherwise might not have the chance to meet you.

• *The board of education.* Accompany your school's athletic director or P.E. department head to meetings with the board of education to discuss school programs and, in your case, the value of your fitness program.

• *Meetings with local business organizations.* Within the past several years, school districts have been seeking supplementary sources of revenue to maintain extracurricular programs. The national increase of girls' programs and the growing participation of both boys and girls in most programs have strained fixed budgets and forced schools to search the community for financial help. Some schools have adopt-

Figure 10-6

COMMUNITY CONTACT

Date

Name of Person
Name of Organization
Address of Organization
City, State, Zip

Dear :

I've been a member of the staff at (name) School for (number) years and have some stories, facts, and figures that you and your group might find interesting. I would enjoy speaking at an upcoming luncheon to provide what I think is valuable and entertaining information.

Did you know, for example

• That a study at a major Midwestern University revealed that steroid use has dropped off by as much as 50 percent?

• That alcohol use is still high in college; almost 88 percent of all college students drink?

• That the use of cocaine has dropped off considerably? Several years ago, 17 percent of all college students used it; the number is now only 1.1 percent.

• That marijuana use has dropped off by as much as 40 percent?

• That you'll find as much cholesterol in fried calamari as in a four-egg omelet?

• That just fifteen to twenty minutes of jogging three times a week can improve your fitness level and promote permanent weight loss?

• That participation in interscholastic sports activity has increased significantly within the past few years?

• That almost a million and a half young athletes incur athletic injuries each year, many of which can be avoided through involvement in effective fitness programs?

More statistics like these are available and could lead to some very interesting discussion during one of your luncheon meetings. Please give me a call to discuss the time and place. Yours is a very important organization in our community; I would enjoy meeting you and your members.

Sincerely yours,

(Your name)

© 1995 by Michael D. Koehler

ed "pay-for-play" programs, soliciting funds from parents to finance their child's sports participation.

Other schools have threatened the elimination of sports programs to scare communities into passing referenda. Still others meet with local businesses to secure sponsorship for specific sports programs or, more relevant to your purposes, for the development of fitness programs that help students and adults and provide valuable PR for the businesses. Use the reproducible in figure 10-7 to initiate contact with one or more businesses in your area.

• *Professional sports team.* Some professional teams have donated funds to inner-city schools to help them maintain sports programs. As with corporate sponsorship, professional teams realize the satisfaction and the public relations value of repaying the community for its support. The players themselves benefit by making their sizable salaries more acceptable to the community when such sponsorship is publicized.

Finally, coaches of fitness programs should consider inviting adults, both teachers and parents, to use the fitness facility on weekends or at times during the day when students are in class. Such a policy is especially appropriate in communities where fitness facilities are unavailable. The parents and other community members who join, particularly once they realize the benefits of total fitness, will support the program with their membership dues and by their willingness to promote the program with school administrators.

Keeping the Program Visible

It may be hard to prove that Coca-Cola is "The Real Thing" or that Ford "has a better idea," but neither company really cares. The important thing is that, from their perspective, these slogans have kept their products visible to you and me. Often, that alone can do much to sell a product or a program. Keep the following ideas in mind, therefore, to publicize your fitness program.

• *Slogans.* Have all the athletes in the school compete to identify the slogan that best exemplifies your fitness program. Some we've seen include: "YAREALLYGOT-TAWANNA," "Fitness for Life," "Mind, heart, and body," and "Performance equals Preparation." Obviously, there are many others. The important thing is that you and your kids develop the one that is most appropriate for you and your program. You might provide a prize for the best slogan and recognize the student in one or more press releases to the local papers.

• *T-shirts.* T-shirts serve two important purposes for your program. They serve as incentives for young athletes and help advertise the slogan that you and your kids created. You might put the name of the school on the front of the T-shirt with the slogan underneath, then put "100% Participation" on the back for those youngsters who showed up for every workout during the summer. Other ideas for the back of the T-shirts include: "Aiming for Perfection," "Nothing Less than Conference Champs," "Win 'em All This Fall," or "One Goal-Be Undefeated." Obviously, the best slogan for the T-shirt is the one that reflects the intentions of your program.

• *Liftathons or runathons.* Have the athletes solicit pledges from teachers, parents, and members of the community for the total amount of weight they lift or the

Figure 10-7

CONTACTING BUSINESSES

Date

Name of Person
Name of Business
Address of Business
City, State Zip

Dear   :

Let me introduce myself. I have been working with the athletes at (name) School for (number) years and have enjoyed watching many of them develop into responsible young adults. Unfortunately, I have also watched many of them incur career-ending injuries, many of which could have been avoided by an appropriate fitness program. Did you know, for example, that almost a million and a half youngsters injure themselves each year playing sports? Fortunately, most of these injuries last for just up to a week; some, however, last a lifetime.

I would like to provide the kind of fitness program at (name) School that will enhance the performance of our young athletes and enable them to avoid the kinds of injuries that curtail careers and leave some of them permanently disabled. I hope you will help.

I would appreciate meeting with you sometime within the near future to discuss your sponsorship of a fitness program for our school. The donation you provide would be tax-deductible, would be recognized by our local and, perhaps, national community, and would do much to help our young athletes participate in sports with increased safety.

Thanks for your time, and I look forward to hearing from you regarding a meeting in the near future.

Sincerely yours,

(Your Name)

© 1995 by Michael D. Koehler

number of miles they run during a specified time. Such competitions promote good training habits, bring in needed finances for equipment, and maintain the visibility of the program.

• *Competitions within the school.* Invite some of the coaches and other faculty members to compete with some of the school's strongest athletes. Bench press, clean and jerk, sit-up, push-up, and other weightlifting competitions promote interest and enthusiasm in the school and can bring students and faculty closer together. You can run the competition after school and charge a modest admission fee, the proceeds to go to the fitness program for equipment.

We saw one such competition where a 56-year-old counselor bench-pressed 390 pounds, beating every football player in the school! The young athletes suddenly developed new respect for the counselor; they also realized how hard they had to work if they ever hoped to compete on the college level. The weight room was suddenly teeming with renewed enthusiasm.

• *Press releases.* Use the form in figure 10-8 to notify local papers of winners in slogan contests, weightlifting competitions, and activities that are taking place in the fitness program. Simply put a short title on the release just above your name and mail it to the local papers. Keep copies of the form on hand; you may want to send releases weekly.

Let's Wrap It Up

Some sports programs across the country have eliminated the handshake after a contest because of fighting. Unfortunately, such a practice seems yet another sign of the times, one that reveals the unwillingness or the inability of some coaches to teach youngsters the values that are so important not only to athletic competition but to their future happiness and success.

We believe in teaching youngsters self-respect and individual responsibility, and no program in the school holds greater potential for teaching both than athletics. The school's fitness program emphasizes hard work as well as the satisfaction to be derived from it. These are larger issues for youngsters, certainly as important as improved performance and the prevention of injuries. That you and I reflect our awareness of these values is critical to the success of our athletic programs.

Recent statistics indicate that crime is exploding in our inner cities. As disturbing, the statistics also indicate that violent crime in many of the nation's *suburbs* has increased by 42 percent. Some metropolitan communities are seeking to provide evening basketball as an alternative to street activity for youngsters. Such a response to crime in the streets may be a good idea. Fitness programs in schools are every bit as good.

Obviously, fitness programs in schools in high crime areas are not the only answer, and they may require intensive supervision to secure the safety of everyone involved. The point is, a youngster's commitment to a sports program gives him or her a present reality and a possible future. In the meantime, it teaches *all* kids the kinds of values our society needs, and it associates them with people who care about them and can give them a sense of direction.

Figure 10-8

PRESS RELEASE

(Title of release here)

FOR IMMEDIATE RELEASE

(NAMES OF LOCAL PAPERS)

Your Name
Your Address
Your Phone Number

(Body of release here)

© 1995 by Michael D. Koehler

Some segments of our society are claiming that an absence of family values has caused the problems in our streets. They may be right, but we are also convinced that the failure of many of our social institutions—welfare agencies, local governments, police departments, courts, and, yes, schools—has contributed in varying ways to the demise of family values. The almost aggressive insensitivity of bureaucratic government and the well-documented inability of *some* schools to promote self-esteem in all their students have contributed as much to the decay of values as the disruptions that are evident in many families across the country.

Athletics really can lead the way in promoting these needed values among youngsters. Currently, the media would have us believe that many athletics programs have simply fallen in step with other segments of society that promote self-indulgence over self-worth. They may be correct—in some instances—but they're not correct in most. Our experience has been that high school and junior high programs are fortunate to have the most dedicated coaches in the country working with young people.

We hope this book helps them continue with their important work.

APPENDIX

The following pages contain information and exercises for your student athletes taken from the body of this resource to create a *Total Fitness Booklet*. Make as many copies as you need for the athletes on your teams or in your classes.

TOTAL FITNESS BOOKLET

Directions: This is your personal fitness booklet. Be sure to have it with you during each workout session and during the summer months or other times when you will be maintaining your off-season fitness levels. We will be referring to the booklet frequently and using it for examples, so *don't lose it!*

See me if you have any questions.

Coaches are reminded that many of the exercises in this booklet are beyond the capability of young or underdeveloped athletes. Be sure to develop booklets accordingly, even mixing and matching the pages to create booklets that may accommodate different strength levels of young athletes. Also be sure to refer to the text of the book for reminders about safety and proper execution. SAFETY FIRST is the primary reminder in the book. Young athletes must always exercise within the framework of their maturity and ability levels.

TABLE OF CONTENTS

Why Physical Fitness? 7
Fitness Training 8
Why Flexibility? 9
The Key Word Is Safety 10
Ten Tips for Effective Stretching 11
Flexibility Exercises 12
Maintaining Your Flexibility 17
Interval Training 18
Off-Season Workout: Soccer, Football, Field Hockey 19
Off-Season Workout: Basketball, Volleyball, Badminton, and Track 20
Off-Season Workout: Baseball, Softball, Field Events 21
Off-Season Workout: Wrestling, Gymnastics, and Swimming 22
Complementary Exercises for Both In- and Off-Season Workouts 23
A Warm-Up Reminder 25
Warming-Up Activities 26
Use a Belt! 27
Pain vs. Fatigue 28
Exercises for the Abdominals 29

Your Complete Workout (Exercise 1-10) 35

Weightlifting Programs. 42

    Level A. 42

    Level B. 43

    Level C. 44

    Level D 45

Descriptions of Exercises (Exercise 1-25). 46

    Football Exercises: Linemen 62

    Football Exercises: Running Backs. 63

    Wrestling Exercises 64

    Basketball Exercises. 65

    Baseball/Softball Exercises 66

    Gymnastics Exercises 67

    Volleyball Exercises 68

    Golf/Field Hockey Exercises 69

    Swimming Exercises. 70

    Tennis Exercises 71

    Track Exercises, Sprinters and Runners 72

    Track Exercises, Field Events 73

Eating Your Way to Improved Performance 74

The Warning Signs of Drug Use 75

Fitness: Exhilaration, not Exhaustion. 76

If You Want Total Conditioning, You Need 77

WHY PHYSICAL FITNESS?

INTRODUCTION

Physical fitness is different from general health. Good health implies an absence of sickness; your general health may be pretty good. But your physical fitness may not be good enough to realize many of the goals you have established for yourself. That's why we offer this fitness program, to enable you to develop the cardiovascular and muscular strength to achieve your goals, many of which deal with sports. Other goals probably deal with community activities and coursework. Physical fitness will provide the energy and strength you need to engage successfully in a wide range of activities. It will also encourage you to develop the self-discipline you may need to improve your athletic performance as well as your success in class.

KEEP IN MIND

If you are a beginner: Don't push yourself too hard right away. You have lots of time to achieve the fitness levels you want. Excellent physical fitness doesn't occur overnight. You can't take a pill to get there in a day or two. Even if such a pill were available, you wouldn't want to take it anyway. The *process* of developing a physically fit body involves a lot of good times. The associations you develop with fellow students, teachers, and coaches will bring you a great deal of pleasure, and the hard work you experience will give you genuine feelings of accomplishment.

So don't look for an easy way. There isn't one, just a lot of enjoyable—and hard—work, but it will involve the kind of experience that will make you proud of who you are and who you are becoming.

ALSO REMEMBER

Work closely with your coach and fellow students. We will be emphasizing some very important safety pointers as we engage in running and lifting exercises. Pay careful attention to them. You don't want an unnecessary injury interfering with your training or performance in one or more areas. And remember that we all have different potential fitness levels. Don't develop the habit of comparing yourself with others. Stay with the program that is right for you. We will work closely with you to develop a program tailored specifically for you. Stick with it. The only person you're competing with is *you*. It's a competition you'll never lose if you work out with the right attitude.

Good luck with your program, and any time you have questions, be sure to contact your coach.

© 1995 by Michael D. Koehler

FITNESS TRAINING
FOR WHAT PURPOSE?

Let's take a look at fitness training and discuss what it means for different people. When most adults join fitness clubs, they usually are interested in losing weight and/or improving their general health and appearance. They want to look good—and have fun. They wear colorful jogging outfits, break a sweat on the treadmill or the bike, watch their diets, and even lift weights. In essence, they do everything athletes do—but less vigorously. They want their workouts to be fun, a total experience that makes them look good and feel good about themselves. When their workouts stop being fun, they don't want to do them any more.

Athletes are involved in fitness training for other reasons. We have gotten involved in our respective sports because we enjoy them; we have fun playing them. But we recognize that the goals we have developed for ourselves in these sports require a kind of training that goes well beyond colorful jogging outfits and 20 minutes on the treadmill. Fitness training for athletic participation is much more demanding than fitness training for general conditioning. We realize that the kind of training we do often is *not* fun; it's hard work. It pushes us beyond our physical limits and often leaves us sore and stiff.

We also realize, however, that, without it, we will never realize our athletic goals. As athletes, we know that "fun" is the byproduct of hard work. We know that when we start running around looking for fun for its own sake, especially if we don't have to earn it, it rarely makes us genuinely happy. Our happiest times provide a deep sense of personal satisfaction and improved self-esteem—and that comes from hard work. That's the way it is with sports now, and that's the way it will be with everything we do later in life.

So for now let's call that hard work a

Full and total commitment to
Useful and vigorous exercise that brings us the
Needed strength to realize our athletic goals.

REMEMBER:
GOOD ATHLETES SEEK OUT HARD WORK;
THEY KNOW THAT THE FUN WILL FOLLOW.

© 1995 by Michael D. Koehler

WHY FLEXIBILITY?

FLEXIBILITY AND TOTAL CONDITIONING

Cardiovascular and weight training are just two of the four components of a good conditioning program. They tend to be the most publicized, so most young athletes overlook the benefits of good nutrition and flexibility. A future section of your booklet explains the value of good nutrition. For now, let's look at the benefits of improved flexibility.

HOW GOOD DO YOU WANT TO BE?

Let's put it this way: you'll never even come close to your true athletic potential if you don't work hard to improve your flexibility. Your performance will be limited because your body won't enjoy a full range of motion, and you'll find yourself injured more often than your more flexible teammates. Flexible muscles have greater elasticity, more snap; they enable you to take longer, quicker strides, to jump further and higher. And they are able to withstand the punishment that athletic competition imposes on your body.

SOME MORE SPECIFICS

Vigorous exercise causes forceful contraction of muscles and tendons. Well-stretched muscles provide greater force in each movement, thereby improving agility and speed. In addition, because flexibility prevents muscles from tightening up quickly, it reduces the potential for injury.

SO WHAT DO YOU DO?

It's simple. Develop the habit of warming up your muscles and stretching them for 20 to 30 seconds *before, during,* and *after* competition. When you improve flexibility before and during vigorous exercise, you improve performance and reduce the possibility of injury to muscles and tendons. When you stretch after vigorous exercise, you help eliminate some of the chemicals in your muscles that make them sore the next day. Stretching, therefore, is a very important, if misunderstood, aspect of total conditioning. Great athletes have developed the habit of warming up and stretching their muscles.

If you want to be a great athlete, remember to do the same thing. And remember not to hurry the exercises. Do them slowly and steadily—deliberately—in order to get the most out of them. I'll help with a periodic reminder.

REMEMBER:
GOOD FLEXIBILITY BEFORE, DURING,
AND AFTER VIGOROUS EXERCISE

© 1995 by Michael D. Koehler

THE KEY WORD IS SAFETY

Flexibility is a significant part of our conditioning program because it promotes the full range of motion that results in improved performance and the reduced potential for injury. Unfortunately, if performed carelessly, flexibility exercises can cause injury. Our job is to make sure that doesn't happen.

Some Information

Following is an explanation of the different forms of flexibility exercises. Your understanding of each one will be the best first step in avoiding injury:

• *Active*. Active stretching involves the kinds of exercises you can peform alone. Study each of the stretching exercises in your booklet carefully before doing them. Your improved understanding of them will significantly reduce any possibility of injury.

• *Passive*. Passive exercises involve the use of a partner, someone who helps you stretch muscles by gradually applying pressure to different parts of your body. Passive exercises do a great job stretching muscles but can result in injury if your partner pushes too quickly or too hard. When we explain passive exercises, we will discuss this potential problem. Remember, *no horseplay* during passive stretching exercises!

• *Static*. Static exercises involve the gradual and deliberate stretching of a muscle or tendon for at least 20 to 30 seconds, sometimes more. The longer the muscle is stretched without pain, the more flexible it will become. *All* the stretching exercises you will be doing should be done statically.

• *Ballistic*. Ballistic exercises involve bouncing or forcing the muscle or tendon to stretch too quickly or severely. We already have emphasized the importance of a gradual and relaxed approach to stretching exercises. *None* of the exercises in your booklet, therefore, should be performed ballistically.

Some Advice

First of all, stretch before, during, and after vigorous exercise. Do it statically, *not* ballistically. And don't do any of these exercises carelessly, especially if you are stretching passively. If you have questions, talk to one of your coaches.

© 1995 by Michael D. Koehler

TEN TIPS FOR EFFECTIVE STRETCHING

The following ten tips provide an excellent summary of the importance of warming-up and stretching exercises. They also provide important pointers. Read this information carefully.

1. Stretching should be preceded by a warm-up. Warming up increases blood flow and raises muscle temperature. Both are very important for muscle elasticity. Without a proper warm-up, stretching could result in sprains, strains, or muscle tears.

2. You should feel slight discomfort during stretching, but it should be mild and brief. If you feel pain—*stop immediately*.

3. Be sure to stretch at least 3 to 4 times a week.

4. Stretching sessions should last at least 15 to 20 minutes. You should hold each stretch for at least 30 seconds, making sure you build up slowly by the end of the 30 seconds.

5. Stretch major muscle groups first, then smaller. This ensures that the smaller groups have been slightly warmed up. Large muscle groups handle shock better than small muscle groups. Small muscles injure more frequently.

6. Stretch within one hour before strenuous exercise or competition to prevent injury and to prepare the muscles for maximum contraction and force.

7. *Don't bounce!* Stretching should be slow, steady, and relaxed.

8. Try to isolate muscles being stretched. You'll be able to feel it when a muscle has been properly isolated.

9. Stretch *during* and *after* vigorous exercise. This prevents muscles from tightening up and reduces the chance of soreness.

10. Don't give up because you are less flexible than others. Flexibility varies from person to person. You may not notice an improved range of motion immediately, but if you keep working at it—*you will!*

REMEMBER:
YOU HAVE TO STRETCH FOR PERFECTION!

© 1995 by Michael D. Koehler

FLEXIBILITY EXERCISES

DIRECTIONS:

The following 33 flexibility exercises are self-explanatory. Look carefully at each diagram and perform the exercise as illustrated. You may perform all or some of them, depending upon your coach's instructions. The important thing is that you increase the flexibility of the muscles you will be using during practice or competition. Talk to your coach about the exercises that he or she wants you to emphasize.

© 1995 by Michael D. Koehler

© 1995 by Michael D. Koehler

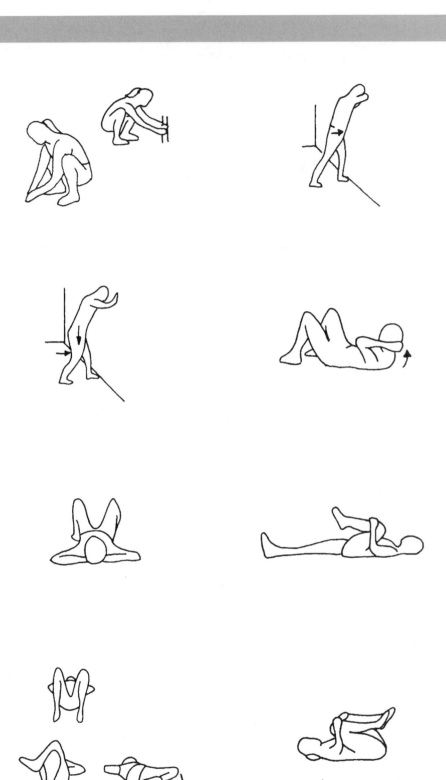

© 1995 by Michael D. Koehler

© 1995 by Michael D. Koehler

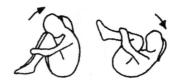

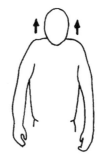

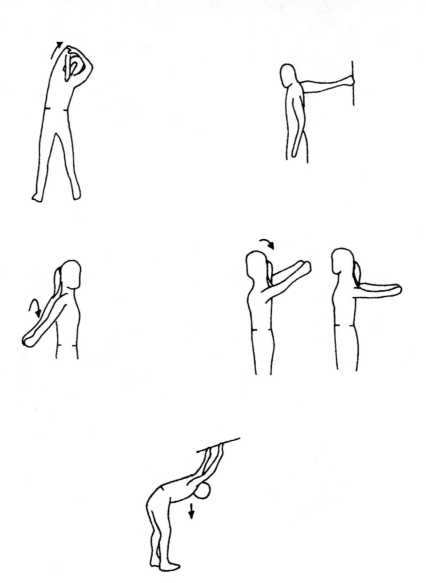

© 1995 by Michael D. Koehler

MAINTAINING YOUR FLEXIBILITY

DIRECTIONS

Perform the following flexibility exercises whenever possible during practice or competition, particularly on hot days. Muscles tend to tighten up during vigorous exercise and can pull if athletes fail to maintain flexibility. The exercises are easy to perform and can be done during any lapse in the action. They are appropriate for all sports; their performance should become a habit for you.

THE EXERCISES

Each exercise is named and referred to by the number it was assigned in figure 2-2. Again, these are exercises that can be performed whenever possible during practice and competition.

Quadriceps Stretch (Exercise 10) - This exercise can be performed while using a teammate for stability. The quadriceps are pulled or strained easily on hot days, Perform this exercise at any time, but especially when you feel your quads tightening up.

Groin Stretch (Exercise 13) - Groin muscles also pull easily. This exercise will avoid that.

Hamstring and Achilles Tendon Stretch (Exercise 15) - These areas of the body are pulled more than any other in sport, especially on hot days. Use a teammate for support while you perform this exercise.

Neck Relaxer (Exercise 26) - This exercise helps prevent neck strains and is relaxing as well. Do it to loosen up your neck and shoulder muscles, especially whenever they feel tight or before you perform a complex skill such as shooting a free throw.

Shoulder Stretch (Exercise 27) - This, too, relaxes the muscles and relieves tension.

Lat Stretch (Exercise 29) - This exercise loosens up the latissimus dorsi, the shoulders, and the rib cage.

Others - You and your coach are advised to look through all the exercises in figure 2-2 to find more that will help during practice or competition. Remember: flexibility *before, during,* and *after* vigorous exercise!

© 1995 by Michael D. Koehler

INTERVAL TRAINING

IMPORTANT: The following program is very demanding and should not be attempted if you haven't discussed it with your coach. Be sure to talk to your coach before engaging in interval training to be sure that the program is right for you.

A General Program

If your coach has given you permission to engage in interval training, read the following program and perform *all* of it very carefully:

1. *STRETCH* yourself completely to guarantee that you don't pull any muscles. Stretch for at least 10 to 15 minutes, maybe more, depending upon how tight you are from previous exercise. Use the stretching and flexibility exercises in your booklet or get some from your coach.
2. *WARM UP* for at least 5 to 10 minutes. It should be a vigorous warm-up, not exhausting. Do it at approximately 60 percent of your maximum heart rate. Again, refer to your booklet or see your coach for specific warm-up exercises.
3. *SPRINT* for 30 to 90 seconds, depending on your particular sport (see your coach for specifics), at 80 percent to 90 percent of your maximum heart rate.
4. *Jog* for 90 to 180 seconds, depending upon the length of your sprint. During this time, be sure your heart rate drops to 70 percent of its maximum. Be sure not to do any more repetitions until your heart rate drops to this level.
5. *Do 4 to 6 more repetitions* of the above program.
6. *Walk very slowly* until your heart rate drops to at least 60 percent of its maximum.
7. *Do another 4 to 6 repetitions* of the entire program.
8. *Cool down* for at least 5 to 10 minutes, using the cool-down activities in your booklet or those suggested by your coach. All cool-down exercises should be done at no more than 60 percent of your maximum heart rate.

REMEMBER:
THIS IS A VERY CHALLENGING PROGRAM.
SEE YOUR COACH BEFORE STARTING IT—
YOUR FAMILY DOCTOR, TOO, IF YOU OR YOUR PARENTS HAVE QUESTIONS!

© 1995 by Michael D. Koehler

OFF-SEASON WORKOUT
SOCCER, FOOTBALL, FIELD HOCKEY

INTRODUCTION

The following activities are designed to accommodate your aerobic and anaerobic needs during the off-season. You will be following a 5-day program. It probably is a good idea to have days one and two on Monday and Tuesday and days three, four, and five on Thursday, Friday, and Saturday. Take Wednesdays and Sundays off to rest your muscles. Remember, these exercises are for your cardiovascular system; they are *not* to replace your weight workout.

See me or your coach for specific examples of skill-related exercises. They will vary according to your sport. Your coach may also have some isolated skills he or she wants you to work on during the off-season. Be sure to write them down and incorporate them into your total workout. If you have any questions, be sure to see me.

YOUR WORKOUT

DAY ONE: 3-mile jog. Remember to take your time; jog within your aerobic range.
DAY TWO: 2-mile jog, followed by 10 to 15 minutes of jumping rope.
DAY THREE: Ten minutes of skill-related activity. This should provide a good warm-up for the next two exercises. Next, run a fast mile; don't sprint it but stride it as strongly as you can. Finally, cycle for 20 minutes.
DAY FOUR: 4-mile jog. Again, run it slowly in order to stay well within your aerobic range.
DAY FIVE: 10 minutes of rope jumping, followed by 10 minutes of skill-related activity. Conclude the workout with 10 minutes of swimming. Swim for 10 minutes. This is a good cool-down for your workout.

MY SKILL-RELATED EXERCISES ARE:

**TAKE SOME TIME TO RELAX YOUR MUSCLES,
THEN DO YOUR WEIGHT WORKOUT. REMEMBER:**

SAFETY FIRST

**IF YOU FEEL TIRED, BE SURE TO REST UP
BEFORE STARTING YOUR WEIGHT WORKOUT.**

© 1995 by Michael D. Koehler

OFF-SEASON WORKOUT
BASKETBALL, VOLLEYBALL, BADMINTON, AND TRACK

INTRODUCTION

The following activities are designed to accommodate your aerobic and anaerobic needs during the off-season. You will be following a 5-day program. It probably is a good idea to have days one and two on Monday and Tuesday and days three, four, and five on Thursday, Friday, and Saturday. Take Wednesdays and Sundays off to rest your muscles. Remember, these exercises are for your cardiovascular system; they are *not* to replace your weight workout.

See me or your coach for specific examples of skill-related exercises; then write them on the bottom of the page. They will vary according to your sport. Your coach may have some isolated skills he or she wants you to work on during the off-season. Be sure to write them down and incorporate them into your total workout. If you have any questions, be sure to see me.

YOUR WORKOUT

DAY ONE: 3-mile jog. Remember to stay well within your aerobic range. Conclude with 20 minutes of sport-related skills.

DAY TWO: 2-mile jog. Again, stay within your aerobic range. Then, climb stairs for 10 minutes, followed by 10 minutes of rope jumping.

DAY THREE: 5-mile jog. Yes, you can do it; just stay within your aerobic range.

DAY FOUR: 1-mile jog, primarily as a warm-up activity. If you are a basketball, volleyball, or badminton player, find some teammates and play a 30-minute game. If a track athlete, practice your starts by taking 10-yard sprints. Do this at least 15 times, then jog another mile.

DAY FIVE: 4-mile jog, followed by 10 minutes of sport-related skill practice. Conclude with a 10-minute swim.

MY SKILL-RELATED EXERCISES ARE:

**TAKE SOME TIME TO RELAX YOUR MUSCLES, THEN
DO YOUR WEIGHT WORKOUT. REMEMBER:**

SAFETY FIRST

**IF YOU FEEL TIRED, BE SURE TO REST UP
BEFORE STARTING YOUR WEIGHT WORKOUT.**

© 1995 by Michael D. Koehler

© 1995 by Michael D. Koehler

OFF-SEASON WORKOUT
BASEBALL, SOFTBALL, FIELD EVENTS

INTRODUCTION

The following activities are designed to accommodate your aerobic and anaerobic needs during the off-season. You will be following a 5-day program. It probably is a good idea to have days one and two on Monday and Tuesday and days three, four, and five on Thursday, Friday, and Saturday. Take Wednesdays and Sundays off to rest your muscles. Remember, these exercises are for your cardiovascular system; they are *not* to replace your weight workout.

See me or your coach for specific examples of skill-related exercises. They will vary according to your sport. Your coach may also have some isolated skills he or she wants you to work on during the off-season. Be sure to write them down and incorporate them into your total workout. If you have any questions, be sure to see me.

YOUR WORKOUT

DAY ONE: 2-mile jog. Take your time and run well within your aerobic range. Follow this with 20 minutes of sport-related skill practice.

DAY TWO: 1-mile jog. Take your time; this is a good warm-up activity. Follow it with 10 minutes of stairclimbing, then 10 minutes of jumping rope.

DAY THREE: 3-mile jog. Again, stay well within your aerobic range.

DAY FOUR: 1-mile jog, followed by 20 minutes of sport-related skill practice.

DAY FIVE: 2-mile jog, followed by 10 minutes of stairclimbing or jumping rope. Conclude with a 10-minute swim.

MY SKILL-RELATED EXERCISES ARE:

**TAKE SOME TIME TO RELAX YOUR MUSCLES, THEN
DO YOUR WEIGHT WORKOUT. REMEMBER:**

SAFETY FIRST

**IF YOU FEEL TIRED, BE SURE TO REST UP
BEFORE STARTING YOUR WEIGHT WORKOUT.**

OFF-SEASON WORKOUT
WRESTLING, GYMNASTICS, AND SWIMMING

INTRODUCTION

The following activities are designed to accommodate your aerobic and anaerobic needs during the off-season. You will be following a 5-day program. It probably is a good idea to have days one and two on Monday and Tuesday and days three, four, and five on Thursday, Friday, and Saturday. Take Wednesdays and Sundays off to rest your muscles. Remember, these exercises are for your cardiovascular system; they are *not* to replace your weight workout.

See me or your coach for specific examples of skill-related exercises. They will vary according to your sport. Your coach may have some isolated skills he or she wants you to work on during the off-season. Be sure to write them down and incorporate them into your total workout. If you have any questions, be sure to see me.

YOUR WORKOUT

DAY ONE: 3-mile jog. Remember to stay well within your aerobic range. This exercise is designed to improve your cardiovascular strength.

DAY TWO: 2-mile jog. Again, jog easily. Follow this with 10 minutes of jumping rope.

DAY THREE: 4-mile jog. Yes, you can do it. Just stay within your aerobic range, no matter how long it takes.

DAY FOUR: 1-mile jog, followed by 10 minutes of stairclimbing. Conclude with 10 minutes of rope jumping.

DAY FIVE: 2-mile jog, followed by 10 minutes of jumping rope. Conclude with 15 minutes of sport-related activity, followed by a 10-minute swim.

MY SKILL-RELATED EXERCISES ARE:

**TAKE SOME TIME TO RELAX YOUR MUSCLES, THEN
DO YOUR WEIGHT WORKOUT. REMEMBER:**

SAFETY FIRST

**IF YOU FEEL TIRED, BE SURE TO REST UP
BEFORE STARTING YOUR WEIGHT WORKOUT.**

© 1995 by Michael D. Koehler

COMPLEMENTARY EXERCISES FOR BOTH IN- AND OFF-SEASON WORKOUTS

SOMETHING TO THINK ABOUT

All athletes require speed and jumping ability. The following exercises are designed to improve both. You may not be able to do all of them. Do the ones you can, making the appropriate adjustments for each. Be sure to talk to your coach to develop a workout program that is just right for you, and ask him or her for demonstrations of all these exercises as needed.

WARM-UP EXERCISES

Perform these exercises deliberately. If you are outside and it is cold, do more of them. If it is warm, do them less frequently.

Walking Toe Up - Walk for approximately 20 yards on your heels, keeping your toes pointing up.

Skipping - Skip for approximately 20 yards, emphasizing the motion. Exaggerate it as much as possible.

Side-stepping - Move as quickly as possible sideways. Don't crossover step but exaggerate the movement of your arms.

Backward Run - Run backwards as fast as you can, bringing your heel up to your buttocks and extending your foot backward as you run.

JUMPING EXERCISES

Don't do all these exercises consecutively; do only those that you can do well. See your coach for the specific exercises for you. If you can't perform them successfully, you won't get much out of them. The purpose of these exercises is to put force into the ground and then get it out of the ground as you perform the jump. Do all these exercises on a relatively soft surface, something that will be easy on your joints. Do *not* do them on concrete or any other hard surface. All these exercises will improve your jumping ability and your speed.

Ankle jump - Keeping your legs straight and your feet together, spring off the balls of your feet, using only your ankles to jump off the ground. Do these for a distance of 10 yards, then come back 10 yards.

Jump-Ups - With your hands on your hips and your feet together, bounce up onto a box that is about a foot high. Be sure it is stable and covered with something soft, like a rug. Do this 10 to 15 times, stepping back down to the ground after each jump.

Backward Jump-Ups - Do the same bouncing motion, only do it backward. Be sure to keep your feet together and step back to the ground after each jump.

Standing Long Jump - Do 10 standing long jumps, pausing after each jump to gather yourself. Jump as far as you can on each jump.

Frog Jumps - These are like standing long jumps, only you will squat down and gather yourself like a frog before jumping again. These jumps are to be done consecu-

© 1995 by Michael D. Koehler

Frog Jumps - These are like standing long jumps, only you will squat down and gather yourself like a frog before jumping again. These jumps are to be done consecutively with little pausing between each one.

Off and On Box - Stand on the box and jump off backward. Use the force of your landing on the ground to jump back on the box immediately. Emphasize the bouncing motion and do this exercise 10 times consecutively.

Hurdle Jumps - With your feet approximately together, jump over a series of hurdles or another obstacle at an appropriate height for you. Emphasize the bouncing motion. Don't jump and stop to gather yourself. You should bounce over each obstacle. Do this approximately 7 or 8 times.

Puddle Jumping - Take 15 to 20 long, bounding strides, as if jumping over a series of puddles on the ground. Emphasize the motion of each long stride.

Again, talk to your coach to determine which of these exercises is best for you and the number of repetitions you should do. If a box is not available, find something that is stable and approximately 12" off the ground. If 12" is too high, lower the height until you can perform the exercise comfortably. The important thing is to use proper form in order to maximize your benefit from the exercise.

RUNNING

Conclude each jumping session with three to five 40-yard runs. Perform each run this way: Get in the starting position that is appropriate for your sport, an upright "ready" position if you play volleyball, basketball, or tennis, a stance if you play football or track. Explode out of the position and sprint hard for 20 yards. After the first 20 yards, stride hard for the remaining 20 yards, running as *relaxed* as possible. Don't run with fists or any strain on your face. Run as relaxed as possible. This final exercise will condition you to run easily and stride out, making you that much faster.

Again, see your coach for explanations of any of these exercises, and be sure to perform only those that you can do properly and comfortably. As always, *safety first* is our slogan. We want you to improve your fitness levels, not injure yourself.

© 1995 by Michael D. Koehler

A WARM-UP REMINDER

As indicated already in the flexibility section, a good warm-up is essential before vigorous exercise. Without it, athletes risk injury to muscles, tendons, and joints. Read the following information—and FOLLOW IT. Our total conditioning program is designed to eliminate injury and improve your performance, not harm it. As usual, if you have any questions, be sure to grab me or one of the other coaches.

ANOTHER LOOK AT THE "WHY" OF WARMING UP

A good warm up:

1. Increases the rate and strength of muscular contractions.
2. Prevents injury.
3. Increases coordination and ease of movement.
4. Gives you a "second wind" faster.
5. Avoids sudden shock to the heart.

THE "HOW" OF WARMING UP

1. A good warm up should be intense enough to increase body temperature and cause mild perspiration, but not fatigue.
2. Warm ups should include large muscle groups. This will increase body temperature faster.
3. Warm ups are mentally as well as physically beneficial if they involve movements that are consistent with the movements you normally perform during competition. See me for examples.
4. A good warm up should take fifteen to twenty minutes.

FOLLOW THESE RULES

WARM UP,
   THEN STRETCH,
      THEN LIFT OR EXERCISE,
         THEN COOL DOWN,
            THEN STRETCH AGAIN.

© 1995 by Michael D. Koehler

WARMING-UP ACTIVITIES

Following is a list of activities that will provide a good warm-up for most weightlifting and other athletic activities. They are complements, not replacements for the sport-specific exercises mentioned in the flexibility section of your booklet. Be sure to start each activity slowly, gradually increase the intensity to about 50% of your maximum heart rate or to a point where you break a sweat, then slow down during the last minute or two in order to cool down.

ACTIVITY	TIME	COOL DOWN TIME
Walking	20 mins.	none
Jogging	10 mins.	2 min.
Stationary bike	12 mins.	1-3 mins.
Rowing	10 mins.	2 mins.
Stair climbing	10 mins.	2 mins.
Jumping rope	10 mins.	2 mins.
Basketball	12 mins.	2 mins.
Handball	12 mins.	2 mins.
Swimming	14 mins.	1 min.
Tennis	14 mins.	1 min.
Baseball drills	15 mins.	none
Skating	15 mins.	none
Calisthenics	12 mins.	none
Ski machine	10 mins.	2 mins.
Soccer	15 mins.	none
Football pregame	15 mins.	none

Cold weather may require a few minutes more for each warm-up activity, warm weather fewer minutes. Just remember to start out slowly and gradually increase the level of intensity until you break a sweat, then slow down to restore your heart rate. If you perform these activities just before competition, don't cool down completely, or you'll tighten up again, especially if it's cold outside. And remember to stretch after the warm-up. Refer also to the information you have on proper stretching exercises.

© 1995 by Michael D. Koehler

USE A BELT!!

Reasons

Belts aid in support of the lower back when lifting weights. They also restrict movement, in essence, to be a constant reminder of proper form when you are doing strenuous exercises.

When to Wear a Belt

Many lifters feel that belts are necessary when lifting heavy weights and doing overhead exercises. Because it takes only 15 seconds to put on, we feel that a belt should be worn *at all times*! It provides the safety insurance you need to prevent unnecessary injury.

In Addition:

Remember to do the proper abdominal exercises to strengthen your stomach even more. Then wear the belt, too. It will provide even that much more support.

Remember:

ALWAYS
WEAR
A BELT !!!

© 1995 by Michael D. Koehler

PAIN VS. FATIGUE

During a vigorous exercise program, every athlete will experience muscle fatigue. The harder you work your muscles, the more they hurt. The pain that results from fatigue is good for you; the pain that results from injury is a sure sign that you should stop exercising immediately. How do you tell the difference? Here are some suggestions:

1. Asymmetrical pain

If you are involved in an exercise that involves both arms or both legs and pain occurs in only one of them, you probably (not necessarily, but probably) have injured a muscle, tendon, or joint in that area of your body. At that point, STOP EXERCISING IMMEDIATELY and see me or one of the other adults in the area.

2. Immediate pain

If a pain hits you immediately in a specific spot, stop exercising and see me. If the pain hits when you start a particular exercise the next day, STOP EXERCISING IMMEDIATELY and see me. You may have injured a muscle, tendon, or joint during the previous day's exercise, and it may be more obvious the next time you exercise.

3. If the pain doesn't go away

As indicated already, muscle fatigue resembles pain that can result from injury. So remember that muscle fatigue will go away during a rest period. If after a rest period, therefore, you still feel a pain in one specific part of your body, DON'T RESUME EXERCISING. See me immediately.

REMEMBER:

We're not exercising to get hurt. We're exercising to PREVENT injury and to improve our appearance and athletic performance. So if you observe any of the above characteristics or are uncertain about a specific pain, see me. Let's not take any chances.

© 1995 by Michael D. Koehler

EXERCISES FOR THE ABDOMINALS

Read this program carefully before starting the exercises. All the exercises in this section are designed to strengthen your abdominal muscles. They range from relatively easy to difficult and are designed to bring you to a high level of fitness. Don't do all of them during your exercise session, just two or three, depending on your abdominal strength. Start with exercise 1 and do 3 sets of 25 sit-ups. Then do the same with exercise 2. STOP. If these two exercises were easy for you, do exercises 2 and 3 the next time you work out, then exercises 3 and 4, and so on until you can do exercises 9 and 10. In other words, you should work on two of these exercises at least three times a week to strengthen this area of your body. And remember: Always start your workout with these exercises. Anyone who wants to be a good athlete or just be physically fit must have a strong center of gravity. That's why these exercises are so important. Depending upon your age, body type, and strength levels, you may not be able to do 3 sets of 25 of exercises 9 and 10. Don't worry about that. The important thing is that you improve your current strength levels. These exercises will help.

Exercise One

NAME - Elevated Leg sit-ups (3 sets of 25)

PROCEDURE - Place legs on stool, chair, or bench and sit up, raising your chin to your knees. Do 3 sets of 25 sit-ups.

ADJUSTMENTS - If these are too difficult, place your legs on the ground with a slight bend at the knees and do 3 sets of 25 sit-ups. If these are too difficult, elevate your legs again on the chair or bench and do "crunchies." Simply raise your head so that your chin touches your chest and reach your hands to the sky. Do 3 sets of these 25 times, each time making sure you feel contractions in your abdominal muscles.

SAFETY HINT- Don't lock your hands behind your head. During periods of exertion, you may pull your head too far forward and damage your spine.

Another hint: If after doing the 3 sets of 25 crunchies, you find that you can't do exercise 2, *don't do it*. Keep doing the crunchies 3 times a week until you can do the elevated leg sit-ups. Then do them until you can do exercises 1 and 2 without back pain or exhaustion. In addition, with any of these exercises, if you should feel back pain, stop the exercise and talk to me immediately.

© 1995 by Michael D. Koehler

Exercise Two

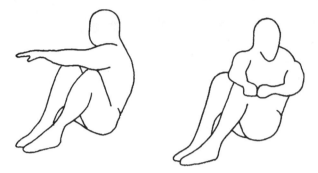

NAME - Seated Bent Knee Sit-up (3 sets of 25)

PROCEDURE - Lie on the floor with your knees bent. Sit up, placing your arms straight out—again, not to hurt your neck—and bring your chest to your knees. A reminder: Once you feel comfortable doing these first two exercises, start your workout with exercise 2 and combine it with exercise 3.

SAFETY HINT- Again, be aware of back pain. In fact, be aware of any pain. These exercises will dramatically improve your strength if you perform them regularly. You need not strain yourself to the point of exhaustion.

Exercise Three

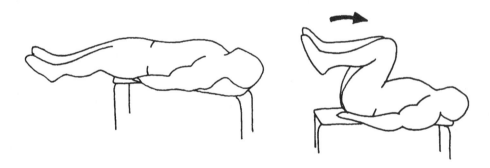

NAME - Flat Knee-ins (3 sets of 25)

PROCEDURE - Lie flat on bench or floor. If on a bench, be sure to let your legs hang down, feet touching the floor. Place your hands under your buttocks for back support and raise your knees until your thighs are at a right angle with the rest of your body.

SAFETY HINT- Be sure to place your hands underneath you. The lower back support is very important to prevent aggravation to your back.

© 1995 by Michael D. Koehler

Exercise Four

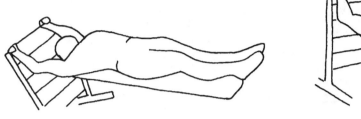 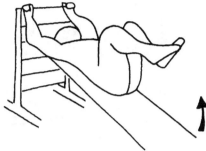

NAME - Slant Board Knee-ins (3 sets of 25)

PROCEDURE - Starting on the lowest incline of the slant board, hang fully extended and bring your knees to your chest until they reach a right angle with the rest of your body.

ADJUSTMENTS - Increase the intensity of the exercise by elevating the slant board. Once you can perform the exercise on the highest incline of the slant board, move on to the next exercise.

SAFETY HINTS - As always, don't push yourself beyond your current strength levels. Don't *start* this exercise at the highest incline of the slant board. Start within your target range; make progress at your own pace.

Exercise Five

NAME - Slant Board Sit-ups (3 sets of 25)

PROCEDURE - Place your feet under the stabilizer, knees bent, with the slant board at its lowest incline. Keeping your arms straight in front of you, sit up, touching your fingers to your toes. Don't lower yourself to a resting position on the board. Your shoulders should not touch the board, just your back. This procedure will keep constant tension on the abdominals. They should be contracted throughout the entire 25 sit-ups.

ADJUSTMENTS - Again, adjust the elevation on the slant board until you can do 3 sets of 25 at the highest level of elevation.

SAFETY HINTS - Don't keep your hands behind your head. As with all sit-ups, such technique can be potentially damaging to your neck.

© 1995 by Michael D. Koehler

Exercise Six

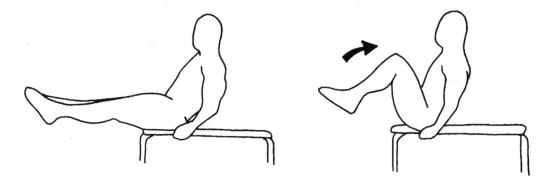

NAME - Bench V Sits (3 sets of 25)

PROCEDURE - Sit on the edge of a bench with your legs extended. Place your hands behind you for support, as in the picture, and grasp the sides of the bench. Bring your legs to a right angle and *slowly* push them back to the extended position. It is important that you bring them up slowly and return them to the extended position slowly.

SAFETY HINT - Grasp the sides of the bench very tightly. The support you provide is very important to prevent back pain.

Exercise Seven

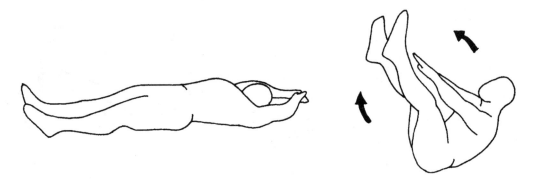

NAME - Lying Flat V Sits (3 sets of 25)

PROCEDURE - At this point, the V stands for Victory. You're making really good progress to have come this far. Keep up the good work. Lie flat on the floor with your arms extended overhead, then bend at the waist, simultaneously raising your arms and your legs. Touch your toes, making a V with your body, then lower back to the prone position.

SAFETY HINT - Perform this exercise slowly in order to prevent a jerky motion that could injure your back. You'll notice that a slow motion will also provide additional control.

© 1995 by Michael D. Koehler

Exercise Eight

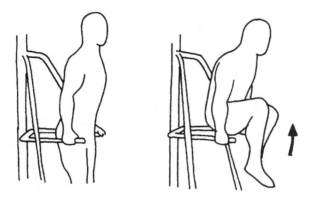

NAME - Straight-arm Vertical Leg Raise (3 sets of 25)

PROCEDURE - Using the dip stand, grip the handles on the end of each bar and raise yourself to an extended position. Raise your legs slowly to a right angle. *Slowly* lower your legs to their original extended position.

SAFETY HINT - Do not drop from the dip stand; use the pegs to step down or slowly lower yourself to the ground to prevent shock to the spine.

Exercise Nine

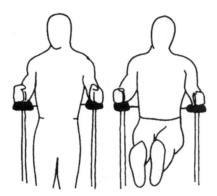

NAME - Vertical Knee-in (3 sets of 25)

PROCEDURE - Again using dip stand, place your arms on the pads and your hands on the grips and push your body against the back pad. Slowly raise your straightened legs to a right angle with your body and slowly lower them to the extended position.

SAFETY HINT - Again, be careful not to drop from the dip stand.

© 1995 by Michael D. Koehler

Exercise Ten

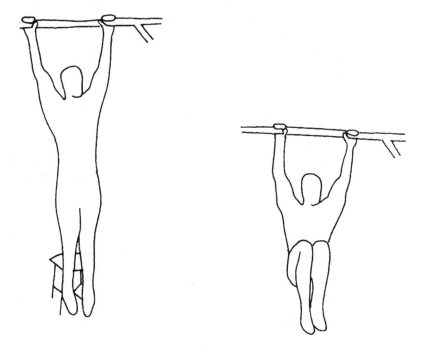

NAME - Hanging from Chin Bar Knee-ups (3 sets of 25)

PROCEDURE - Grasp the bar at shoulder width or a little wider. Be sure you're comfortable. Fully extend your body and raise your knees until they form a right angle. Be sure to raise and lower your legs slowly in order to realize maximum benefit from the exercise.

SAFETY HINT - Be sure to use a chair or a stool to get down from the bar. Unnecessary jumping from the bar, especially if you're tired, may injure your back.

REMINDERS

These exercises are designed to provide a natural progression from easy to difficult. Don't force yourself to do the more advanced exercises until you're ready for them. You probably will start with the first and second exercises but may progress quickly to a combination of 3 and 4 or 4 and 5. Ultimately, you will want to be doing exercises 9 and 10 and, if you progress beyond them, exercises 9 and 10 followed by another set of any one of the other eight. Recognize as well that you may never get to exercises 9 and 10. Such a progression is especially difficult for junior high school students.

If you are interested in improving your appearance or athletic performance, however, you will work hard at each of these exercises and *will* realize definite strength increases. It's unimportant which of the sets you are doing; it is important that you benefit from the experience.

© 1995 by Michael D. Koehler

© 1995 by Michael D. Koehler

YOUR COMPLETE WORKOUT

Like the abdominal exercises, these exercises involve a progression from easy to difficult and will meet all your strength needs without using weights. In fact, this is a very difficult program and may require as much as three months work for you to master it. You may never master it because of your age, but if you stay with it, you will improve your strength and appearance considerably. Again, stay within your own range. Goals for girls will be different from those for boys. For some girls, 3 sets of 25 will always be too difficult. Don't worry about that. Just work to accomplish your own goals by focusing on the adjustments contained within each exercise. The important thing is not that you master the program but that you improve your strength, appearance, and/or athletic performance. This program will do all of them for you. It's important that you determine your goals and stick with them. And, remember, you don't have to do every exercise in this program every day, or even every other day. Make the right combination to guarantee the program that's best for you. I will help you.

Exercise One

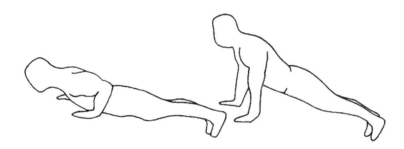

NAME - Push-ups

PROCEDURE - Position your body parallel to the ground with your weight on your toes and the palms of your hands as illustrated in the drawing. For the first part of the exercise, position your hands approximately shoulder width. Keep your body as straight as possible throughout the exercise. Slowly lower yourself until your chest touches the floor, inhaling as you go down. Then slowly raise yourself as you exhale. Repeat the process for 3 sets of 25 or as many as possible.

ADJUSTMENTS - The goal is 3 sets of 25. You may not be able to do this many. If you can't do many at first, adjust your original position so that your knees are on the ground and do everything else the same way. Also, keep your hands close together if you want to emphasize work on your triceps (the muscles in the back of your upper arm), relatively far apart (wider than your shoulders) to work your pectorals (your chest muscles).

SAFETY HINT - Report shoulder or elbow pain to me immediately, and when you complete the exercise, lower yourself slowly; don't just drop to the floor!

Exercise Two

NAME - Free Squat

PROCEDURE - Stand erect with both arms crossed over your chest. Keep your head and back straight and your feet planted about shoulder width. Inhale as you squat down. When your thighs are approximately parallel to the floor, stop. Your head and knees should remain straight throughout the entire exercise. Exhale as you push yourself back to an erect position. Repeat the process until you complete 3 sets of 25 or whatever goals you have set for yourself.

SAFETY HINT - Do not squat beyond the point where your thighs are parallel to the ground. If you go beyond the parallel, you may stress your knees. Also, as with all exercises, do not push through knee pain. If you experience pain, see me immediately.

Exercise Three

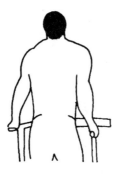

NAME - Dips

PROCEDURE - Using a dip stand, grip the ends of the bar and position yourself straight-armed. While you inhale, slowly lower yourself by bending at the elbows, keeping them as close to your body as possible. Try to touch your biceps to your forearms to get the maximum benefit from the exercise. Then exhale as you slowly raise yourself back to an erect position.

ADJUSTMENTS - If you are unable to lower yourself to the point where your biceps touch your forearms, go down as far as you can. Remember, work within your own range. Girls may want to bend the elbows only slightly and then return to the original position.

© 1995 by Michael D. Koehler

SAFETY HINTS - Call me over the first time you do this exercise or have a teacher or another coach watch you. We will want to check the proper form and make sure you are experiencing no pain. Again, establish your own personal goals regarding the number of times you do this exercise.

Exercise Four

NAME - Ballet Squat

PROCEDURE - Stand erect with your head and back straight, your arms crossed over your chest, with a wide stance, maybe 4 to 5 inches wider than your shoulders. Turn your feet out and slowly bend at the knees until your thighs are parallel to the floor, your knees over your toes. While exhaling, push up to your original starting position. Try to work up to 3 sets of 25.

SAFETY HINT - Do not bend beyond the parallel position, or you will risk damage to the knees. If you have pain the next time you try this exercise, see me immediately.

Exercise Five

NAME - Declining Push-ups

PROCEDURE - Place your feet on a bench or chair and assume the same position as in exercise 1. While inhaling, lower your body slowly until you touch your chest to the floor. Exhaling, slowly push yourself back to the original position.

ADJUSTMENTS - If you do not want to do this exercise, at least at first, simply focus on exercise 1 and progress to this exercise as it becomes possible.

SAFETY HINT - Keep your head and back straight in order to get the full benefit from the exercise and to reduce lower back strain.

© 1995 by Michael D. Koehler

Exercise Six

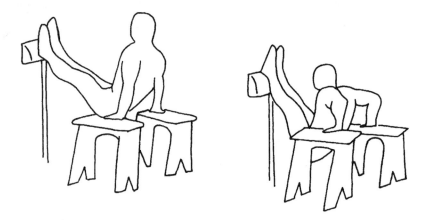

NAME - Triceps Push-ups

PROCEDURE - Place your feet on a chair or other support that elevates them at least parallel to the floor. Position yourself straight-armed between two benches or chairs and slowly lower your body, keeping your elbows together. Exhale as you push up. Again, the ultimate goal is 3 sets of 25. Go at your own pace and do only as many as you can.

ADJUSTMENTS - A simple adjustment is to sit on the ground, your hands placed approximately a foot behind you. Lean back so that your arms are bent at the elbows. Then do the push-ups by straightening your arms. Progress to the more difficult exercise outlined above by placing your hands on the benches or chairs but by keeping your feet on the ground instead of elevating them.

SAFETY HINT - Be sure the benches or the chairs are stable. You might have someone hold them for you.

Exercise Seven

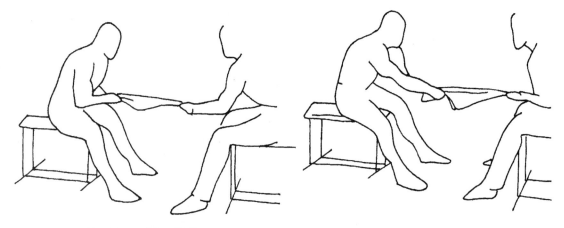

NAME - Seated Lat Pull

PROCEDURE - Sit on a bench, your partner seated opposite you. Each holding one end of a towel or rope, slowly pull it back and forth, not with the attempt to pull your partner off the bench but to offer enough resistance to exercise the back muscles.

© 1995 by Michael D. Koehler

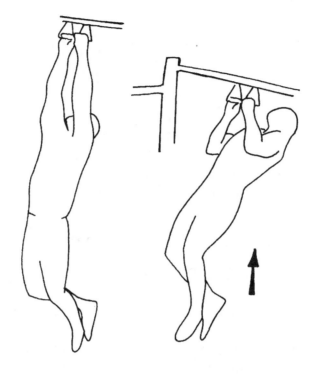

© 1995 by Michael D. Koehler

NAME - V Bar Chin-ups

PROCEDURE - Attach a V bar to the chin-up bar. The V bar should be positioned higher than your extended reach. Use a stool or a chair to reach it and pull yourself slowly to a position where your chin touches the chin-up bar. Inhale as you lower yourself to a hanging position and repeat the process, exhaling as you lift yourself.

ADJUSTMENTS - If a V bar is unavailable, grasp the chin-up bar with both hands, one in front of the other, and pull yourself up the same way. You may not be able to pull yourself up high enough to touch your chin on the bar. If need be, simply flex your arms and hold that position for 10 to 15 seconds. Try for as many 10-second intervals as possible.

SAFETY HINT - Don't fall to your original starting position; lower yourself slowly. Falling can damage your shoulders or elbows. In addition, use the stool or chair to get off the chin-up bar. Dropping from the bar can damage your back.

Exercise Nine

NAME - Front Chin-ups

PROCEDURE - Use a stool or chair to raise yourself to a chin-up bar. Grasp the bar with a closed grip (palms facing down), hands about 18 to 20 inches apart. Inhale then exhale as you pull yourself to a point where your chin touches the bar. Slowly lower yourself to your original hanging position. Don't swing; execute the exercise slowly and deliberately to keep your body steady, and don't kick your feet. Let your legs hang straight down during the entire motion.

ADJUSTMENTS - As with the V bar chin-ups, you may want to start by doing flexed arm hangs instead of chin-ups. If this is the case, try to find a chin-up bar that is low enough to grasp from the ground. Grip the bar, flex your arms, and hang for as many 10-second intervals as possible.

SAFETY HINT - As already mentioned, don't drop from the bar. Use a stool or chair to step down, making sure the stool is stable.

Exercise Ten

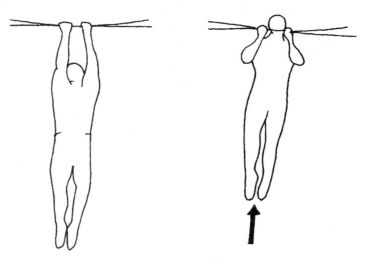

NAME - Reverse Grip Chin-up

© 1995 by Michael D. Koehler

PROCEDURE - Same as front chin-ups but with hands in an open grip (palms facing up). Execute the exercise in the same way and observe the same safety hint. Make the same adjustments as with the other chin-ups if this exercise is too difficult.

REMINDER

This program involves some very difficult exercises. You probably won't want to do all of them during each exercise session. And you probably won't be able to do 3 sets of 25, at least initially. In fact, you probably will have to make many of the adjustments suggested in each exercise. But that's OK. When you develop your goal sheet, establish an initial program that you can perform and set target goals that will mark your improvement. I will help you with this. Let's also be sure to incorporate an aerobic workout, flexibility exercises, and the proper diet. I will help you with this, too.

© 1995 by Michael D. Koehler

WEIGHTLIFTING PROGRAMS

Level A

Sequence 1

This first sequence should be followed three times a week and should take roughly 40 to 45 minutes to complete. Do 3 sets of each exercise with 10 repetitions at 60% of your maximum strength (3 x 10 x 60%).

Maximum Strength x .60 = Weight Used

Two Abdominal Exercises
Bench Press
Military Press
Triceps Extensions
Chin-ups
Barbell Curl
Leg Extension
Leg Curl

Sequence 2

Do 4 sets of these exercises with 10 repetitions at 70% of your maximum strength (4 x 10 x 70%).

Maximum Strength x .70 = Weight Used

Two Abdominal Exercises
Bench Press
Upright Row
Triceps Kickback
Barbell Curls
Leg Press
Leg Curl

Sequence 3

Do 3 sets of these exercises with 10 repetitions at 70% of your maximum strength. This sequence may take an hour or longer (3 x 10 x 70%).

Maximum Strength x .70 = Weight Used

Two Abdominals
Bench Press
Inclined Bench Press
Military Press
Upright Row
French Curl
Triceps Extension
Barbell Curls
Dumbbell Curls
Chin-ups
Squats
Leg Curls

REMEMBER: SAFETY FIRST

© 1995 by Michael D. Koehler

Level B

This program is more aggressive than the previous one. Be certain that you use proper form, wear a belt, and follow all our rules of safety. Remember: Safety First! All these exercises should consist of 4 sets of 10 repetitions at 70% of maximum strength.

Sequence 1

Maximum Strength x .70 = *Weight Used*

Two Abdominal Exercises
Bench Press
Behind Neck Press
Bent-over Row
French Curl
Barbell Curl
Squat
Leg Curl

Sequence 2

Maximum Strength x .70 = *Weight Used*

Two Abdominal Exercises
Bench Press
Inclined Bench Press
Behind Neck Press
Upright Row
Bent-over Row
Barbell Curl
Dips
Squat
Leg Extension
Leg Curls

Sequence 3

Maximum Strength x .70 = *Weight Used*

Two Abdominal Exercises
Bench Press
Inclined Bench Press
Military Press
Behind the Neck Press
Lateral Raise
French Curl
Triceps Extensions
Chin-ups
Bent-over Row
Barbell Curls
Dumbbell Curls
Lunge
Leg Curls

REMEMBER: SAFETY FIRST

© 1995 by Michael D. Koehler

Level C

These exercises will work your muscles to and through fatigue, so be sure to work with a partner. Watch each other closely. This is a very strenuous program. Do not perform these exercises on the day *before* or *of* a contest.

Sequence 1 (3 x 10 x 70%)

Monday and Thursday
Two Abdominals
Chin-ups to 30 or Max
Bent-over Rowing
Triceps Kickbacks
Barbell Curl
Dumbbell Curl
Squats
Straight Leg Dead Lift

Tuesday and Friday
Two Abdominals
Bench Press
Inclined Bench Press
Military Press
Upright Rowing
French Curl
Triceps Kickbacks
Dips

Sequence 2 (3 x 10 x 70%)

Monday and Thursday
Bench Press
Inclined Bench Press
Dumbbell Flies
Military Press
Behind the Neck Press
Upright Rowing
French Curl
Triceps Extensions
Triceps Kickbacks

Tuesday and Friday
Maximum chin-ups (try for 30)
Bent-over Rowing
T-Bar Rowing
Barbell Curls
Dumbbell Curls
Preacher Curls
Squat
Lunge
Straight Leg Dead Lifts

Sequence 3 (3 x 10 x 70%)

Mon./Wed./Friday
Two Abdominals
Bench Press
Inclined Bench Press
Military Press
Upright Rowing
French Curl
Triceps Extensions
Dips

Tuesday/Thur./Sat.
Two Abdominals
Squat
Lunge
Straight Leg Dead Lift
Leg Curl
Bent-over Row
Barbell Curl
Dumbbell Curl

Level D

This is the toughest program in the booklet. Once you master it (and it won't be easy!), get one of the coaches to make adjustments to increase the intensity. Each sequence is done with 3 sets of 10 repetitions at 70% of your maximum strength. Do not perform these exercises on the day *before* or *of* a contest.

© 1995 by Michael D. Koehler

Sequence 1

Mon./Wed./Friday
Two Abdominals
Bench Press
Inclined Bench Press
Behind the Neck Press
Dumbbell Press
Lateral Raises
French Curls
Triceps Extensions
Triceps Kickbacks
Dips

Tues./Thurs./Sat.
Two Abdominals
Max. Chin-ups to 30
Dead Lift
Barbell Curls
Dumbbell Curls
Preacher Curls
Squat
Leg Press
Leg Curl

Sequence 2

Mon./Wed./Friday
Two Abdominals
Bench Press
Inclined Bench Press
Dumbbell Flies
Upright Row
Lateral Raise
French Curls
Triceps Extensions
Triceps Kickbacks
Dips

Tues./Thurs./Sat.
Two Abdominals
Chin-ups to 30
Dead Lift
Barbell Curls
Preacher Curls
Military Press
Squat
Lunge
Leg Curls

Sequence 3

Mon./Wed./Friday
Two Abdominals
Bench Press
Inclined Bench Press
Military Press
Upright Row
Behind the Neck Press
French Curls
Triceps Extensions
Triceps Kickbacks

Tues./Thurs./Sat.
Two Abdominals
Chin-ups to 30
Cleans
Barbell Curls
Dumbbell Curls
Squat
Lunge
Straight Leg Dead Lift

© 1995 by Michael D. Koehler

REMEMBER: SAFETY FIRST

© 1995 by Michael D. Koehler

DESCRIPTIONS OF EXERCISES

Each of the exercises mentioned in the previous four programs is illustrated and explained on the following pages. Study each exercise carefully and pay particular attention to the proper form and the safety points. In addition, the coaches will explain each exercise before you actually start the program.

Exercise 1

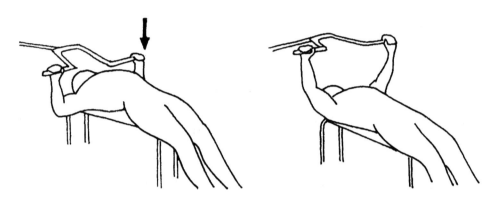

NAME: Bench Press

PROCEDURE: If a Universal machine is available, use it first. The machine makes the spotter's job easier and it provides better balance for the lifter. When you feel you have become sufficiently strong, ask me or another coach to introduce you to the free-weight bench press. The technique is similar to both the machine and the free weights: Lie flat on the bench with your legs hanging off the side of the bench, your feet flat on the floor. Positioning your hands about six inches wider than your shoulder width, your thumbs inside, grab the bar. Lower the bar to your chest, just below your pectorals and push the bar back to arm length.

ADJUSTMENTS: Narrow your grip on the bar (place your hands closer together) to emphasize work on your triceps; place them farther apart to emphasize work on your pectorals. You can also—with the help of a spotter!—lie on the floor, arch your back to do a neck bridge, then do bench presses. This exercise is particularly helpful for wrestlers.

SAFETY HINTS: Do not relax or drop the weight onto your chest; lower it in a controlled fashion. Inhale as you lower the bar to your chest; exhale as you push it back to arm's length. Always keep your head on the bench and do not arch your back too sharply or raise your hips off the bench.

Exercise 2

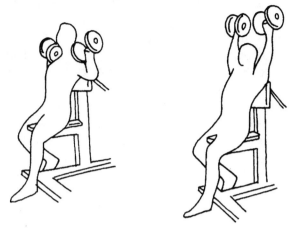

NAME: Seated Back-supported Military Dumbbell Press

PROCEDURE: Raise the barbells to your shoulders and sit on any kind of structure that will give support to your back. Be sure that your elbows are facing out and that the palms of your hands are facing forward. Slowly push the dumbbells upward until your arms are fully extended. Then lower the dumbbells slowly to the original position.

ADJUSTMENTS: You can also use a barbell for this exercise. It may be easier the first time you do it. Once your deltoids become stronger, switch to the dumbbells. They will challenge the entire muscle group.

SAFETY HINTS: As with all exercises, inhale when you lower the weight and exhale forcefully when you raise it. Keep your feet on the floor at all times and your back against the support. Keep your body as straight as possible. This way, you will prevent injury to your back.

Exercise 3

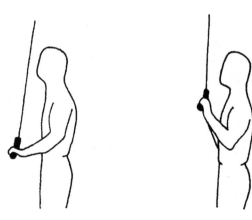

NAME: Standing Triceps Extensions

PROCEDURE: Face the machine bar with your feet approximately shoulder width. Grip the bar with your palms down, your hands at shoulder width. Emphasize a full range of motion by having the bar almost as high as your neck. Slowly lower the bar,

© 1995 by Michael D. Koehler

exhaling forcefully throughout the motion. Inhale as you allow it to raise back to neck height. Remember to lower and raise the bar slowly and deliberately.

ADJUSTMENTS: Use a barbell if the lat machine is unavailable. Raise the barbell over your head, your palms facing the ceiling and your elbows slightly in front of your face. Allow the barbell to *slowly* lower behind your head, making sure your elbows stay slightly in front of your face. Inhale while you lower the bar; exhale forcefully while you raise it.

SAFETY HINTS: Keep your arms tight to your sides throughout the exercise or, if using a barbell, keep your elbows slightly in front of your face, tight to your head. Be sure your hands are approximately shoulder width throughout the exercise, and if you feel any pain during or after the exercise, be sure to see a coach. You may have to use less weight. Always remember: any pain—at any time—*stop the exercise immediately!*

Exercise 4

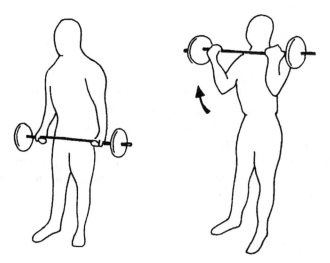

© 1995 by Michael D. Koehler

NAME: Standing Barbell Curl

PROCEDURE: Stand with your back against a wall. Using the appropriate weight for your level of conditioning, grasp the barbell with your palms facing forward—your thumbs facing out. Keeping your back against the wall, slowly raise the barbell, exhaling forcefully throughout the motion. Slowly lower the barbell to its original position at arm's length, inhaling throughout the motion. Remember: both the raising and the lowering should be done slowly and deliberately.

ADJUSTMENTS: You may use dumbbells for this exercise instead of a barbell, and you may alternate the lifts—first one arm, then the other. You can also sit with your back supported, using dumbbells, either simultaneously or alternately.

SAFETY HINTS: Don't allow the weight to fall ballistically after lifting it to the height of your shoulders. You might drop it or pull a muscle. If you find that the weight is too difficult to lift or tires you too quickly so that you are unable to perform the exercise safely, *use less weight*. See a coach first.

Exercise 5

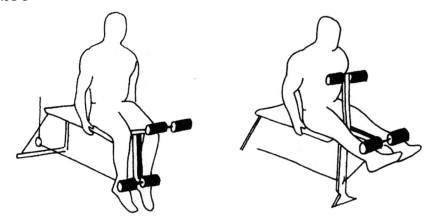

NAME: Leg Extensions

PROCEDURE: Place the top part of your ankles under the pads of a leg extension machine as shown in the illustration. Be sure the front of the seat is tight against the backs of your knees. Grip the seat as illustrated and exhale while raising the weights to the point where your legs are parallel with the floor. Inhale as you lower the weights.

ADJUSTMENTS: If a leg extension machine is unavailable, have a partner provide steady resistance by applying pressure to the fronts of your ankles as you sit on a bench.

SAFETY HINTS: If sitting on a bench, be sure to put a towel on the front part of the bench so that you don't scratch the back of your knees during the exercise. Again, be sure to use an appropriate amount of weight; see a coach if you have any questions.

Exercise 6

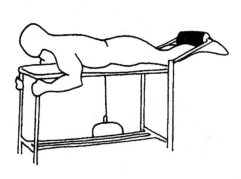 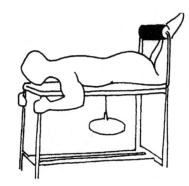

NAME: Thigh Curls

PROCEDURE: Lie face down on the leg extension machine and place your heels under the top pads. Your legs should be parallel to the floor. Slowly bend your legs as you grip the sides of the table for leverage. Exhale as you lift; inhale as you lower your legs to the starting position.

ADJUSTMENTS: If the leg extension machine is unavailable, have a partner apply pressure to the back of your legs as you perform the exercise as described above.

SAFETY HINTS: To avoid injury, be sure the partner applies pressure to your heels, not your Achilles tendons. Also, be sure to place a towel under your legs if using a bench to avoid possible abrasions to your knees and thighs.

© 1995 by Michael D. Koehler

Exercise 7

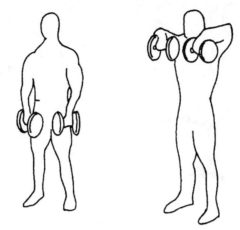

NAME: Standing Upright Rowing with Dumbbells

PROCEDURE: Using a closed grip (your thumbs facing each other), grip two dumbbells, your arms to your sides, the dumbbells resting on the outside of your thighs as in the illustration. Exhale forcefully while lifting the dumbbells straight up as in the illustration. After lifting, your elbows should be as high as your head. Pause for a second at the top of the lift, then slowly lower the dumbbells, inhaling through the motion.

ADJUSTMENTS: The same exercise can be performed with a barbell. Be sure to adjust your grip on the barbell so that your palms are facing your body and your hands are resting on your thighs.

SAFETY HINT: Avoid injury by being sure not to drop the dumbbells ballistically after each lift. They must be lowered slowly to their original position. Use the right amount of weight for your level of conditioning. You're not competing with anyone else to lift the most weight; you're working to improve your own strength levels.

Exercise 8

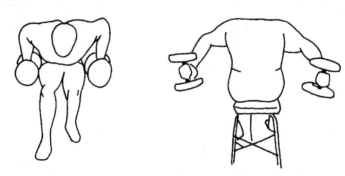

NAME: Triceps Kickbacks

PROCEDURE: Grasp two dumbbells with your palms facing your body. Sit on a bench with your feet solidly on the floor and bend over so that your chest is resting on the tops of your thighs, allowing the dumbbells to hang at your side. Kick the dumbbells back deliberately until the biceps part of your arms and your forearms are parallel

© 1995 by Michael D. Koehler

to the floor. Exhale forcefully as you perform the exercise. Hold the dumbbells in the kicked back position for a second, then slowly return them to the hanging position, inhaling as you do so.

ADJUSTMENTS: This exercise may also be done from a standing position, and the dumbbells may be kicked back alternately. Do it initially from the sitting position, however, because of the support it provides.

SAFETY HINT: If you prefer to do kickbacks from a standing position, find a bench or the arm of a chair to support your head while performing the exercise. It will help provide better leverage.

Exercise 9

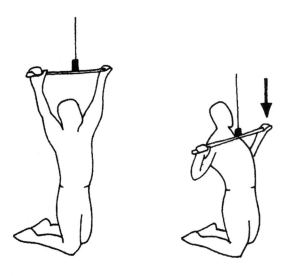

NAME: Lat Pulldowns

PROCEDURE: Kneel underneath the bar of a lat machine and grip the outside ends of the bar so that your thumbs are facing each other. Your arms should be fully extended and your hands about two feet apart. While exhaling forcefully, pull the bar straight down to your chest. Inhale as your return it to its original position. This exercise is designed to work on the upper lats.

ADJUSTMENTS: You can work on your lower lats by closing your grip on the bar so that your hands are only 7 or 8 inches apart. Perform the exercise the same way. Another variation for upper lat work is to grip the bar so that your hands are 2 feet apart and lower the bar behind your head. If the lat machine is unavailable, modified chin-ups can provide many of the same benefits. Refer to that section of your booklet or see your coach.

SAFETY HINTS: Place a folded towel under your knees to avoid soreness. If pulling the bar down behind your head, be sure to execute the exercise carefully and deliberately so that you don't hit your head with the bar. This is a common problem with this particular exercise.

© 1995 by Michael D. Koehler

Exercise 10

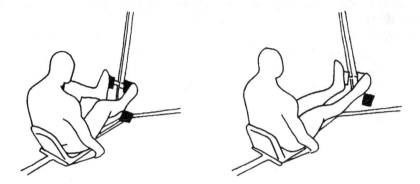

NAME: Leg Press

PROCEDURE: Adjust the seat on the machine so that your thighs are vertical to the floor when your legs are bent. Firmly grasp the handrails under your seat, then press the weight until your knees are in the locked position, exhaling through the motion. Inhale as you slowly lower the weights to their original position.

ADJUSTMENTS: If a leg press machine is unavailable, see your coach for alternatives or refer to the squat exercises illustrated later in this section.

SAFETY HINTS: Be sure to adjust the seat to maximize the benefits of the exercise and never use more weight than you can lift throughout the number of repetitions in your individual program.

Exercise 11

NAME: Inclined Bench Press with Barbell

PROCEDURE: Lie down on an inclined bench, holding the barbell with as wide a grip as possible. Depending upon the width of the bar, your hands should be approximately 4 to 6 inches inside each weight. The wide grip will enable you to work on your outer and upper pectorals. Push the bar to arm's length, exhaling forcefully through the strain, then slowly lower it to a point just below your neck. Keep your elbows back, in line with your head. Repeat the procedure.

ADJUSTMENTS: If you are doing this exercise at home or if the inclined bench is unavailable, do regular bench presses, using the wide grip as described above.

© 1995 by Michael D. Koehler

SAFETY HINTS: Always use a spotter with this exercise; never do it alone! After raising the bar, lower it slowly. Use an appropriate amount of weight; too much weight increases the chance of injury. Also, keep your head on the bench and do not arch your back. Again, *use a spotter!*

Exercise 12

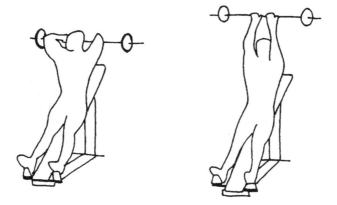

NAME: Seated Closed-grip French Curl

PROCEDURE: Sit on the end of a bench, your back straight and your feet on the floor. Grasp the middle of the bar, your hands in a closed grip (your palms facing you), approximately 5 to 7 inches apart. Hold the bar above your head at arm's length and slowly lower it behind your head, keeping your upper arms as vertical as possible throughout the exercise. Slowly raise the bar to arm's length, exhaling through the effort and keeping your elbows close to the side of your head.

ADJUSTMENTS: You can perform the same exercise while standing. Be sure to keep your legs straight throughout the exercise.

SAFETY HINTS: Again, use a spotter and be sure to use an appropriate amount of weight.

Exercise 13

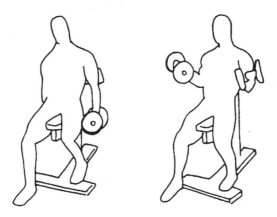

NAME: Seated Dumbbell Curl

PROCEDURE: Sit on a chair with a back support or on the bench with your back against the wall. Keep your back straight and your feet on the floor. Allow the dumb-

© 1995 by Michael D. Koehler

bells to hang at your side, then slowly curl them to shoulder height, exhaling through the strain. Slowly lower them, inhaling through the motion. Keep the dumbbells close to your sides throughout the exercise.

ADJUSTMENTS: Curl the dumbbells alternately, concentrating on your biceps throughout the exercise.

SAFETY HINTS: Be sure you have adequate support from your chair or bench. Set the dumbbells on the floor between each repetition.

Exercise 14

NAME: Wide Stance Squat

PROCEDURE: Place a bench behind you, your heels even with the end. With the barbell on your back, your hands gripping it as wide as possible and your feet a little wider than shoulder width, slowly bend your knees and lower the weight until your buttocks touch the bench. Exhaling, raise yourself to a standing position. Keep your head up and your back straight throughout the exercise, your feet flat to the floor. Do not sit on the bench during the exercise. Simply touch it, keeping tension on your thigh muscles.

ADJUSTMENTS: A wider stance, as in this exercise, enables you to work on your inner thigh muscles. Adjust the exercise by closing your stance to work on the outer thigh muscles. You also can perform the same exercise without a barbell by crossing your arms in front of you and executing the same motions.

SAFETY HINTS: Never bend lower than the height of the bench. Lowering yourself to a point where your thighs are not parallel to the ground places undue stress on the knees. Always use the bench as a reminder. You will also want to be sure you use a belt during this exercise. As we have said repeatedly, however, the use of a belt is wise during *every* exercise in this booklet.

© 1995 by Michael D. Koehler

Exercise 15

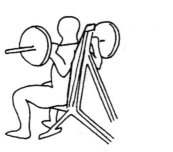

NAME: Behind-neck Barbell Press

PROCEDURE: Sit on a bench or a chair that will provide safe support for your back while you perform this exercise. Be sure your back is straight and your feet firmly on the floor. Gripping the barbell as wide as possible, lift it overhead to arm's length and lower it slowly behind your head. Push it back to arm's length, exhaling forcefully through the motion.

ADJUSTMENT: If a bench or chair is unavailable, the exercise can be performed in a standing position. Use an appropriate amount of weight when standing. This is a difficult exercise.

SAFETY HINTS: Use back support whenever possible to provide a solid base while performing this exercise. Also be sure to have a spotter behind you in the event you need help lifting the weight.

Exercise 16

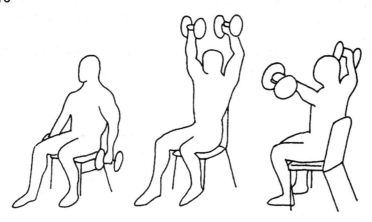

NAME: Dumbbell Raises

PROCEDURE: Sit on a bench or chair that provides support for your back. With your feet flat to the floor, allow a dumbbell in each hand to hang at your sides. Keeping your arms straight, raise the dumbbells in front of you until they are directly overhead. Exhale forcefully through this motion. Inhale while lowering them to your sides, then raise them laterally—straight out to each side—until the dumbbells are approximately shoulder high. Exhale through this motion, then inhale while lowering them again. Continue with the forward motion and the lateral motion as you complete your repetitions.

© 1995 by Michael D. Koehler

ADJUSTMENTS: The exercise can be performed while standing or sitting without back support. It is best, however, to support your back while performing this exercise.

SAFETY HINTS: If in doubt, use less weight while performing this exercise. The number of repetitions you do will provide enough benefit, even if the weight is less than you are accustomed to.

Exercise 17

NAME: Front Lunge

PROCEDURE: Rest a barbell on your shoulders as if you were going to do some squats. With your feet approximately shoulder width, step forward first with your right leg, keeping your left foot planted firmly on the floor. You should step forward far enough so that your right thigh is almost parallel with the floor. Next, step back to your starting position and repeat the motion with your left leg. Continue through the appropriate number of repetitions.

ADJUSTMENTS: This exercise can be performed without a barbell. If you decide to do it without a barbell, place your hands on your hips and execute the exercise as described above.

SAFETY HINTS: Do not use too much weight and be sure to have a spotter with you when you perform this exercise.

Exercise 18

NAME: Barbell Rowing

PROCEDURE: Grasp a barbell on the floor in front of you, your hands just less than shoulder width (close grip) and your thumbs facing each other. With your legs bent and

© 1995 by Michael D. Koehler

your back approximately parallel to the floor, exhale while you lift the barbell straight up until it touches your lower chest. Inhale as you lower the bar almost to the floor. Do not allow it to touch the floor. Continue as described throughout the proper number of repetitions.

ADJUSTMENTS: Perform the same exercise as described above with the following adjustments:

1. Place your hands approximately two feet apart on the bar (medium grip).
2. Place your hands as wide as possible on the bar (open grip).
3. Perform the same exercise with the same variety of grips while lying face down on a bench, the bar lying on the floor underneath you. Lift it until it touches the underneath part of the bench.
4. Perform the same exercise with the same variety of grips with your back bent, your forehead resting on a bench in front of you.

SAFETY HINTS: When supporting your forehead, be sure to use a bench with a soft seat or place a towel under your forehead to avoid abrasions. Also be sure to keep your knees bent and your back straight.

Exercise 19

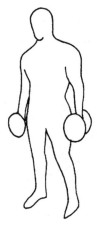

NAME: Dumbbell Dead Lift

PROCEDURE: With your feet 8 to 10 inches apart and holding dumbbells at your sides, bend at the waist until the dumbbells almost reach the floor. Keep your head up and your legs straight throughout the exercise. Inhale while lowering yourself and exhale while returning to the standing position. This is an excellent exercise for the lower back and thighs.

ADJUSTMENT: Grasp the dumbbells at your sides and do a dead lift (bend at the knees) instead of bending at the waist straight-legged. Both exercises—the dead lift and the stiff-legged dead lift—can also be performed with a barbell.

SAFETY HINTS: Be sure to stretch your hamstrings sufficiently before doing the stiff-legged dead lift. You want to stretch before doing *any* exercise, but it is especially important with this exercise.

© 1995 by Michael D. Koehler

Exercise 20

NAME: T-Bar Rowing

PROCEDURE: Place one end of an empty barbell in a corner of a room or some-where that will stabilize it. Place the desired amount of weight on the other end. Straddle the bar and bend until your back is parallel to the floor, your head directly over the weighted end of the bar. Grasp the bar just inside the weights and lift it until the plates touch your chest, exhaling through the effort. Inhale as you lower it. Don't let the weighted end touch the floor once you begin the exercise.

ADJUSTMENTS: Using the appropriate amount of weight, perform the same exercise using only one arm at a time.

SAFETY HINTS: Keep a slight bend in your legs throughout the exercise to keep some of the pressure off your back and hamstrings.Use the proper technique, stretch yourself, and warm up first.

Exercise 21

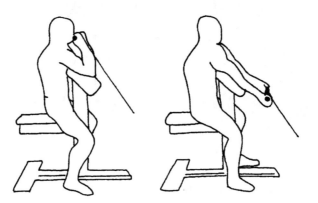

NAME: Preacher Curls

PROCEDURE: Sit behind the Scott Bench or an improvised inclined board holding a dumbbell in each hand as illustrated. Extend your arms completely with your palms up. Slowly raise the dumbbells until they are almost touching your chin. Exhale force-fully through the motion and inhale as you lower them to their original position. Concentrate on each motion, trying to isolate the effort in the biceps.

ADJUSTMENTS: The same exercise can be performed with a pulley or a barbell. If you use either, have your spotter help you get set up before the exercise.

SAFETY HINTS: No matter what piece of equipment you use, be sure you work with a spotter. This exercise is designed to exhaust the biceps. You may need the spot-ter to take the weight at the end of a set.

© 1995 by Michael D. Koehler

Exercise 22

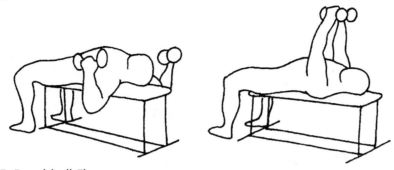

NAME: Dumbbell Fly

PROCEDURE: Lie on your back on the floor or on a bench. Hold two dumbbells at arm's length directly above you, your palms facing inward. Keep the dumbbells almost directly in front of your shoulders. Use the appropriate amount of weight so that you can keep your arms as straight as possible as you lower the dumbbells so that they are in line with the side of your head. Raise the dumbbells on the same path, exhaling forcefully through the motion. Inhale as you lower them.

ADJUSTMENTS: This exercise can be performed as well on an inclined bench.

SAFETY HINTS: Work with a spotter and use only as much weight as you can lift with the proper technique.

Exercise 23

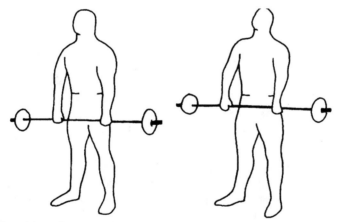

NAME: Shoulder Shrug

PROCEDURE: Hold two dumbbells, thumbs inward, alongside your thighs. Keep your arms relaxed and slowly shrug your shoulders, raising them forward, then rolling them backward as you lower the weights. When you have completed each shrug, you should be standing "at attention," your shoulders back, prepared for the next repetition.

ADJUSTMENT: You can use a barbell instead of two dumbbells. If using a barbell, grasp the bar so that your thumbs are facing each other, your hands a little wider than shoulder width.

SAFETY HINTS: Be deliberate with the motion. Raise and lower the bar slowly; do not drop it back to its original position. Because this exercise allows the use of a considerable amount of weight, be sure to bend your knees when you return the weight to the floor.

© 1995 by Michael D. Koehler

© 1995 by Michael D. Koehler

NAME: Heel Raises

PROCEDURE: Resting a barbell behind your head on your shoulders as in the illustration, slowly raise your heels off the floor so that you are on your tiptoes, then slowly lower your heels back to the floor. Continue with the proper number of repetitions.

ADJUSTMENT: To maximize the benefits of the exercise, place the ball of each foot on a two-by-four and slowly raise and lower yourself as explained above.

SAFETY HINTS: Don't place the balls of your feet on anything higher than 2 inches. The inch and a half side of a two-by-four is generally about the right height. You want to exercise the muscle, not strain it. Also, have a spotter stand behind you to provide support by simply placing his or her hands on your back as you perform the exercise. That will help you maintain balance. The spotter can also help you put the weight on and off your shoulders.

© 1995 by Michael D. Koehler

NAME: Cleans

PROCEDURE: Place a barbell on the floor in front of you. With your feet approximately shoulder width and your shins almost touching the bar, grasp the bar—palms down. Your hands should also be shoulder width and your legs bent so that your thighs are almost parallel to the floor. Keep your head up and your arms straight, then inhale forcefully as you pull the bar straight up until you stand in an erect position. As illustrated, after you have flipped the bar so that your hands are under the bar, your palms are facing up, the bar should be shoulder height and resting on your chest when the movement is completed. Exhale as you return the bar to the floor.

SAFETY HINTS: Be sure to use an appropriate amount of weight. If you try to lift too much, you can damage your back. As always, make sure you have a spotter with this exercise and that you use a belt.

**NEVER—WITH ANY OF THESE EXERCISES—
NEVER FORGET OUR SAFETY FIRST PRINCIPLE.
YOU ARE PERFORMING THESE EXERCISES TO IMPROVE YOUR HEALTH
AND FITNESS, NOT TO INJURE YOURSELF!**

FOOTBALL EXERCISES
LINEMEN

To the Athlete: About a month before the start of the season, perform each of the following exercises at 70% of your maximum strength. Gradually increase the intensity each week. By the start of the season, you should be lifting at 80% to 85% of your maximum strength, concluding each exercise with one or more 100% efforts. Be sure to see me for periodic strength testing to determine maximums and to guarantee safety.

During the season you should follow the same regimen, but at 50% of your maximum strength, doubling the number of repetitions, if you can do so with the proper form. Remember, these exercises are limited. They are specific to your playing position and are not substitutes for your total conditioning program.

Exercises	Muscle(s)	Purpose(s) & Qualifications
Two abdominals	abs	Maximum mobility
Bench press	pectorals and deltoids	Blocking strength particularly pass blocking Emphasize wide-grip to maximize benefits
Upright row	deltoids	Hand shiver during pass blocking
Military press	deltoids	Pass and run blocking
Shoulder shrug	upper trapezius	Forearm shiver and protection for shoulders
Dead lifts	all back muscles	Blocking efficiency. Perform this exercise only after you have mastered the Level D program
Behind-neck press	trapezius	Protection for neck
Triceps extension	triceps	Pass and seal blocking
Squats	quadriceps	Lateral mobility and upward thrust
Leg press	quadriceps and gastrocnemius	Leg drive during blocking
Heel raises	gastrocnemius	Driving power during run blocking

More as prescribed by coach. . . .

ALWAYS USE BELTS AND PROPER FORM

© 1995 by Michael D. Koehler

FOOTBALL EXERCISES
RUNNING BACKS

To the Athlete: About a month before the start of the season, perform each of the following exercises at 70% of your maximum strength. Gradually increase the intensity each week. By the start of the season, you should be lifting at 80% to 85% of your maximum strength, concluding each exercise with one or more 100% efforts. Be sure to see me for periodic strength testing to determine maximums and to guarantee safety.

During the season you should follow the same regimen, but at 50% of your maximum strength, doubling the number of repetitions, if you can do so with the proper form. Remember, these exercises are limited. They are specific to your playing position and are not substitutes for your total conditioning program.

Exercises	*Muscle(s)*	*Purpose(s) & Qualifications*
Three abdominals	abs	Improved mobility
Dumbbell curls	biceps	Reduction of fumbles
Preacher curls	biceps	Reduction of fumbles
Push-ups and triceps flybacks	triceps	Forearm strength while running and blocking
Palms-up wrist curls	forearm flexors	Hand strength for holding ball
Neck flexion and neck extension	neck muscles and upper trapezius	Blocking strength and neck protection while running ball
Bent-over rowing	latissimus dorsi, teres major, and biceps	Upper-body strength for warding off tacklers
Military press	deltoids and triceps	Upper-body strength to ward off tacklers and improve speed
Squats	quadriceps, gluteus, and leg abductors	Explosion from start and high-knee drive
Heel raises	gastrocnemius	Leg drive while blocking and running

More as precribed by coach. . . .

ALWAYS USE PROPER FORM

© 1995 by Michael D. Koehler

WRESTLING EXERCISES

To the Athlete: About a month before the start of the season, perform each of the following exercises at 70% of your maximum strength. Gradually increase the intensity each week. By the start of the season, you should be lifting at 80% to 85% of your maximum strength, concluding each exercise with one or more 100% efforts. Be sure to see me for periodic strength testing to determine maximums and to guarantee safety.

During the season you should follow the same regimen, but at 50% of your maximum strength, doubling the number of repetitions, if you can do so with the proper form. Remember, these exercises are limited. They are specific to your sport and are not substitutes for your total conditioning program.

Exercises	*Muscle(s)*	*Purpose(s) and Qualifications*
Three abdominals	abs	Improved general mobility
Squats and leg presses	quadriceps, gluteus, and leg abductors	Improve power from bottom position and for driving through opponent
Heel raises	gastrocnemius	Driving through opponent
Bench press	pectorals, deltoids, and triceps	Take-downs and pushing opponent away
Triceps extensions	triceps	Keeping opponent at arm's length
Dead lift	entire back, legs, and biceps	Improved pulling power
Upright and bent-over rowing	latissimus and biceps	Improved strength to control opponent
Palms-up and palms-down wrist curls	hands and forearm muscles	Gripping strength
Shrugs	trapezius	Neck strength for bridging
Bridge bench press	neck muscles	More bridge strength

More as prescribed by coach. . . .

AWAYS USE PROPER FORM

© 1995 by Michael D. Koehler

BASKETBALL EXERCISES

To the Athlete: About a month before the start of the season, perform each of the following exercises at 70% of your maximum strength. Gradually increase the intensity each week. By the start of the season, you should be lifting at 80% to 85% of your maximum strength, concluding each exercise with one or more 100% efforts. Be sure to see me for periodic strength testing to determine maximums and to guarantee safety.

During the season you should follow the same regimen, but at 50% of your maximum strength, doubling the number of repetitions, if you can do so with the proper form. Remember, these exercises are limited. They are specific to your sport and are not substitutes for your total conditioning program.

Exercises	Muscle(s)	Purpose(s) and Qualifications
Three abdominals	abs	Improved general mobility
Heel raises	gastrocnemius (calves)	Quick jumping ability
Squats	quadriceps	Improved vertical jumping ability
Lunges	quads and gluteals	Jumping
Military press	deltoids and triceps	Increased ability to hold arms over head for quick rebounding
Behind-the-neck press	trapezius and deltoids	Arm strength for rebounding
Dumbbell raises	deltoids	Arm strength for rebounding and shooting
Front chin-ups and reverse-grip chin-ups	biceps, forearm, and hands	Improved hand strength for rebounding and shooting
Leg extensions	quadriceps	General leg strength for defensive movements
Leg curls	hamstrings	General leg strength
Upright rowing	latissimus dorsi, rhomboids, and biceps	Upper-body strength for rebounding and defensive maneuvering

More as prescribed by coach. . . .

ALWAYS USE PROPER FORM

© 1995 by Michael D. Koehler

BASEBALL/SOFTBALL EXERCISES

To the Athlete: About a month before the start of the season, perform each of the following exercises at 70% of your maximum strength. Gradually increase the intensity each week. By the start of the season, you should be lifting at 80% to 85% of your maximum strength, concluding each exercise with one or more 100% efforts. Be sure to see me for periodic strength testing to determine maximums and to guarantee safety.

During the season you should follow the same regimen, but at 50% of your maximum strength, doubling the number of repetitions, if you can do so with the proper form. Remember, these exercises are limited. They are specific to your sport and are not substitutes for your total conditioning program.

Exercises	*Muscle(s)*	*Purpose(s) and Qualifications*
Three abdominals	abs	Improved general mobility
Front chin-ups and reverse-grip chin-ups	biceps, forearms, and hands	Arm strength for bat speed
Modified preacher curls	forearms and hands	Position your arms on the board as if doing regular curls. Instead, lift the weight by bending your arms only at the wrists, putting all the strain on the forearms This exercise will improve your hand and forearm strength for better bat speed
Leg extensions	quadriceps	Leg strength for improved throwing
Squats	quadriceps	Leg strength for throwing and running
Heel raises	calves	Improved base running
Dumbbell dead lift	quadriceps, gluteals, and erectors (back)	Improved stance for defensive positioning, especially for catchers.
Inclined bench press	pectorals, deltoids, and triceps	Upper-body strength for initial speed
Lat pulldowns	latissimus dorsi and biceps	Upper-body strength for quickness
T-Bar rowing	rhomboids, deltoids, lats	Upper-body strength for batting power

More as prescribed by coach. . . .

ALWAYS USE PROPER FORM

© 1995 by Michael D. Koehler

GYMNASTICS EXERCISES

To the Athlete: About a month before the start of the season, perform each of the following exercises at 70% of your maximum strength. Gradually increase the intensity each week. By the start of the season, you should be lifting at 80% to 85% of your maximum strength, concluding each exercise with one or more 100% efforts. Be sure to see me for periodic strength testing to determine maximums and to guarantee safety.

During the season you should follow the same regimen, but at 50% of your maximum strength, doubling the number of repetitions, if you can do so with the proper form. Remember, these exercises are limited. They are specific to your sport and are not substitutes for your total conditioning program. Because of gymnastics' unique demands, you may need to supplement this workout with exercises specific to your event(s). See me to discuss these additional exercises. You will also need to work intensively on your flexibility. Refer to that section of your booklet.

Exercises	Muscle(s)	Purpose(s) and Qualifications
Three abdominals and more as needed	abs	General mobility; exceptionally important for gymnasts
Dips	deltoids, pectorals, and triceps	Arm strength for horizontal and parallel bars
Push-ups	deltoids, pectorals, and triceps	Upper-body strength for floor exercise
Military press	deltoids and triceps	Upper body strength for floor ex and other events
Chin-ups	hands, forearms, biceps, and lats	Pulling strength for all bars
Squats	quadriceps	Leg strength for floor ex
Heel raises	gastrocnemius (calves)	Improved jumping ability
Dumbbell fly	pectorals, triceps, deltoids	Upper-body strength for rings, pommel horse, and others
Lat pulldowns	latissimus dorsi and biceps	Upper-body strength for bars and rings
Preacher curls	hands, forearms, and biceps	Grip and arm strength for bars and rings
Triceps extensions	triceps	Pushing strength for bars and floor exercise
Behind-neck-press	trapezius, deltoids, and triceps	Upper-body strength for bars, rings, and floor exercise

More as prescribed by coach. . . .

ALWAYS USE PROPER FORM

© 1995 by Michael D. Koehler

VOLLEYBALL EXERCISES

To the Athlete: About a month before the start of the season, perform each of the following exercises at 70% of your maximum strength. Gradually increase the intensity each week. By the start of the season, you should be lifting at 80% to 85% of your maximum strength, concluding each exercise with one or more 100% efforts. Be sure to see me for periodic strength testing to determine maximums and to guarantee safety.

During the season you should follow the same regimen, but at 50% of your maximum strength, doubling the number of repetitions, if you can do so with the proper form. Remember, these exercises are limited. They are specific to your sport and are not substitutes for your total conditioning program.

Exercises	*Muscle(s)*	*Purpose(s) and Qualifications*
Three abdominals	abs	Improved general mobility
Leg extensions	quadriceps	Leg strength for jumping
Squats	quadriceps	Leg strength for jumping
Heel raises	gastrocnemius (calves)	Lower leg strength for jumping
Front lunge	quadriceps and gluteals	Improved quickness
Upright rowing	lats, rhomboids, deltoids, and biceps	Arm strength for hitting ball
Military press	deltoids and triceps	Arm strength for killing ball
Barbell rowing	lats, deltoids	Upper-body strength for jumping and blocking shots
Dumbbell dead lift	quadriceps, gluteals, and erectors	Jumping ability and quickness
Cleans	deltoids and rhomboids	Upper body strength for jumping

Others as prescribed by your coach. . . .

ALWAYS USE PROPER FORM

© 1995 by Michael D. Koehler

GOLF/FIELD HOCKEY EXERCISES

To the Athlete: About a month before the start of the season, perform each of the following exercises at 70% of your maximum strength. Gradually increase the intensity each week. By the start of the season, you should be lifting at 80% to 85% of your maximum strength, concluding each exercise with one or more 100% efforts. Be sure to see me for periodic strength testing to determine maximums and to guarantee safety.

During the season you should follow the same regimen, but at 50% of your maximum strength, doubling the number of repetitions, if you can do so with the proper form. Remember, these exercises are limited. They are specific to your sport and are not substitutes for your total conditioning program.

Exercises	Muscle(s)	Purpose(s) and Qualifications
Three abdominals	abs	Improved general mobility
Modified preacher curl	hands and forearms	Hold a barbell on board as if to do preacher curls. Instead, lift the weight by bending the hands at the wrists, concentrating on the muscles in the forearms. This will improve grip strength and ability to control the stick/club.
Dead lift	quadriceps, gluteals, and erectors (back)	Improved back strength to control ball while running downfield and to increase power of stroke.
Bench press	pectorals, triceps, and deltoids	Upper-body strength for improved stroke.
Military press	deltoids and triceps	Same as above.
Squats	quadriceps	Upper-leg strength for improved speed.
Heel raises	gastrocnemius (calves)	Lower-leg strength for quickness.
Front lunge	quadriceps and gluteals	Total leg strength for quickness.
Thigh curls	hamstrings	Improved quickness.
Dumbbell fly	pectorals and deltoids	Upper-arm strength for stronger stroke.

Others as prescribed by coach. . . .

ALWAYS USE PROPER FORM

© 1995 by Michael D. Koehler

SWIMMING EXERCISES

To the Athlete: About a month before the start of the season, perform each of the following exercises at 70% of your maximum strength. Gradually increase the intensity each week. By the start of the season, you should be lifting at 80% to 85% of your maximum strength, concluding each exercise with one or more 100% efforts. Be sure to see me for periodic strength testing to determine maximums and to guarantee safety.

During the season you should follow the same regimen, but at 50% of your maximum strength, doubling the number of repetitions, if you can do so with the proper form. Remember, these exercises are limited. They are specific to your sport and are not substitutes for your total conditioning program. In addition, be sure to do flexibility exercises at least 20 minutes *before* and *after* doing these exercises. For a swimmer, flexibility is as important as strength.

Exercises	Muscle(s)	Purpose(s) and Qualifications
Three abdominals	abs	Improved general mobility
Leg extensions	quadriceps	Leg strength for improved kick
Leg curls	hamstrings	Leg strength for improved kick
Lat pulldowns	latissimus dorsi and biceps	Upper-body strength for stroke
Shoulder shrug	upper trapezius	Same as above
T-bar rowing	latissimus dorsi, deltoids, and rhomboids	Back strength for stroke
Dumbbell fly	pectorals and deltoids	Shoulder strength for stroke
Upright rowing	latissimus dorsi, rhomboids, and biceps	Same as above
Triceps kickbacks	triceps	Pulling strength for stroke
Dumbbell raises	deltoids	Shoulder strength for stroke
Dips	deltoids and triceps	Shoulder strength for stroke

Others as prescribed by coach. . . .

ALWAYS USE PROPER FORM

© 1995 by Michael D. Koehler

TENNIS EXERCISES

To the Athlete: About a month before the start of the season, perform each of the following exercises at 70% of your maximum strength. Gradually increase the intensity each week. By the start of the season, you should be lifting at 80% to 85% of your maximum strength, concluding each exercise with one or more 100% efforts. Be sure to see me for periodic strength testing to determine maximums and to guarantee safety.

During the season you should follow the same regimen, but at 50% of your maximum strength, doubling the number of repetitions, if you can do so with the proper form. Remember, these exercises are limited. They are specific to your sport and are not substitutes for your total conditioning program.

Exercises	Muscle(s)	Purpose(s) and Qualifications
Three abdominals	abs	Improved general mobility
Dead lift	quadriceps, gluteals, and erectors (back)	Improved ability to stay in crouch
Leg extensions	quadriceps	Improved upper-leg strength
Squat	quadriceps	Improved upper-leg strength
Leg curls	hamstrings	Improved quickness
Heel raises	gastrocnemius (calves)	Improved foot speed
Dumbbell raises	deltoids	Upper-arm strength for improved stroke
Dumbbell fly	pectorals and biceps	Total arm strength. This exercise simulates stroke motion and helps prevent tennis elbow
Lat pulldown	latissimus dorsi and biceps	Improved upper-back strength for stroke
Front lunge	quadriceps and gluteals	Leg strength for stretching for shots
French curls	triceps	Improved strength for serve

Others as prescribed by coach. . . .

ALWAYS USE PROPER FORM

© 1995 by Michael D. Koehler

TRACK EXERCISES
SPRINTERS AND RUNNERS

To the Athlete: About a month before the start of the season, perform each of the following exercises at 70% of your maximum strength. Gradually increase the intensity each week. By the start of the season, you should be lifting at 80% to 85% of your maximum strength, concluding each exercise with one or more 100% efforts. Be sure to see me for periodic strength testing to determine maximums and to guarantee safety.

During the season you should follow the same regimen, but at 50% of your maximum strength, doubling the number of repetitions, if you can do so with the proper form. Remember, these exercises are limited. They are specific to your sport and are not substitutes for your total conditioning program.

Exercises	*Muscle(s)*	*Purpose(s) and Qualifications*
Three abdominals	abs	Improved general mobility
Leg extensions	quadriceps	Upper-leg strength
Thigh curls	hamstrings	Pulling strength in legs
Squat	quadriceps	Power out of the blocks
Heel raises	gastrocnemius (calves)	Pushing power during running motion
Lunge	quadriceps and gluteals	Power for improved stride
Military press	deltoids and triceps	Upper-body strength for power out of the blocks
Upright rowing	latissimus dorsi, rhomboids, and biceps	Upper-body strength for power during running motion
Dumbbell raises	deltoids	Upper-body strength for running motion
Triceps kickbacks	triceps	Increased power for running motion
Cleans	deltoids and rhomboids	More upper-body strength

More as prescribed by coach. . . .

ALWAYS USE PROPER FORM

© 1995 by Michael D. Koehler

TRACK EXERCISES
FIELD EVENTS

To the Athlete: About a month before the start of the season, perform each of the following exercises at 70% of your maximum strength. Gradually increase the intensity each week. By the start of the season, you should be lifting at 80% to 85% of your maximum strength, ending each exercise with one or more 100% efforts. Be sure to see me for periodic strength testing to determine maximums and to guarantee safety.

During the season you should follow the same regimen, but at 50% of your maximum strength, doubling the number of repetitions, if you can do so with the proper form. Remember, these exercises are limited. They are specific to your sport and are not substitutes for your total conditioning program. Because of the variety of field events, be sure to see your coach for additional exercises that are specific to your event.

Exercises	*Muscle(s)*	*Purpose(s) and Qualifications*
Three abdominals	abs	Improved general mobility
Bench press	pectorals, triceps, and deltoids	Improved push for shot and other throwing events
Upright rowing	latissimus dorsi, rhomboids, and biceps	Good for throwing events and arm lift for jumping events
Dumbbell raises	deltoids	Also good for throwing events and for arm lift for jumping events
French curl and triceps kickback	triceps	Both good for running motion and all throwing events
Military press and behind-the-neck military press	deltoids, trapezius, and triceps	Excellent for throwing events and for arm lift for jumping events
Squat	quadriceps	Leg power for throwing and jumping
Heel raises	gastrocnemius (calves)	Lower-leg power for both throwing and jumping events
Lunge	quadriceps and gluteals	Excellent for jumping events; also good for throwing events
Dumbbell fly	pectorals and biceps	Good for throwing events
Cleans	deltoids and rhomboids	Upper-body strength for all events

More as prescribed by coach. . . .

ALWAYS USE PROPER FORM

© 1995 by Michael D. Koehler

EATING YOUR WAY TO IMPROVED PERFORMANCE

THE BODY'S NUTRIENTS

The basic nutrients of the body are proteins, carbohydrates, fats, vitamins, and minerals. Look at the following chart to understand how they work:

NUTRIENT	NEEDED FOR	CAN BE FOUND IN
Fat	Continuing energy	Meat and dairy products
Carbohydrates	Energy, especially quick energy. Also help to burn fat	Preworkout: Apples, ice cream, raw carrots. Postworkout: Bananas, honey, raisins, bread. Most fruits, vegetables, and grains
Proteins	Muscle growth and repair	Meat, (including fish and poultry), eggs, and most beans
Minerals and vitamins	The body's metabolism	A well-balanced diet

All athletes who eat well-balanced diets, including appropriate servings from the bread, vegetable, fruit, milk, and meat groups, will take in all the vitamins and minerals they need to sustain their growth and promote their athletic performance. They also will consume the carbohydrates and the proteins they need for practice and competition. Athletes or their parents who have specific questions are encouraged to see the family doctor.

© 1995 by Michael D. Koehler

THE WARNING SIGNS OF DRUG USE

INTRODUCTION

Coaches, parents, and students should all be aware of the warning signs of drug use. We must know them in order to recognize symptoms, then to help the drug user in whatever way we can. We all know that drugs, no matter how desirable they may seem to us, have the potential to kill. Parents, coaches, and *real* friends don't want teammates and close friends taking such chances with their lives. A friend who lacks the pride and self-confidence to avoid drugs needs our help. Please read this sheet very carefully so you will be in a better position to provide that help. Your coaches already are familiar with these signs.

NAME OF DRUG	WARNING SIGNS
Alcohol	Slurred speech, unsteady walk, slowed reflexes, relaxed inhibitions, glazed eyes
Cocaine	Restlessness, increased excitement, glass vials, glass pipe, razor blades, syringes, needle marks
Marijuana	Red eyes, dry mouth, excitement, laughter, increased hunger, rolling paper, pipes, odor of burnt hemp rope
Hallucinogens	Focus on detail, anxiety, panic, nausea, capsules, tablets, blotter squares
Inhalants	Nausea, dizziness, headaches, poor coordination, drowsiness, poor muscle control, smell of inhalant on clothing and breath
Narcotics	Nausea, dizziness, drowsiness, inability to feel pain, pinpoint pupils, cold and moist skin, needle marks
Stimulants	Alertness, talkativeness, loss of appetite, weight loss, irritability
Depressants	Drowsiness, lack of coordination, capsules, confusion, slurred speech, needs more sleep
Steroids	Significant weight gain, acne, altered moods, increased anger, puffiness in face, hair loss for men, increased facial hair and deeper voice in women

© 1995 by Michael D. Koehler

FITNESS: EXHILARATION,
NOT EXHAUSTION

SOMETHING TO THINK ABOUT

- Almost 70 percent of adult Americans discontinue fitness programs within one month of starting them.
- Recently, there was a 6 percent drop in the percentage of Americans who stay away from cholesterol and fatty foods.
- The numbers of people who smoke in this country has leveled off in recent years. This leveling off has concluded a 26-year decline in the number of smokers in America.
- Sixty-six percent of the people in this country were overweight last year.
- Only 10 to 20 percent of 18- to 64-year-olds in this country have developed appropriate aerobic exercise habits.
- Most people reach their biological prime at age 30, but that prime can be extended to age 60 with regular exercise.
- People need lose only 5 percent of their endurance with each decade of age.
- Raking, walking briskly, even gardening can provide aerobic exercise—and actually delay the aging process.
- Sedentary people tire and weaken faster than their active friends.

Get in on the action! Develop a regular exercise program for yourself. Better yet, join our fitness program. You'll be doing yourself a big favor!

© 1995 by Michael D. Koehler